# Witchcraft
## Myths in
## American Culture

# Witchcraft

## Myths in
## American Culture

## Marion Gibson

Routledge
Taylor & Francis Group
New York   London

Routledge
Taylor & Francis Group
270 Madison Avenue
New York, NY 10016

Routledge
Taylor & Francis Group
2 Park Square
Milton Park, Abingdon
Oxon OX14 4RN

© 2007 by Taylor & Francis Group, LLC
Routledge is an imprint of Taylor & Francis Group, an Informa business

Printed in the United States of America on acid-free paper
10 9 8 7 6 5 4 3 2 1

International Standard Book Number-10: 0-415-97977-3 (Softcover) 0-415-97978-1 (Hardcover)
International Standard Book Number-13: 978-0-415-97977-1 (Softcover) 978-0-415-97978-8 (Hardcover)

### Library of Congress Cataloging-in-Publication Data

Gibson, Marion, 1970-
    Witchcraft myths in American culture / Marion Gibson.
        p. cm.
        ISBN 0-415-97977-3 (hardback : alk. paper) -- ISBN 0-415-97978-1 (pbk. : alk. paper)
        1. Witchcraft--United States. I. Title.

    BF1573.G53 2007
    133.4'30973--dc22                                    2006037153

**Visit the Taylor & Francis Web site at**
**http://www.taylorandfrancis.com**

**and the Routledge Web site at**
**http://www.routledge.com**

# CONTENTS

# INTRODUCTION

This is a book about the writing of the history and literature of witchcraft in the United States of America, from the first prosecution for the crime in the 1620s to the present day. In some ways the history of witchcraft in the English colonies in the "New World" is a well-worn theme. In 1970 the great American historian John Demos apologized to his audience for calling them together yet again for a paper on a favorite topic:

> it is faintly embarrassing for a historian to summon his colleagues to still another consideration of early New England witchcraft. Here, surely, is a topic that previous generations of writers have sufficiently worked, indeed overworked.[1]

Yet Demos went on not only to deliver a thoughtful paper, but to write the five-hundred-page study *Entertaining Satan*, the best book of its generation on just this topic. And scholars, journalists, genealogists, and students have continued to write and read about the witchcraft events of early New England with undimmed enthusiasm ever since. Yet there are very few books and articles written *about* writing about witchcraft in America. Bernard Rosenthal's illuminating *Salem Story* (1993) is the only major example, and it deals — as its title suggests — solely with the most famous of American witch prosecutions.

Was Demos right, then, in his self-deprecating remarks in 1970? Have scholars scraped the barrel clean? If so, why does witchcraft continue to occupy the American mind? Demos was certainly right to suggest that there was limited scope for new discoveries of fact to be made about the participants in the better-known witchcraft trials — but what about those less well known? And, as his own new readings of his material showed, it was also a different matter when it came to interpretation. Here there was ample room for new thought and research. Records of witchcraft have been read as demonstrating both the probity and the viciousness of Puritanism; the superstition and the enlightenment of the clergy; the frailty and the strength of American women; the merits of theocracy, democracy, and aristocracy; the dangers of governmental power; the dangers of devolved power; the triumph of the human spirit; and the corruption of humanity in general. It is, then, the interpretation of texts about American witchcraft that is the subject of this book. It is a literary historiography rather than another retelling of the story of Salem or any other American community afflicted by accusations of witchcraft. And by "literature," I mean everything written about witchcraft, from the tiniest scraps of seventeenth-century notation in the Essex Institute at Salem through the fat histories of the nineteenth century to the poems of modern Wiccans and the recent filmic adventures of Nicole Kidman as Isabel Bigelow and Samantha Stevens in *Bewitched* (2005).

The basic question that motivated the writing of the book was, "What does witchcraft mean to Americans?" But this is, of course, a hopelessly ill-defined question, and the book comes out of the realization that it is also the wrong question to be asking. Witchcraft may mean something very different, and an interest in it may be sustained for completely different reasons, depending on one's cultural heritage, politics, age, ethnicity, sexual orientation, and gender, or simply on whether — like L. Frank Baum's witches in *The Wizard of Oz* — one is from North, South, East, or West. America's diversity means that it might be hard even to agree on a working definition of "witchcraft" with a Bostonian descendant of Lowells and Mathers, a Pennsylvanian Wiccan influenced by "Dutch" *hexenmeisters*, a parent challenging the inclusion of a Harry Potter book on a school syllabus, a practitioner of African-American "hoodoo" in Alabama, a Harvard historian, a lesbian Dianic Witch from San Francisco, a Jewish New

Yorker playwright, and a teenage Floridian goth. So I have limited myself, initially, to a consideration of the English colonies of the northeastern and central eastern United States, where witchcraft was defined by legal codes based on English law and biblical quotation and was prosecuted as a crime in the seventeenth and early eighteenth centuries. Even here, there are many problems of definition and differences of emphasis, and one of the aims of the book is to tease these out. The first two chapters, therefore, examine the records of witchcraft from Virginia in the south to Maine in the north, in the period of circa 1620 to 1730, and discuss the interpretation of them by historians, politicians, and interested communities internationally, nationally, and at local levels, from state down to town or village.[2]

Just as definitions of witchcraft differ greatly among modern Americans, so they have greatly altered over time. As a war of liberation was fought and won, and expansion westward drew in new Americans of all kinds, what "witchcraft" meant changed and was contested. Decriminalization in English law in 1736 and the widely held opinion that witchcraft prosecution had simply been persecution gave it a new life in romance. Witchcraft was psychologized, pathologized, and sociologized, often with a focus on gender and race — categories of American experience largely ignored by the political theoreticians and historians of Chapter 1 and 2. Chapter 3 examines this process of reimagining. While a focus on the east is maintained — as is to some extent inevitable because of the disproportionate and iconic prominence afforded by historians to the witch trials at Salem, Massachusetts, in 1692 — attention is also given to interventions from across America and from the wider world. Witchcraft is not, however, conflated with the African- and Caribbean-American religions that came to America with slavery in the eighteenth and nineteenth centuries. While white colonists and planters often thought they recognized their own demonic paradigms in what Native Americans, slaves, and freed black Americans were doing when they performed rituals or chanted songs, this was always a misreading, and usually a racially discriminatory one. The misreadings of scholars and politicians will therefore be examined, but the actual nature and cultural history of obeah, santeria, vodoun, *candomblé*, and other spiritualities is a subject for another book — and one that concentrates in particular on the American South, where such traditions and mythic reworkings of them are strongest. This book focuses instead on reimaginings of the very different, precisely defined, and previously criminalized tradition of European-American witchcraft as it and its decriminalization were incorporated into a vision of the United States as a free and tolerant new nation — but one in which women and non-white citizens might still experience demonization.

However, while decriminalizing witchcraft was usually seen in the tradition of Enlightenment reform of the irrational, bigoted, and superstitious past, it also had other implications for modern America. If practicing witchcraft was not illegal, was it still wrong? Where were God and the devil in all of this rethinking of America's past? Anticlerical and even liberal Christian movements in nineteenth-century America began to redefine witchcraft as beneficent paganism, or feminism, or — paradoxically — a kind of liberating, nature-worshipping theology of individualism, running curiously parallel to the "official" myth of the frontier and manifest destiny. Chapter 4 therefore continues the focus on reimagining, charting the rise of Witchcraft as a new religion, beginning in the northeast but with enormously important input from both the American West and from Britain. Interests in American sublime, the mystic West of King Arthur, *Hiawatha,* and finally California, melded unexpectedly to turn the musings of transcendentalists and suffragists into a worldwide religious revolution. I should explain that where I use a capital *W*, I mean Witchcraft the modern religion and its affiliates in Wicca and related traditions, while a small *w* denotes the historic crime and the practices associated with it. Chapter 4 ends with an examination of the portrayal of Witchcraft and Wicca in American popular culture, especially film and television, which is often surprisingly negative.

Finally, Chapter 5 considers the more positive portrayals of witches in popular culture since the 1930s. Not all witches on the big or small screen, in comic books and cheap novels, are wicked, and they are often actively good. The rehabilitation of the witch in modern America runs alongside the gradual growth of feminism and the acceptance of women in the workplace and political life. But in order to be accepted, witches in popular culture often have to be framed by the traditional setting of marriage and family, which sometimes undercuts their metaphorical significance as empowered women. The traditional American family offers strength but also containment to a witch, and it is hard to imagine a portrayal of a witch as a single working woman who will not succumb to motherhood (and apple pie).

What does the future hold for American witches? The book traces their representation in early records and argues that some of the traits of that representation seem likely to continue in future portrayals: an anxious conscientiousness of approach due to a sense that the subject is a special and controversial one; a belief that important issues of morality and justice are associated with witches; and a belief that the United States' national destiny is somehow, mythically and confusedly, linked to her approach to satanic conspirators whom only witch hunts can eradicate. In the past, the witch has become part of two major discourses in American history: of political development, with a special focus on the dangers and benefits of democracy (ca. 1760–1930), and of social history, with a special focus on gender and race (ca. 1880–2006). It seems to me that there is still some mileage left in the second approach — the portrayal, perhaps, of a completely empowered *and* completely virtuous female witch, especially if that witch happened not to be white, which has not yet been achieved. But beyond that the linkage between race and witchcraft seems likely to grow stronger, both because of the continuing racial divisions in American society and the ethnic implications of the more hawkish attitudes toward the "war on terror."

Since this book deals in part with the way in which an author's background and cultural location influences his or her reading and reconstruction of past events, a word about the author herself also seems necessary — in fairness both to the reader and the other writers discussed here, and to explain the wider framework of argument that informs the book. For sixteen years I have been reading accounts of witchcraft, having almost by chance encountered them during my undergraduate study. I found myself unable to put them down until I had come to some kind of understanding of them — especially how the people who had narrated and written them had thought about activities I personally believed to be impossible, or, if you like, at some level "fictional." This book is part of a journey, therefore: from the English news pamphlets about the crime, with which I began, into the wider context of Puritan writing on witches. Beyond that, it also became an exploration of modern popular culture, for which I have to thank my students at both Exeter's Streatham and Cornwall campuses, and at the University of Plymouth. They were far more likely to imagine witchcraft in relation to an episode of *Buffy the Vampire Slayer* or a graphic novel than a set of musty documents in a library, and I found that I had to abandon my snobbery and acknowledge that they were right. The portrayal of witchcraft in film and other popular modern genres was just as worthy of study as its embodiment in early modern depositions and letters, and in fact the two were very closely related. Because of its often American origin, too, the televisual representation of witches that I saw owed a great deal to American understandings of the witchcraft trials at Salem, Massachusetts, in 1692. Hence I broadened my reading to New England, and there experienced a growing realization that America's witchcraft history was much broader and more complicated than I could possibly have imagined.

It was a shock to discover that it was not Massachusetts or even Connecticut but Virginia that was the first colony to produce and preserve the record of a prosecution for witchcraft — and the discovery was a long time coming because of the intense concentration of scholarship and popular writing on New England and its witchcraft history. It meant a rethinking of the godly focus of the work, and a greater concentration on what I thought of as "Americanness" instead. But what did this term mean? I first visited the United States at the age of twenty-seven, and began pondering the differences between the different Americas I had seen. There was Cleveland, Ohio, where I stayed with a friend from university, with its leafy suburbs and — to the English eye — vast lots, hopping with squirrels and cardinals. Then there was Chicago, which appeared to be two cities: white and black, shiny skyscrapers and shattered sprawl. We got innocently lost on the south side one night, having taken the wrong bus, and were shocked by the terror of the black taxi-driver who came to our rescue. Was she right to think we were lucky to be alive, or was I witnessing a kind of demonization that seemed oddly familiar? And then there was New York, where European Jews, Koreans, and Indians had poured in to become Americans, and the streets were filled with protestors and celebrants in marches against police practices and in favor of lesbian pride. And all this packed into only about a quarter of North America's land mass; and all the unvisited territory beyond and between . . . Further visits only provoked more questions.

This sense of indeterminacy is one that has become important for this study. Plural as they are, Americans choose and remake their identities, and perhaps more consciously and visibly than the people of any other culture they have done so since the early seventeenth century. Each choice is also — as Robert Frost pointed out — a "road not taken," and choices are often made for reasons untheorized, prejudiced, or imaginative rather than reasoned.[3] Many of the Americans discussed in this study had or have a stronger identification with the seventeenth-century witches and their prosecutors than has hitherto been explored. Some historians and other writers were and are literally descended from those who are the subject of their research, while genealogically unconnected people have formed a variety of mythic and emotive bonds with them, building on these to draw some surprisingly pointed and personal lessons for themselves and their fellow Americans. As an English outsider to these processes, I wanted to offer some readings of these formations of American identity. I also found, as the study progressed, that I wanted to question the preoccupation of American academia with New England history, at the expense of the histories of non–New England colonial witchcraft cases, and the subsequent development of the image of the witch in American culture. What witchcraft, and its successor Witchcraft, have in my view meant to a

number of prominent American communities will become clear, and it is
for the reader to add to this discussion his or her own understandings of
what witchcraft means to them. I hope that the book will provoke thought
and debate about how witches, Witches, and America's historic witch trials were and are represented.

The book could not have been written without the help and generosity
of many people, and I would like to dedicate the book to all of them.

Most prominent, because they often gave their time freely or under the
great pressure of other commitments, are the librarians and archivists of
the historical societies, museums, and libraries across New England and
the Tidewater states whom I visited in 2003, 2005, and 2006. These are:
Fairfield Historical Society, CT (especially Dennis Barrow); the Connecticut Valley Historical Museum, Springfield, MA; the Historical Society
of Pennsylvania, Philadelphia, PA; the Virginia Historical Society, Richmond, VA; the Library of Virginia, Richmond, VA; "Historic Northampton," Northampton, MA (especially Kerry Buckley and Bridget Marshall);
Dutchess County Historical Society, Poughkeepsie, NY; the Franklin D.
Roosevelt Presidential Library, Hyde Park, NY (especially Karen Anson);
the New Haven Colony Historical Society, New Haven, CT; Wethersfield
Historical Society, Wethersfield, CT; Williams College, Williamstown,
MA; the Connecticut State Library, Hartford, CT; Stamford Historical
Society, Stamford, CT; the Maryland Historical Society, Baltimore, MD;
Frederick County Historical Society, Frederick, MD; the Massachusetts
Archives, Boston, MA; and the Phillips Library, Essex Institute, Salem,
MA (especially Kathy Flynn); the New York Public Library (especially
Melanie Yolles); and Boston Public Library (especially Eric P. Frazier). The
librarians of Brown and Harvard Universities, as well as the Fogler Library,
University of Maine, were especially helpful in subsequently supplying
reproductions of key documents. I would also like to thank the Salem
Witch Museum, Colonial Williamsburg, and the Matilda Joslyn Gage
Foundation, Fayetteville, NY. The project could never have been begun
or completed without the generous funding from the British Academy
(2003) and the Arts and Humanities Research Council (2005–06). Pro-

fessor Ronald Hutton has offered his unstinting support to the project throughout. I would also like to thank the anonymous readers of the proposals to the AHRC and Routledge, as well as readers of part of the project that appears in the *European Journal of American Culture*: their criticisms and comments have made this a better book. Exeter University Library provided outstanding support. The Franke Institute, University of Chicago, and the Western Conference on British Studies both provided early opportunities to give papers in the United States. Many people have talked or corresponded with me about witchcraft over the years, pointed me in the direction of new ideas, reviewed my work, and given me the opportunity to explore and mature my ideas in print. I am especially grateful to Dr. Harry Bennett, the late Dr. Gareth Roberts, Professor James Sharpe, Dr. Jonathan Barry, Professor Betty Travitsky, Professor Anne Lake Prescott, Professor Brian Levack, Dr. Becky Munford, Dr. Juliette Wood, Dr. Daniel R. Rolph, Dr. Sally Roesch Wagner, Dr. Owen Davies, Dr. Rob Fish, Dr. Rachel Moseley, Dr. John Newton, Dr. Amy Hale, Spencer and Allyson Reese, Gelly McAlinden, Emma Wilby, April Letsch-Bogert, Lesley Jones, Deborah Neild — and all the people who chatted in bookshops and at museums, historical societies, and libraries. Finally, thanks to the many students and colleagues who have been interested in the project and offered help, insight, and support throughout, to my parents, to Harry, Hoppy and Lucille, and to my editor at Routledge, Kimberly Guinta, and project editor, Marsha Hecht, for their commitment to the project.

# 1

## E PLURIBUS UNUM? MYTHIC AND MISSING HISTORIES AND THE POLITICS OF AMERICAN WITCHCRAFT

"Stop" says the seventeenth century, "stop, my conceited nineteenth, before you fling your stones at me. . . . Every century, my vainglorious nineteenth, has its own glasshouse; and yours may yet be spacious enough to merit the name of a crystal palace."

"The project of memorializing the New England past . . . became, in the long run, more of a rattling of the skeletons in the closet."[1]

### Witchcraft in the New World

In the century and a quarter after the founding of the Jamestown colony announced the arrival of large numbers of European settlers on America's northeastern shores, we know that at least three hundred and fifty cases of witchcraft were reported to the colonial courts of the "New World."

Many more people were accused or believed guilty of the crime without the matter ever coming to court: statements made by and against them as well as scattered references in contemporary records remind us of their existence, but without revealing to us the true number of those suspected. It is almost certainly much larger, over five hundred — and many people undoubtedly carried on magical practices without ever thinking of them as witchcraft, until it appeared that their neighbors thought differently. The records of many courts are also incomplete, which allows us to imagine that accounts of other trials may have been lost and makes the events of some trials very difficult to follow. Surviving documents show that between thirty-eight and forty people were hanged for witchcraft offenses (witches were not burned in America, contrary to one of many persistent myths). Yet even here it is quite possible that the true number was higher. Some executions are known only through a chance reference, and sometimes it is not made clear even in otherwise complete records whether a convicted witch was executed as was legally warranted, or not. We know, then, that witchcraft was a subject of great interest to early Americans, and that they took pains to record its occurrence among them. But we can also see that the information we have about the place of witchcraft in their differing colonial cultures has built-in unreliabilities and gaps, in which conflicting interpretations, myth, and confusion can flourish.

There are great stories to be told about American witches and their accusers — and also some unexpected contradictions lurking behind the stereotypes to which we have all become accustomed. The surprises start with the first person we know to have been accused of witchcraft in America. She was not from Massachusetts, which has become famous for its "Salem" witchcraft trials and has a reputation for enthusiastic witch-hunting. She was not from Connecticut, which executed the highest number of witches. She was not even from Puritan New England. Joan Wright, who was accused of witchcraft in the surprisingly early year of 1626, was from Virginia. In fact, even with the massive loss of records during the Civil War, Virginia is not that far behind Connecticut in the number of people whom we know were suspected of witchcraft in the colony during the time that witchcraft was a criminal offense.[2] Before 1730 Connecticut proper, excluding New Haven and New York territories, saw at least forty-three cases in which a text was created detailing the crimes of a suspected witch: Virginia had thirty, including the last known case. Massachusetts had the largest number: eighty-two without the "Salem" or more properly "Essex County" cases, which by themselves totaled just over 140 for whom formal records remain. One contemporary source speaks of up to two hundred more accused. Maryland, meanwhile, has only ten recorded witches. New Hampshire, in the period of its judicial union with Massachusetts and afterward, has twelve, while Maine (with a similar political history) has four. Many of its residents were displaced by "Indian" wars and returned to Massachusetts, where, as Mary Beth Norton has shown, they took part in the Essex County witch trials, so that these figures are certainly distorted. Plymouth, later part of Massachusetts, had two cases. New Haven, before its absorption by Connecticut, had nine, and the parts of New York governed by Connecticut five, with three elsewhere in the colony or under English rule. North Carolina had one; Rhode Island had one, and was a place to which witches accused elsewhere traditionally fled; and Pennsylvania had six.[3]

Witchcraft was defined in two ways, in practice if not formally in law — and, as we shall see, laws and their enforcement differed between colonies. The first definition involved the making of a pact or covenant with Satan or a familiar spirit by the suspected witch, which was in itself a hanging offense. But second, that pact enabled the witch to cause harm to people, animals, and goods, and such unexplained misfortune was often the way in which the presence of a witch could initially be identified. Suspicion might then fall on a person who was known to wish ill to the victim, and evidence of this could be given in court, from which it might be inferred that the accused had made a demonic covenant. But other magical offenses also came under the umbrella of "witchcraft," although they seldom involved the death penalty. Included in the figures above are also witchcraft-related cases: accusations of practicing divination, of fortune-telling, or of reading and using magical books, and also cases where those who had hastily executed a suspected witch on board ships bound for America were themselves tried. These all add information about the culture of witchcraft prosecution in America. Finally, there are further details about who was suspected and why, even if their cases never came to court, in the substantial number of records of slander suits brought by those who had been called "witch" and had decided to fight back. After 1730, witches were no longer being formally accused, and slander suits had tailed off, too, although clearly magical beliefs and even lynchings and other kinds of antiwitchcraft violence persisted. In Virginia, the last case that I have identified (in 1730) resulted in a woman being convicted of using witchcraft to find treasure or lost goods and being whipped. But 1730 was also the year in which Benjamin Franklin published in the *Pennsylvania Gazette* a satirical account of a fake witchcraft trial in which four people (accused and accusers) were tried by being weighed against a Bible and swum to see if they would float. Among their supposed crimes were making sheep dance and hogs sing psalms. Attitudes were changing decisively, and 1730 will be the end date of this chapter's account of early American witchcraft texts.[4] It must also be said that new cases of witchcraft are being uncovered quite frequently in repositories and libraries: the subject is by no means cut-and-dried, and all the documents that we have can only give us a provisional understanding of the offense and its appearance in the courts.[5]

How, then, can we best explore this vast, incomplete, and complex body of texts — telling the stories of early American witches and their accusers while acknowledging the importance of local differences among the original American colonies, the fragmentary nature of the texts about witches, and the multiplicity of theories and interpretations of what witchcraft meant? This book attempts to do just that, focusing on differences, gaps, and interpretive choices not just as problematic but rather as important and interesting in their own right. The first chapter explains the colonial legal systems that tried the witches, before exploring the ways in which their stories were recorded, delving into the importance of lost records and untold histories, and finally analyzing how American historians began in the mid-nineteenth century to think about their country's witchcraft history in the (rather unexpected) terms of local politics and interstate rivalry.

## *American Law, Courts, and the Records of Witchcraft Prosecutions*

The whole tenor of American courts was very different to that of English Assizes, where the mother country usually tried her witches. Where England had a largely unified, fixed system, Americans embraced difference, inclusivity, and flexibility as rights. So when someone was accused of witchcraft in one of the American colonies, his or her path to court, the verdict, and the sentence depended to a great extent on where he or she lived, on the circumstances of the accusation, who was involved in accusing and judging him or her, and on the period in which the trial took place.[6] Each colony had its own legal code, most of them specifying particular demonic or magical crimes, and offenses of slander that could be applied to witchcraft cases. Massachusetts and Connecticut and the territories that they governed based their fundamental laws on biblical injunctions concerning witches, notably that they should not be suffered to live, as did New Haven and Plymouth. The laws did not concentrate on the harm witches were thought to do to their victims (*maleficium*) but rather on witches' offenses against God. Virginia, Rhode Island, and Maryland adopted English witchcraft laws, which were more worldly in their focus on *maleficium*, as did the colonies later under English rule, such as New York. Meanwhile Pennsylvania, and New York when it was under Dutch rule, had no witchcraft laws at all. Pennsylvania adopted a mass of English statutes in 1718 and the Witchcraft Act was among them. This was one of a number of surprisingly late adjustments to colonial laws on witchcraft: in 1712, for example, South Carolina adopted English witchcraft law but no evidence of formal proceedings against witches there has yet been found.

The importance of apparently dry legal forms to the history of witchcraft and its literature becomes obvious when we see that no sooner had previously witch-free New York adopted English laws, in the form of the "Duke's Laws" in 1665, than a witchcraft trial was recorded.[7] Although the Duke's Laws did not specify the crime, English law did, and it seems that therefore witchcraft was accepted as an offense worthy of investigation. Ralph and Mary Hall of Long Island were immediately indicted at an Assize court. Ralph, a substantial freeman, was acquitted and Mary was found to be suspicious but not guilty to the extent that she should be executed. Yet this was hardly a regular English verdict (which should have been "guilty" or "not guilty"), and the penalty was also unusual (imprisonment or hanging were the English penalties for conviction).[8] Neither acquitted nor condemned, Mary Hall was sentenced to appear for monitoring before each subsequent court session for as long as the couple continued to live in New York. They were released from further court appearances and bonds by the governor three years later.[9] Another witchcraft matter also came to the English governor's attention in New York in 1670. The inhabitants of Westchester petitioned him that a woman newly arrived in their town from Connecticut be asked to leave because she had previously been suspected of witchcraft. This woman, Katherine Harrison (of whom we will hear more later), refused to leave despite her neighbors being granted their petition, and a month later the governor agreed to meet her and her opponents to resolve their differences. There was no trial, and Harrison was allowed to stay.[10] New Yorkers prosecuted very few witches — but when they had a legal process in place, however shakily, complaints and prosecutions did occur.

Even where there were no witchcraft laws, however, a way might be found to indict witches. In 1683 in Pennsylvania, which completely lacked witchcraft statutes, two suspected witches were referred to the governor and council: Margaret Mattson and Yeshro Hendrickson, accused at Philadelphia. The allegations against them were taken as far as a trial, although since the indictment itself is lost it is not clear how the charges were legally (or illegally?) expressed. Like Mary Hall, Mattson was found guilty only of having the "Comon fame" of being a witch and not of the crime itself. This was not the complete acquittal that some historians have supposed: as we have seen, it still indicated suspicion, and might lead to further legal measures. In 1695, too, the Quakers of the Chichester and Concord meeting in Pennsylvania also investigated two of their members for practicing astrology and other magic, and took the matter as far as court, where one was admonished and fined. In 1701 two more Philadelphia "witches," Robert Guard and his wife, brought what was in effect a slander suit against accusers by petitioning the governor and council, but the case was dismissed as "trifling" and the accusers went unpunished. Despite their lack of a law, then, Pennsylvanians brought witchcraft and witchcraft-related cases almost as often as New Haven's inhabitants and more often than the people of Plymouth, Rhode Island, or New York.

A witchcraft case and the records that went with it began when someone felt strongly enough that a neighbor was a witch to complain to the magistrate about him or her. The suspect would be questioned by the magistrate or "assistant" (so called in some colonies because magistrates assisted in colonial government). Testimony would be collected from the suspect's accusers and written down to be sent to a higher court. But the constant proliferation of new communities in America meant that pragmatic modifications to this process and the trial itself were inevitable. Court systems took time to develop when the priorities were finding food and building homes, and if a person was accused of witchcraft in a new colony or town then judicial processes had to take that into account. So, for example, in Springfield, Massachusetts, in the 1630s, a court specific to the new town was given power over all offenses including capital crimes. There was no requirement for a higher court to become involved. No witchcraft cases were tried, as far as we know, but they could have been if necessary, in a way unprecedented in English law.[11] New settlements were also often far from the centers of colonial governance, easily cut off by winter or "Indian" wars. In such cases, the local magistrate might be given the power to hold further hearings in his own court, and to delay the transportation of the suspect to a higher court that would eventually judge him or her. Some colonies also suffered periods of turbulence that made normal judicial processes impossible, such as Maryland's mini–civil war, known as "the plundering time," in the mid-1640s, or the northern Pequot wars.[12] Even a mild version of this kind of disruption would influence the making and keeping of records, and it is almost certain that some undocumented witchcraft cases from early America have simply disappeared.

This is made more likely because written evidence was intended only an aide-mémoire. The spoken word had more power than the written one, and the story had to be told verbally in court. To this end, courts enforced attendance strictly. In 1656 the County Court of Hampshire, into which Springfield was eventually incorporated, was not impressed by accuser Sarah Bridgeman's written testimony or her excuse that she could not attend court because she was "weeke and with childe"— even though the constable endorsed it with the statement that she "is not abele to a peare at this court with out hassard to her life."[13] The Massachusetts Court of Assistants jury and the General Court prevented the conviction for witch-craft of Hugh Parsons of Springfield in 1652 partly because evidence against him had not been given in person in Boston.[14] So important was verbal testimony that commissioners might even be deputed by a superior court to investigate a case locally, so that the suspect and witnesses could be interviewed initially without leaving their hometown. Commissioners were sent to hear Eunice Cole's accusers at Hampton, New Hampshire, in 1673 because there were no resident assistants, and Hampton was a long way from Boston, where the Court of Assistants met.[15] In such cases, the suspect might take several months to progress to the next stage of the legal process, or he or she might never reach it at all if the case could be resolved locally. Any records might at this stage be lost, or pared down. But as the colonies grew and became more stable, increasingly the assumption was that the local magistrate would pass on all written depositions to a higher court that would continue the case.

In the early years of each colony, this was generally the highest (and often only) colonial court. But as the colonies developed, the court to which the magistrate would forward the less serious depositions — such as those in slander cases or where there were accusations that a suspect had been heard muttering magical words — was often at town, county, or equivalent level.[16] Since the 1620s Virginia, for example, had had county courts, which could hear capital cases until 1628 and for a brief period during the English interregnum. This provision was, however, unusual and county courts normally dealt with lesser offenses.[17] The testimonies taken by the original magistrate would be sent to the place where the court was meeting, and indictments would be drawn up based on the depositions. These would usually be examined first by a grand jury to see if they were worthy of the court's attention, and then determined by a petty jury and the panel of magistrates. If a witchcraft case was not judged to involve a capital offense, the matter would in most cases be resolved here. For example, John Bradstreet, presented to Essex County Court, Massachusetts, for reading a magic book and conversing with the devil, was judged (he was found guilty only of lying) and sentenced at Ipswich and that was the end of the matter.[18]

When a case involved a capital crime, however, it usually went straight to the higher judicial level. The higher courts were, essentially, the governing body of the colony in one of its forms, and they were roughly equivalent to the English Assizes in the witch-trial procedure: indeed, some of them were renamed "Assizes" in Massachusetts and Connecticut in the 1680s, and they were also so called, as we have seen, in English-governed New York. But in each colony there were important differences from Assizes. In England these were circuit courts held by royal authority, with one or at most two autocratic and highly trained judges and a grand and petty jury, which heard all felony cases in each area that they visited. After judgment, the Assizes regularly carried out death sentences for witchcraft without further ado. Massachusetts is a good example of American difference. The Bay Colony often led judicial practice in New England, and before the loss of its charter the magistrates' Court of Assistants heard witchcraft cases. Here juries also operated, giving verdicts, but a large panel of magistrates presided and often determined the final outcome of cases by amending sentences or demanding further trial. If there was disagreement among the magistrates, who had no legal training, or between them and their jury, they appealed to the General Court. The assistants also sat here, but so did deputies (the elected representatives from individual towns) and by voting on the original verdict these representatives of government and the governed together determined the outcome of the appealed case. This included cases from Maine and New Hampshire before their separations. So it was the General Court that, for example, reviewed Hugh Parsons's case when the Court of Assistants was unable to reach a clear verdict.[19] Thus there was a two-stage process in difficult witchcraft cases that greatly benefited some defendants, and at each stage a number of officials and laymen were involved in a way that was much more consensual than in England.

Each colony had its own version of consensual justice. In Virginia, after the period of martial law from 1609–19, the main court was the General Court, which despite its name acted rather like the Court of Assistants in the northern colonies. It thus heard major cases such as witchcraft accusations, and there was a right of appeal from it to the General Assembly, of which the magistrates of the General Court formed the upper house. They and the lower house, the elected burgesses, could vote together to reverse verdicts or decide difficult cases. In 1655, amid complaints of reckless slander from the county courts, the General Assembly passed a law stipulating that anyone who accused another of witchcraft but could not prove his or her case would be subject to a fine of a thousand pounds of tobacco.[20] In Maryland the highest court was the Provincial Court. It began life as a county court, but as new counties developed in the early 1640s it became the upper tier of these new governmental units. It was thus an appeal court for the county courts, but it also tried all capital cases. In other respects Maryland closely resembled Virginia.[21] Plymouth had a General Court and a Court of Assistants, but they found their respective roles as legislature and judicature hard to define correctly, and several times reorganized themselves. In 1660 and 1676, when Plymouth heard its witchcraft cases, the Court of Assistants was handling capital crimes. But Plymouth's system had, unusually, no right of appeal to the General Court.[22] Some colonies, therefore, were less judicially inclusive than others. New Haven, exceptionally, had no trial juries at any level of the judicial process. New

Haven's magistrates based their practice more on biblical than English precedent and took all weighty decisions in their Magistrates' (the equivalent of the Assistants') Court unaided. But magistrates still decided cases consensually, and they and the colony's deputies both decided General Court appeal cases, as elsewhere.[23] Thus in America witchcraft suspects had a right to have their cases examined by a wider range of people than in comparable English cases.

The most important long-standing anomaly in American witchcraft trials was in Connecticut, and it went somewhat against the spirit of consensual decision-making that characterized many of the other colonial processes of the "Old Colony." Connecticut did not follow Massachusetts in setting up county courts until thirty years after its northern neighbor, in the mid-1660s, and it did not separate out its higher judicial functions in the same way either. Instead of a Court of Assistants, Connecticut held Particular Courts. The Particular Court was set up to try all serious cases against individuals, as opposed to the general public business that was the concern of the General Court. It thus handled a lot of cases—anything too important for a town court to try was forwarded to it. It operated as a kind of cross between a County Court and the Court of Assistants for the whole colony, which the Hartford court eventually became. As the records of the Hartford court show, colonists struggled to find a stable official title for this mixed entity: their "county courts," they said, were "called sometimes Quarter Courts, sometimes a court of Magistrates and Sometimes particular Courts."[24] This system was in the process of change in 1662–5 when Hartford experienced its "witch-panic," a series of at least thirteen trials that led to two certain and two probable executions and caused half a dozen suspects to flee the colony in fear for their lives. The witch trials began in the Particular Court but by the time the last suspect was freed from "further suffering or imprisonment" the court had been reconstituted as a Court of Assistants.

Many of the important documents are now lost, including some paperwork from the Particular/Assistants Court itself, and there is reason to believe that the built-in oddity of the system and the attempts to reform it had an impact on the witch trials and their outcome. The overgrown and overworked Particular Court at Hartford was judging both felonies and other crimes, including sensitive matters in its own immediate locality, and while persons convicted by the Particular Court could appeal to the General Court, it too was in Hartford and was composed of many of the same men. Even if appeals had been made, the assistants and deputies in Connecticut voted separately in appeal cases. This meant that in effect the assistants had the ability to uphold their own original verdict in a Particular Court case even if the deputies wanted to reverse it. As Edgar J. McManus puts it: "appeals were vitiated by what amounted to a magistrates' veto." They were rare, and seldom successful, and there is no record of appeals being forwarded in any of the witchcraft trials. The General Court and Assembly meetings — also at Hartford — were filled instead with business relating to the merger of New Haven with Connecticut, and negotiations over the colony's New York territories' future after the arrival of the new charter in 1662. William K. Holdsworth also suggests that the practice of using grand juries as trial juries, and magistrates' unwillingness to overrule juries before 1666 may have contributed to the high number of convictions in the Particular Court.[25] The same small group of people made all the important decisions in the trials of the Hartford witches, and indeed in the trials of the "witches" that the Particular Court and its deputed magistrates had tried and executed before 1662, and during the "witch-panic" they did so in a legal system, a city, and a colony in internal flux. Uncontested executions and lost paperwork were, perhaps, more likely than usual to be the result, and most of the texts that do survive were preserved by one magistrate and a minister.

Here one can find echoes of another moment when judicial practice is thought to have influenced America's history of witchcraft and where record-keeping certainly has: the peculiar legal circumstances of the Essex County witchcraft trials in Massachusetts in 1692, which led to the executions of nineteen people and the pressing to death of another, who had refused to plead. Because Massachusetts had no Royal Charter during the period of the early accusations, and was in judicial limbo even once the new charter arrived, those accused of witchcraft were tried by a Special Court of Oyer and Terminer based at Salem itself, instead of by the now-defunct Court of Assistants at Boston or any regularly constituted assembly. When the Court of Oyer and Terminer was replaced with a Superior Court of Judicature, the new court backed away from the decisions of its predecessor — as did the Connecticut Court of Assistants in the 1660s. Thus while a wide cross-section of people at Salem were involved in the trials, decisions were once again made by relatively few of them and once again in circumstances of unusual strain.[26] However, unlike the scrappily recorded 1662 Hartford trials, the "Salem," or Essex County, cases of 1692 are the best documented in American history — not just because we have records from over one hundred trials, but because the records are uniquely detailed, even to the extent that there are three or four separate accounts of some of the pretrial examinations and accusers' statements, made by interested parties. It was probably the unusual legal nature of the Salem court, its location in a small community right at the heart of the accusations, and the involvement of a number of ministers and other godly and literate people that led to the creation of so many records, and this was very conducive to later historical research. In later years, someone quietly lost the texts produced by the Court of Oyer and Terminer itself. But they did not dispose of the mass of pretrial and informal records, and it is for this reason as well as the scale of the accusations that the Essex County trials are the only witchcraft trials that most Americans know: they were written about in most depth, studied first and most frequently by scholars, published first, and can now even be viewed on the Internet.[27] Meanwhile, a full history of the Hartford "witch-panic" has yet to be written.[28]

Likewise, the history of witchcraft in the colonies that prosecuted fewer witches and preserved fewer records has been left largely unexplored. Interest in witchcraft history grew out from Salem across New England, as historians rediscovered other documents in their localities. In some cases, they met insuperable barriers. Most of the records of Virginia's General Court were destroyed during the Civil War when Richmond was burned. In Maryland, too, almost all the early records were lost, leaving only minimal traces. The case of a woman probably executed for witchcraft in 1685 is a striking example. Nothing is known of her trial except for a single entry copied into the records of the General Assembly in 1723. This reads "Same Court Rebecca Fowler for Witchcraft and Conclusion Contra formam Statuti." The one-line record was only preserved because a clerk was instructed to trawl through the then-existing records to find examples of the ways that English law had been absorbed into colonial law.[29] In both states County Court records of witchcraft-related trials survive and have now begun to receive attention, however.

In some states the lack of interest in witchcraft history seems to stem from the perception that certain American cultures were too sensible or tolerant to prosecute witches. In 1908 Amelia Mott Gummere put into print the widespread approbation of Pennsylvania and New York, writing "to call attention to the sanity of an entire community" of Quakers and "the sensible Hollanders." The apocryphal story that Governor William Penn himself told Margaret Mattson that "she was at perfect Liberty to ride on Broomsticks, for he knew of no Law against it" and thereby ended her trial was repeated frequently. Of New York, two Connecticut historians wrote ruefully: "evidently, the New Yorkers with their civil process of bail-bond, handled 'the witch' with more wisdom and better success than the Yankees with their 'expert' ministerial opinions and jury trials."[30] Yet New York and Pennsylvania in fact have some of the most celebrated supernatural traditions in America — think of Washington Irving, and the *hexenmeisters* and pow wow magic of the Pennsylvania "Dutch" and Appalachian communities.[31] True, local governmental traditions of religious tolerance and refusal to enact witchcraft laws kept witchcraft largely out of the courts, but each colony did prosecute witches in small numbers. It was not that the populace and their leaders did not believe in the possibility of magic and witchcraft, only that its prosecution was not felt to be a defining cultural imperative. This has greatly influenced their portrayal in the mythic history of American witchcraft.

### Cases of Conscience in New England and Beyond

The colony that tried the most witches, and so created and was able to preserve the greatest number of records of witchcraft, was, as we have seen, Massachusetts; and thus the Bay Colony became the target of most reproach in future times. Charles Wentworth Upham in his *Salem Witch-craft* (1869) regretted that "those who know nothing else of our history or our character will be sure to know, and tauntingly to inform us that they know, that we hanged the witches." The blame extended over New England: in 1892 Charles H. Levermore sympathized with "the Yankee whose Southern and Western friends half seriously try to make him responsible for hanging Quakers and burning witches . . . if he knows enough to deny that witches were ever burned in New England, he will be met with an incredulous smile."[32] Important, though, as the statistics of trials and record numbers can be to the history of American witchcraft, it is just as vital to examine the content of the records that do remain. Massachusetts left the most texts about witch trials, but paradoxically the more records were created, the greater was the colonists' emphasis on proof, conscience, and consensus in judgment. As accusers and the recorders of accusations, the Massachusetts — and other New England — Puritans created records not as a means of integrating events into a preexisting legal and cultural system, as must those colonies that had adopted English law and practice, but rather as an individualized response that would continue into an individualized hearing and verdict. This was intended to ensure careful community consideration of offenses, and complete justice in their punishment. If we look closely at their texts, we can see colonists struggling with their consciences and memories to recollect evidence and represent their beliefs precisely. Their narrations, and the texts embodying them, are not smooth and finished but are still processing complex considerations as the deponents speak and recorders write. One finds frequent scribblings-out and insertions above lines and in the margins. An accusation of witchcraft was not made lightly, as has sometimes been assumed, and although the Bay colonists harassed and killed many of their neighbors as witches, they did so, ironically, as part of a culture of ultra-conscientious recording and minute self-examination.

For example, in the Massachusetts college town of Cambridge in 1659 to '60, John Gibson Jr. made extensive notes about the witchcraft that he believed was being practiced on his daughter Rebecca Stearnes by her neighbors Winifred and Mary Holman. He drafted and redrafted evidence, which he eventually presented to the Middlesex County Court in an uncorrected form, with several versions of the same story recorded alongside the names of those who could testify about them. The document appears to be a kind of brief for Gibson, the magistrate Thomas Danforth, and others, in response to the Holmans' claim that Gibson and Stearnes were defaming them. What is most interesting is first Gibson's demonstrable anxiety about the presentation of the stories he and others had to tell, but also his scrupulous care not to overstate or oversimplify matters so that his narration mutated into an untruth. For example, he had himself been troubled by Winifred Holman's hens, which repeatedly got into his barn and ate his corn. One day he threw a stone at one of them and killed it, "and after that" his narration records "{shee calld here hens away} Thay troubled me no more." The deleted phrase in my curly brackets, "shee calld here hens away," suggests that Gibson had proof of Mrs. Holman's power over her chickens, which he believed to be a supernatural one. Of course, he did not have such proof, and so he substituted the phrase "Thay troubled me no more," which is an objective piece of evidence rather than a circumstantial inference.

Other evidence from the slander case further demonstrates the care that Massachusetts people devoted to the evidence against the accused. Elizabeth Bowers came forward to offer a nonmagical explanation for some of the evidence that Gibson had presented against the Holmans. It had been alleged that Mary Holman had been pouring water from one vessel into another in a suspicious way, which coincided with an episode of violent weeping by her supposed victim. Bowers said that she had been in court when the "pasag" about it had been read, and had "thought to speak herein." However, she had been prevented at the time and now wished to say that Mary and Winifred Holman had lacked water on their property because their well was "frossen up." Accordingly they had fetched water in dishes, which explained Mary's unusual actions. The court's documentation reflected a similar concern for justice. A sentence is recorded that Rebecca Stearnes, the supposed victim, must acknowledge at court or meeting her "scandalos and unadvised speches" defaming Winifred Holman — but it was then crossed out and instead a marginal note substituted, explaining an apparent change of the court's determination because Stearnes had spoken "when shee by Gods hand [was] deprived of the use of reason." Thus the jury's original verdict against the defendant was modified to a requirement that she simply pay the court costs. Finally, codefendant Gibson offered a fulsome apology to Mary Holman, saying that he acknowledged his legal conviction for slander and was "heartily sorry for his evill thereby committed ag[ain]st god and wrong dew to ye said Mary Holman and her freinds and doth crave forgivenes of ye s[ai]d Mary." His behavior in court was an extension of the hair splitting care with which he had constructed his potentially lethal evidence against her and her mother.[33]

It was not even necessary for witnesses to be literate for there to be evidence of their care in having testimony recorded. Many accusers could not write, or not confidently enough to record their stories. They could, however, give verbal evidence to a scribe — who might not be highly literate himself — and many such texts exist, with careful revisions as the story was told. Bethiah Carter, reconstructing the long and vexed chain of events that led the accusation of Ann Burt of Lynn as a witch by Carter and her sister Sara Townsend, told the recorder of her testimony for Essex County Court that "the said Sara townsan Being sorely afflicted with sad fits {this said Goodwife Burt coming to the} crying out and Rayling against me saying my father carryed me to boston But carryed her too Lin too an owld wich." There was clearly another story competing for attention in Bethiah Carter's text, which probably involved a visit by Burt to Townsend at her home. This story was deleted and did not get told, perhaps because it was inaccurate, or inopportunely disordered the plain narration of Carter's accusation.[34] Care in recording also meant care in demonstrating the guilt of the accused, however. Some colonists were so keen to have their stories recorded so as to make the best possible case against the suspect that they wrote them, often with difficulty, themselves. Anthony Morse, who thought his brother at Newbury was being attacked by the witchcraft of Caleb Powell, wrote painstakingly that "I anthony mores: ocationally being at my brothars Mores hows my brothar showid me a pece of a brik which had severall tims come down the chimne . . . this was about 10: deayes a goo."[35] Richard Lyman, the brother of Sarah Bridgeman whom we have already seen as an accuser, was so keen to defend her from the resultant slander suit that he counter-accused the recorder who had taken testimony against her of bias. Edward Elmore, he said, "did Conster the meaneing of there wordes and writt downe what he thought good; and when he read it the witnesses denyed what he writt." Lyman either collected further evidence himself or brought in his own tame scribe: someone certainly interpolated his comments on the "witch" Mary Bliss Parsons's guilt into his testimony, such as "Its a made [proven] ly of Goodwife Persons."[36]

Small details can, therefore, be important evidence that in Massachusetts, and New England, many colonists told stories of witchcraft and recorded them with great care, whether they sought to make clear what they saw as evident guilt, or to offer a balanced narrative of events. But blanket condemnation of their all-too-successful efforts has been the frequent response, as we shall see. More objectively, the New England colonists created a uniquely revelatory set of pretrial records, an approach that, while we might deplore its consequences, suggests anything but reckless malice. And this careful approach continued into the courtroom. Although American court systems were often in flux, especially in the early colonial period, and their members often acted without much regard for the letter of law, governors and their deputies, magistrates and their juries freely exercised a right that they must have considered superior to any legal formality: the power to make creative and idiosyncratic decisions. These included split verdicts, postponements for further deliberation, or a modification of sentence that was not warranted by any writ-ten law but seemed the right thing to do.[37] Magistrates considered cases together, called in ministers, and discussed the subject with a wide range of ordinary witnesses, often over several months, which was unthinkable in England. Juries often defied convention to reach unique determina-tions. Sometimes this flexible approach was disastrous, as at Salem, where in contravention of all law and precedent those who confessed were kept alive to give further evidence, while those who pleaded not guilty were condemned almost automatically. But sometimes it distinctly advantaged the accused.

So, for example, in the case of our old acquaintance Katherine Har-rison, indicted at the Connecticut Court of Assistants on 11 May 1669: "the Jury finding difficulty in the matter given them in Charge . . . cannot as yet agree to give in a Verdict." Stumped, the court adjourned the case until the fall and released Harrison, provoking her neighbors to petition the court that "the greater part" of the jury had believed her guilty. To the next court, on 12 October, Harrison, who was a wealthy woman, brought an attorney and — in the first item minuted at the new session — she also agreed to pay the costs of witnesses who had traveled once again from her hometown of Wethersfield. This time the jury found her guilty, but the magistrates had had time to reflect. There is every indication that Har-rison and her lawyer had argued strongly for her innocence, impressing upon the magistrates the importance of the jury's doubts, in the period between May and October. Harrison was imprisoned, therefore, but not condemned. Meanwhile, the magistrates sought the opinion of local min-isters. Armed with a response that could be construed as ambiguous, they obtained a special order (in effect, from themselves) to reconvene the Court of Assistants. And at this final, special session on 30 May 1670 the secretary minuted that "the court having considered the verdict of the Jury respecting Katherin Harrison cannot concur with them so as to sentence here to death or to longer continuance in restraynt." Instead, they released her from prison with the revealing requirement "to minde [remember, act upon] the fullfilment of removing from Weathersfield" for her own safety and the satisfaction of her neighbors — implying an agreement reached in earlier discussion. Harrison left the state a free woman and, as we have seen, moved to New York.[38]

This was far from being the only split verdict returned by the jurors of this or other courts, and the result was not always good. In the case of Andrew and Mary Sanford, indicted in the Particular Court at Hartford on 6 June 1662, the jury returned the following verdict: "they cannot agree, some find Indictment against Sanford, the rest strongly suspect." But it was not even clear from this legally indefensible determination which of the Sanfords was being referred to, and the inadequacies of the Particular Court's last days are evident. In Massachusetts such a case would have been referred to the General Court, but we have no evidence that this was done with the Sanfords. The Particular Court determined the case itself, in a manner inconsistent with precedent: a similar verdict in the case of Nicholas and Margaret Jennings in the same court in 1661 had led to their release. But in 1662 Hartford was in the midst of the "witch-panic" and Mary Sanford was indicted separately from her husband on 13 June and found guilty. She was probably executed.[39] Elizabeth Seager, accused at the same time, was luckier. She was accused of witchcraft three times, and twice the Particular Court jury acquitted her. On 26 June 1665 her latest accusation arrived at the new Court of Assistants. But again the jury were unsure, and found Seager guilty only of familiarity with the devil, stopping short of a proper conviction for witchcraft. The Court of Assistants delayed sentencing Seager at the request of the colony's governor, John Winthrop junior, and — just as with the Harrison case five years later — a special Court of Assistants reconsidered the jury's verdict. They found that in evading the precise terms of the indictment, it did not meet legal requirements. Again the process of recording uncertainty, delay, and review worked in favor of the accused, and Seager was released.[40]

What is distinctive about these cases is not just their outcomes but how they were recorded. The secretary's conscientious reflection of the questionably legal internal deliberations of the courts is strikingly full.[41] And such thoroughness was normal in New England practice. One finds, for example, a constitutionally important minuteness of recording in the case of Elizabeth Morse of Newbury, the wife of the William mentioned above, who was condemned for witchcraft in 1680. The Court of Assistants repeatedly reprieved Mrs. Morse. But the deputies rebuked them, and the rebuke was recorded. "The deputys . . . ," reads one note "doe not understand the reason why execution of her sentence given ag[ain]st her by the s[aid] Court is not executed . . . her 2d repreivale seemes to us to be beyond what the law will allow." The assistants were determined, however, and recorded that their implied request was "not Consented to by the Magist[rate]s" — after which Morse was released.[42] Because of this precision, transparency, and pride in recording conflict and uncertainty, the original records of New England witchcraft with all their marginalia and scribbling-out are an important collection for understanding how these early modern Americans thought about the crime, weighing arguments and agonizing over verdicts in ways not usually recorded in other jurisdictions. Modes of writing about such cases were unfixed in America. It was not until 1650 that Essex County Court, Massachusetts, minuted that because of "the inconvenience of takeing verball testimonyes in Court by reason of many imp[er]tinencyes in their relations, so that the clarke cannott well make a p[er]fit record there of, testimony must be given in writing."[43] This had been the rule in England for over a century, and the forms of the accusers' and witnesses' "informations," the suspect's "examination," and court documents were accordingly rigid.[44] In contrast, the flexibility of the New England systems and the lack of immediate literary precedent meant that individual people had considerable leeway to write their own stories of witchcraft as they liked, free from the usual generic constraints of legal paperwork.[45]

How much were the famous New England records of witchcraft — the stories they told and the manner of the telling — like those of the rest of early America? As we have seen, cases from New York and Pennsylvania were treated in remarkably similar ways: recorded carefully, judged with Solomonic balance. Plymouth has left too few records to judge fairly, but New Haven certainly conformed to the conscientious New England

model. And even in the colonies furthest from New England both culturally and geographically, the Anglican and Catholic mercantile ventures
of Virginia and Maryland, where records do survive they do not suggest
a radically different approach to trial and judgment. For example, in 1705
the County Court of Princess Anne County, Virginia, heard the case of
Grace Sherwood. She was accused of witchcraft by Luke and Elizabeth
Hill, although their precise charges are not specified, which is rather odd.
The court ordered her to be searched for witch marks by a jury of women
and then dropped the matter for several sittings: they seemed to be hoping
that it would go away. Frustrated, Luke Hill petitioned the colony's governing council. He complained that the county court had taken no action,
"not knowing how to proceed." The council asked the attorney general to
give a legal opinion, upon which he referred the matter back to the county
court, stating that the accusation was "too general" for the matter to go to
the General Court. Thus pressured, the county magistrates searched Sherwood's house and recalled the jury of women who, unexpectedly, refused
to attend court. Matters were becoming strained: the court's dilemmas are
not disguised. As a final resort, in order "to have all means possible tryed
either to acquit her or to Give more strength to ye suspicion," it was determined that Sherwood should be asked if she would consent to be ducked,
in the traditional test of magical guilt. Those who floated were strongly
presumed guilty, those who sank innocent. It was a desperate step: ducking was highly controversial. The magistrates were greatly concerned with
demonstrating in writing both Sherwood's willingness to risk her life and
their care for her well-being. The ducking was even postponed, "ye weather
being very Rainy soe yt possibly it might endanger her health." On 10 July
she was at last ducked, and searched again. Since she floated, the women
stated that they had found unusual marks on her *and* evidence had been
sworn against her by several witnesses, Sherwood was then committed
to jail, although it was not stated what was to become of her, perhaps this
time with deliberate taciturnity. Maybe Sherwood proceeded to a General Court trial, but the court's records were destroyed, and we will never

know. Apparently she survived to pay debts in 1708, and to make a will that was proved in 1740.[46]

This is a late, post-"Salem" case, of course, which might make the recorder particularly likely to display the court's care for the rights of the accused. Indeed, the records of the case of Joan Wright, America's first recorded witch, are rather less thorough. Half a dozen people accused Wright of witchcraft offenses at the court of 11 September 1626: making a family ill and killing a child, telling fortunes, impeding hunting, threatening people, and telling stories about witches, including one whom she had known in England. A typical story is that of Alice Baylie, who said that "she asked goodwief wright whether her husbande should bury her, or she burye him To whom good wiefe wright answered, I can tell you yf I would, but I am exclaimde against for such thinges and Ile tell no more." Her husband Robert Wright was, however, called as in effect a defense witness, stating, "that he hath beene maried to his wiefe sixteene years, but knoweth nothinge by her touchinge the Crime she is accused of."[47] And no determination seems to have been made on 11 September. Instead the matter was revisited at the court of 28 September, where another two witnesses against Wright were heard, probably because they were able to confirm evidence offered only as hearsay by others on 11 September. This suggests a concern for justice, although no reasons for the adjournment are given. We also have no record of Joan Wright's fate: no verdict, no reasons given, no sentence. There is no particular indictment, just a string of accusers' stories. The lack of detail is probably due to the fact that Wright's case, unlike many in New England, is only documented in fair copy court records, while the original pretrial documents are lost. It is a miracle that even the court book survives, and this is attributable only to someone's having borrowed it from the archives, probably Thomas Jefferson for his historical researches, and having not yet returned it. On the night of the great Richmond fire, therefore, it was safe. What it records is clear and full, if not complete or detailed, but it is not enough evidence to suggest real differences in approaches to witches in the southern courts.

One textual difference, however, does offer some justification for the excoriation of the culture of Massachusetts and Connecticut as particularly to blame for witch persecution. The Puritans of these colonies were much more likely than the people of the Dutch, Quaker, Independent, Anglican, and Catholic colonies to keep personal notes about suspected witchcraft, in addition to court records. There was a compulsion in godly culture not only to examine all apparent manifestations of God's providence, but to write about them, write to others about them, reflect on and debate them, and keep the texts. So from New England and especially Massachusetts we have, as well as court records, the notebooks and letters of magistrates, clergymen, and other literate people. Most famous are the published works of Increase and Cotton Mather, especially *Cases of Conscience Concerning Evil Spirits Personating Men, The Wonders of the Invisible World* and *Memorable Providences, Relating to Witchcrafts and Possessions.*[48] There is John Hale's *A Modest Inquiry*, which despite its penitence draws attention to his role in forwarding witchcraft prosecutions. There are other "Salem"-related texts — published and private narratives, transcripts of examinations, reflections in private journals, letters — by ministers and godly participants in the trials, such as Deodat Lawson, Samuel Sewall, and Samuel Parris. There are accounts of other witchcraft accusations and apparent demonic possessions in Massachusetts and Connecticut by Joshua Moody, John Whiting, Nathaniel Mather, Samuel Willard, and many others.[49] There are the archival collections of magistrates such as William Pynchon and Samuel Wyllys, preserving important witchcraft testimonies. As far as we know, nothing comparable survives — indeed, may seldom have been created — in Rhode Island, Pennsylvania, New York, or the Tidewater states, even though the latter began to prosecute witchcraft over twenty years before the first records of prosecution appear in New England.

What we can say, then, about early modern texts on American witches is that where evidence is available it appears that colonists from Virginia to New Hampshire were careful to record stories about witches and careful to judge those accused. In New England, with its bible-based laws, creative adaptations of process and verdict were often made. But in the colonies bound by English laws, the same was — unexpectedly — true, although it is less well recorded. Americans judged witchcraft differently from contemporary Englishmen, whether they were in Philadelphia, Hartford, New York, or Salem. New Englanders, especially ministers, often documented witchcraft cases as important providences of God and became involved in witchcraft prosecutions as a matter of course, creating a large body of writing on the crime and on unprosecuted cases as well. Meanwhile, Southern and non–New England colonists were not uninterested in witchcraft, but they seem to have created a bare minimum of purely official records about them, many of which were later destroyed. Here, surely, is a real cultural difference, as well as a regrettable historical accident.

But it is one that has had a disproportionate impact on the writing of American witchcraft history. The inhabitants of colonies other than Massachusetts and Connecticut may not have written demonologies and exchanged long letters about witches, and some of them refused to enact statutes forbidding witchcraft at all. But their approach when confronted with a case that had to be tried in court because a complainant insisted upon it was quite similar to that of their Puritan neighbors. The cultural differences between the Puritan colonies and their Anglican, Catholic, Independent, and Quaker neighbors are in the number of cases brought and thus the number of texts surviving, rather than a distinction between an indifference to witchcraft and a fanatical pursuit of satanic conspirators. But in the Puritan areas of the north more pretrial documents are preserved, as well as more informal records of court proceedings and the private papers of ministers and magistrates. Because of these, it became fashionable to accuse Massachusetts and Connecticut of feverish delusion and to contrast this with the supposed good sense of Quakers, Virginians, and other early Americans, who were thought either to have prosecuted no witches at all or to have contemptuously dismissed such nonsense from their courtrooms. In fact, the crime was almost universally portrayed as a debatable matter of conscience to be taken most seriously. It behooved each participant in a witch accusation to express his or her views fully *and* after his or her own fashion — rather than be bound by convention or kept silent by authority. Experimental and consensual American justice as well as Puritan conscience demanded such an approach, and it is one that is still present in the unusual weight of moral significance attached to witchcraft in America ever since.

*Democrats, Ministers, and Witch-Hunting: Accusatory Histories*

Discussing early modern Scotland, the sociologist Christina Larner argued that:

> it was not possible in the sixteenth and sevententh centuries (and is, indeed, difficult now) to put a barbed wire fence round newly acquired or consolidated borders and police them. Instead, you built churches on your borders, sent priests and ministers to instruct your subjects and stamped out heresy and witchcraft — false belief and apostacy — with particular ferocity in those vulnerable border areas.[50]

The formulation of witchcraft laws, and ways of trying, punishing, and publicizing the crime were, for Larner, intimately connected to the identity of a people and the building of their national culture. What they thought witches did reflected, indeed inverted, their sense of what a Christian people ought to do, and in creating internal laws and policing frontiers with other kinds of people they were defining themselves as much as these demonic "others." In America, Kai T. Erikson made a similar case, featuring witches as "deviants."[51] If this was true in Scotland, how much more might it be true in Maryland, Massachusetts, or Maine, where an entire continent populated by tribespeople and various religious antagonists lay on the other side of the real or imagined border?[52] America's new inhabitants — "a People of God settled in these, which were once the Devil's Territories" as Cotton Mather put it — had great need of definition in their polities in every way. The early American emphasis on accusation and relative uninterest in the viewpoint of the suspect, to the extent that hardly any witches' examinations were written and preserved, is thus suggestive of an attitude of relentless self-assertion against demonic others.

And a look at the historiography of American witchcraft makes the point in even more interesting terms. Witchcraft became a matter of self-definition for Americans in ways that have nothing to do with belief in the reality of magic, or a fear of Native Americans, Catholics, or Quakers. Instead, the *history* of witchcraft has been used as a stick to beat other groups of Americans — northeners, southerners, the people in the next state, ministers, magistrates, the New England "brahmins," the Pennsylvania Germans, Native Americans, Unitarians, Congregationalists, freethinkers, Democrats with and without a capital *D*, Republicans, physicians, psychiatrists, African-Americans, teenagers, men, and women. The politics of representing witchcraft has moved on over time from differences in court practices and hairsplitting in records into major dissension in history books, textbooks, novels, plays, and films. At its mildest, it expresses itself in parochial pride, a touching if sometimes partial belief in American virtues, and in minor interstate rivalries. But at its most ferocious it is an all-out showdown between liberal and conservative, northern and southern, American and un-American, religious and Rationalist visions of America in the most stereotypical and aggressive terms.

And in the process of this warfare, the conscientiousness of the stories recorded in such detail and with so much soul-searching by early modern colonists has often been lost, replaced by mistake, misrepresentation, partiality, and fudge — in short, by myth. Nineteenth-century historians, in particular, preserved the accusatorial emphasis of early records without much concern for their detailed content. They preserved, too, an anxious concern with the inclusive and (as they saw it) worryingly democratic nature of American justice, as we shall see. But they buried the actual texts under thick layers of myth that have proved almost impossible to remove. Most strident are the myths of "Salem," but these are related to wider myths of American witchcraft that are equally reluctant to die. This surprising and depressing state of things is recognized and deplored by insightful historians. John Demos has argued that much of the historiography of American witchcraft "can be viewed, in large measure, as an unending effort to judge the participants — and, above all, to affix blame."[53] But efforts to combat the trend and rise above it are rare. And while discussion of mythmaking has begun at localized level — Chapter 3 discusses, among other questions, who is blamed for the deaths at Salem and why — what has not often been discussed is its larger geographical operation and the intersection of such mythmaking with the development of American political culture well into the twentieth century.[54]

After the "Salem" witch trials New Englanders in particular internalized a now rather well-known dialogue of self-accusation and self-defense.[55] It was begun as soon as the trials were over. The first combatant to identify a particular culprit (or, depending on one's view, scapegoat) for New England's witchcraft-prosecuting past was the Boston merchant Robert Calef, in his 1700 *More Wonders of the Invisible World*. He blamed his fellow-townsman Cotton Mather, especially for failing to learn the lessons of 1692 and becoming involved in the case of the young Boston woman Margaret Rule, thought to be afflicted by devils in 1693. Calef saw Mather's endorsement of Rule's claims as an attempt to start another witch hunt, and so he detailed for the public what he saw as the cruelty and absurdity of many of the original Essex County prosecutions with as much emotive starkness as possible. Calef printed the heartrending words of the executed, such as Mary Esty: "I Petition to your Honours not for my own Life . . . but the Lord he knows it is, if it be possible, that no more Innocent Blood be shed, which undoubtedly cannot be avoided in the way and course you go in." He described the execution of a dog for witchcraft in Andover, the accusation of the minister John Hale's wife, which (Calef suggested cynically) soon changed his mind about the truth of the charges in general, and the depredations of the sheriff on the estates of those accused. Some of his stories are verified by other documentation, but others cannot be checked. This is not to suggest that Calef lied, but a reminder that like all the historiographers of "Salem" he had an opinion that manifests itself in his writings. Calef began the "*j'accuse*" tradition of American witchcraft history, which lasted into the early twentieth century.

His arraignment of Mather has, accordingly, been debated with blistering heat. Mather did not actually attend any of the Salem trials, although like other New England ministers he believed that witchcraft attack was one of God's providences designed to awake a sinful world, and he publicized his opinions. He contributed to a carefully weighed report of ministerial opinion about witchcraft, which could have been used to stop the convictions if it were not for its last paragraph, which advised the vigorous prosecution of suspects. But, fatally for his reputation, he subsequently published his justification of the proceedings and executions. Calef regarded this as contemptible and refuted *Wonders of the Invisible World* point by point. He also, even more damningly, described Mather's attendance at the execution of George Burroughs, a fellow-minister. Burroughs's innocence, said Calef, was amply demonstrated by his speech and prayers from the gallows, and "it seemed to some, that the Spectators would hinder the Execution," which included several other condemned witches. But "as soon as he was turned off [hanged], Mr. Cotton Mather, being mounted upon a Horse, addressed himself to the people . . . to possess the People of his guilt . . . this did somewhat appease the People, and the Execution went on."[56] Mather's reputation never really recovered from this vignette.[57] The debate over his role was not, however, an academic one. Instead it was carried on by public men and occasionally women in genres that appealed to educated, middlingly wealthy Americans of all kinds: general history books and periodicals, public lectures and pamphlets. It was thus made and kept continuously relevant to America's cultural and political development. Two important books set the tone of writings during the eighteenth and early nineteenth centuries.

In 1765 the Massachusetts Governor Thomas Hutchinson wrote the history of his state and the first major history of "Salem." He suspected fraud and superstition, especially in the "afflicted" women and girls, and while he named no names among the ministers and judges, he regarded them as dupes of these girls. Then, following Calef closely, in 1834 the Democrat diplomat George Bancroft returned to the attack on Cotton Mather, accusing him directly of credulity, vanity, and selfishness, in his

*History of the Colonization of the United States of America.* Mather's pernicious activities had begun, said Bancroft, in promoting the execution of a
"friendless emigrant," Goodwife Glover, who was accused by the Goodwin family of Boston in 1688. Mather had ministered to the supposed victims of her witchcraft, and written an account of the case. That Glover
was "a wild Irish woman, of a strange tongue" (Gaelic) and a Catholic had,
Bancroft suggested, made her an ideal sacrifice for a Puritan leadership
made anxious by threats to its power. "The rapid progress of free inquiry
was alarming," he believed, adding that "the cry of witchcraft has been
raised by the priesthood rarely, I think never, except when free inquiry was
advancing." Fears of schism and atheism had prompted further interest in
Satan and his supposed attacks on Christianity, and as soon as accusations were made at Salem another outsider, the Native American "Indian"
Tituba, was beaten into confession. The gallows were then set up, "not for
those who professed themselves witches, but for those who rebuked the
delusion." The trials were a campaign against free thought and liberalism,
led by ambitious ministers and "despotic" magistrates of whom "not one
held office by the suffrage of the people."[58] Hutchinson's deluded oligarchs
had become for Bancroft malignant and xenophobic oppressors, manipu-
lating accusation for their own ends.

Here, viewed through late-eighteenth and early-nineteenth century
eyes, were — fascinatingly — reworkings of all the traits of the original
records, except tentative moderation. The emphasis was still on accusers,
but now the interest was in why had they been so horribly mistaken or
perjured. The tone, too, was accusatorial: now the "afflicted" girls or "the
priesthood" stood arraigned instead of the witch. There was no interest
in the actual "witches" and their viewpoint, except as hapless victims.
And Bancroft in particular ignored the inclusivity of the records while
paradoxically claiming to focus on the issue of whether or not it was an
early form of democracy that was to blame for the trials. He made no
attempt to identify the social or political status of accusers — had he done
so, he would have found both substantial freemen and servants, literate
and illiterate men and women consensually accusing others and joining

with magistrates and ministers to condemn them. Instead, he bypassed the records themselves in pursuit of a didactic myth that built on their concerns and textures but twisted them out of all recognition. But he was not alone in this, for he was responding, as Philip Gould's analysis of early historical romances and minor histories of Salem shows, to almost universal assertions that democracy in the sense of mob rule was to blame for the witchcraft trials. Discussions of colonial witchcraft prosecutions in the period from the French Revolution to the 1830s such as those in the general histories of America, New England, or Massachusetts by Hannah Adams, Jedidiah Morse and Elijah Parish, Abiel Abbot, and Charles A. Goodrich all to some extent blamed "delusion" and "ignorance," which together drove "popular" emotion against witches in a kind of proto-Terror.[59] After Hutchinson, the idea of delusion had become a commonplace, and by 1830 shorthand for public ignorance and "democratic" ambition.

By the time that Bancroft offered his more direct and lengthy consideration, then, histories of witchcraft had turned into proxy meditations on the dangers of mobs and their leaders. There was, says Gould,

> a problem in early republican culture concerning the nature of patriotism itself. Anxieties about people's "passions" were particularly acute for conservatives, who were witnessing the gradual rise of democratic, popular parties. . . . These anxieties were inscribed upon the record of Puritan witch-hunting, particularly the famous (or infamous) episode at Salem in 1692, where the people's zealous passions destroyed social and political order.

Because of this perception of a kind of revolutionary zeal at Salem, in the early nineteenth century the witchcraft trials there became "a historical trope displaying the supposed danger of an emergently popular politics in America" — politics both imported from Europe and homegrown. Novels such as the anonymous *Salem Witchcraft* (1820), *The Witch of New England* (1824), and John Neal's *Rachel Dyer* (1828), as well as James Nelson Barker's *The Tragedy of Superstition* (1824) all echoed this trope.[60] Curiously, when it came to witchcraft and democracy American Federalists, Republicans, Whigs, and Democrats "spoke the same conservative language," says Gould. It was this view that Bancroft tried to counter in 1834 with his attack on Massachusetts's ministers and unelected rulers and his statement that "the common mind of Massachusetts was more wise" than they.[61] His highly successful book set the tone and theme of debate thereafter precisely because it was so polemical.[62]

But it was the Salem mayor, congressman, and Unitarian pastor Charles Wentworth Upham who most effectively articulated the belief that the Salem trials had been the fault of just those solid citizens and public men who were most interested in them: especially the New England clergymen among them. In 1867 Upham published the most professionally researched history of Salem to date, basing it on a series of lectures originally delivered in the 1820s and creating a community history that is still in print. He read the records carefully, unlike most of his predecessors except Hutchinson, but he drew from them a polemical argument that once again blamed some accusers and judges while ignoring others. In one strand of argument, Upham attacked some of the most respectable citizens of 1692 for their quarrels over money and land, which, he suggested, could be seen to predict the patterns of witchcraft accusation. And when he came to discuss Mather and the role of the church in the most controversial passages of the book, he spoke of "perverse misrepresentation," secrecy, and "cunning" in a "purpose of restoring and strengthening the influence of the clerical and spiritual leaders" by fomenting witch-hunting. Upham believed that a cynical political motivation lay behind the conduct of the Mathers, both Cotton and Increase, who were trying to "get up" cases of witch accusation for their own ends. Boldly, he then likened this political manipulation to the "horror and folly" of the panic over the supposed New York "Negro" plot of 1741. Salem's accusers were thus indicted together with the conservative forces of modern "fanaticism" and "superstition" while the defenders and accused were associated with "real and thorough reformation" and "justice." It was an old argument, and — as we have seen — there was justice in the statement that New England ministers were especially interested in witchcraft, just like the English godly from whom they had recently sprung. But Upham's interpretation of that interest was openly hostile to the early Congregational ministers, and because it was backed by a vast weight of new evidence it became the standard history. It displaced decisively the anti-democratic histories of the period before 1830 and, as Bryan F. Le Beau sums up, "Upham established the metaphoric role the Salem witchcraft trials . . . would assume in American history" — one where innocent people fell victim to the schemes of ministers.[63]

But Upham's modernizing restatement of Calef's and Bancroft's view was extreme enough to be challenged by William F. Poole, the librarian of the Boston Athenaeum and a direct descendant of the founders of Cambridge. Poole was incensed by Upham's work. Ignoring its pioneering attempt to reconstruct the community of early Salem, he read it simply as an anti-Mather polemic: a betrayal of the expected American loyalty, to locality, religion, and gentlemanly ancestry. Poole published two answers to Upham, one in the *North American Review* (to which Upham replied) and one anonymous republication of two of his own reviews of *Salem Witchcraft*. The reviews summed his position most pithily. The first was titled "Upham v. Mather," as if the debate were an adversarial lawsuit — an accurate reflection of the bitter accusatorial nature of the debate. It criticized everything about Upham's works, which included the answer to Poole's original article: their length ("many persons . . . will . . . feel their utter inability to wade through the ninety-one pages of small type in double columns"), method ("tangled mass of historical detail"), style ("heavy and monotonous . . . redundant phraseology"), but most of all their conclusions. Poole described the representation of Cotton Mather simply as a "falsification of history." He did indeed convict Upham (and other historians like Abner C. Goodell, who agreed with Upham) of a number of errors of fact and interpretation in statements about the Mathers.

In addition, seeming to forget Calef and Bancroft, Poole complained that "during his life, and for a hundred years after his death, no name in the annals of the Province of Massachusetts, was held in more reverence than that of Cotton Mather, unless it be that of his father." Now, he said, historians were trying "to reverse this contemporaneous record, and to heap reproach upon his name." Upham and his friend Goodell were simply the latest, engaged in a witch hunt that "would hang all the eminent clergymen of the present day." In Upham's mind, said Poole, "they are responsible for all the crimes and outrages in the community." And he dated the beginning of the attack on the Mathers to the "development of 'liberal Christianity' in Massachusetts," by which he meant primarily Unitarianism such as Upham's, and Universalism.[64] Traditional Congregationalism was pitted in Poole's account against more radical churches, in a dispute broadly along conservative/liberal lines. A fear of democracy had been blended with, and to some extent replaced by, a dislike of activist religion that promoted social change. This development was important for future historiography: soon America would see freethinkers and pagans disputing with traditional Christians. But in the mid-nineteenth century it was further complicated by the growth of local American histories of witchcraft.

### State Histories and Their Implications

Whether one blamed democratic mobs or scheming clerics, the liberal-conservative division that shaped the Upham-Poole argument was often inflected, for individual historians, by a tendency to deflect blame from the localities that they favored and to give that deflection a political spin. Forrest Morgan in his "Witchcraft in Connecticut" of 1906 spoke of "other American colonies considering themselves entitled to throw stones at the Puritans," while others felt that the nation's witchcraft history had "been exploited by writers abroad."[65] But some brought the blame game down to the level of individual states. Connecticut writers were especially prone to comparing their history favorably with that of others. The Connecticut historian J. Hammond Trumbull wrote in 1850 that the case of Elizabeth Garlick was the first to be tried by the colony's General Court, taking the trouble to note that it was "(an *imported* case, by the way)," because Garlick was from Long Island, then part of Connecticut but now in New York State.[66] Connecticut had acquired a reputation as "the straight man" of

American witchcraft history, "stable and tranquil," "the Land of Steady Habits," ever since Benjamin Trumbull (ancestor of J. Hammond) had emerged triumphantly from his pioneering study of its records in the late eighteenth century having found no cases of witchcraft there. Even once it had been realized that, what with the turmoil of famines, "Indian" wars, epidemics, and religious controversies, the early colony was neither stable nor tranquil, the belief that few witches had been prosecuted there remained. By 1904, Sherman W. Adams and Henry R. Stiles could still argue that only two people were believed to have been executed for witchcraft in Connecticut, that even these executions were not certain, and that even if they were substantiated "it is certain that the *Connecticut* colony was not swept by the whirlwind of superstition which disturbed the Massachusetts colony."[67] John M. Taylor likewise wrote of the "contrasts" between Massachusetts's record of prosecution and "the more cautious and saner methods of procedure that obtained in the government of Connecticut."[68]

Yet some of the same historians often also offered acidic critiques of their past. Speaking of Katherine Harrison, it was Adams and Stiles who wrote that "the New Yorkers . . . handled 'the witch' with more wisdom and better success than the Yankees." As we have seen, they might rather have chosen to argue for the strong element of merciful conscience evident in the lengthy and minute records of Harrison's trial at Hartford. Despite her imprisonment and eventual removal from the state, they might have seen her comparatively as one of the most scrupulously treated suspects in the history of American witchcraft. What they saw, however, was shame and injustice, despite their desire to defend their state. Sometimes these contradictory impulses of sheepish admission and hopeful rebuttal even jostled each other in the same sentence: Wethersfield "enjoys the unenviable distinction of having furnished a majority of the *proven* (?) cases of witchcraft occurring in Connecticut." What does that emphasis and question mark mean?[69] In the late nineteenth century the internal New England dialogue about witchcraft thus uneasily spanned both the arraignment of particular historical figures and a more pointed focus on the polities and state cultures that had produced the witch trials. State historians wrestled with conflicting impulses of guilt and pride, and often resolved this discomfort by accusing other polities of ignorance or religious mania. The rhetoric of superstition versus enlightenment thus often included reference to New York Spiritualism and the "transparent Jugglery . . . which has peopled the Salt Lake Regions."[70] The unspoken theme of the debate was what modern America might learn from different state cultures as she rebuilt herself after the Civil War and entered the twentieth century. Usually it remained unspoken.

The most overt statement of the political arguments being aired in an apparently obscure antiquarian enquiry into comparative colonial injustice is in Charles H. Levermore's "Witchcraft in Connecticut" of 1885. Levermore was a prominent scholar and educator, the founder of Adelphi College, New York, and president of the New York Peace Society from 1917 to '24. He wrote extensively on New England history and politics, and was an important figure across the region and nationally. When he came to write about witchcraft, his first impulses were to defend New England against accusations of credulity and cruelty, and then to rank and judge the relative guilt of various colonial cultures. But from this initially provincial-sounding beginning came some political conclusions that were not favorable to his chosen subject, Connecticut, at all:

> the panic of 1692 was not an event peculiar to Massachusetts, or to New England . . . Anywhere in the Christian world . . . neighbourhood gossip, joined to the manifestations of "nervous force" . . . produced similar results. But let it be remembered that the New England Puritans were the first of Englishmen to disregard accusations of witchcraft, and that the typical colonies of Puritan New Haven, Separatist Plymouth and Independent Rhode Island, never knew a conviction for witchcraft within their borders. . . . Doubtless a larger number of people suffered in Massachusetts for the fictitious crime of "Familiarity with ye Devill" than in any other of the thirteen colonies, but the majority of the victims were sacrificed at one time and place to an uncontrollable popular frenzy. Prior to that time it is historic fact that public instances of this delusion had occurred most frequently in the colony of Connecticut.[71]

The information is mostly true, although New Haven colonial magistrates at the Fairfield court must have been responsible at least for the execution of "Goodwife" Knapp in 1653, but the interpretation and use made of it are highly debatable.[72] What is interesting, therefore, is not Levermore's accuracy, but his anxious desire to reapportion blame.

Levermore was motivated by two separate beliefs in his drive to defend Massachusetts against "an ill-report beyond the measure of its deserts" and to shift some blame to Connecticut. The first was a religious one: his feeling that Massachusetts's Puritanism was being used as a "scapegoat." The second was related, but more politically complex. It was that, as he put it in a reworking of his original article in 1892, "the theocratic system of New Haven proved to be safer than the democracy of Connecticut or the aristocracy of Massachusetts" for accused witches. If Massachusetts had been "stained with witches' blood" it was a historical accident due to "a bevy of malicious girls and a group of stupid or scheming ministers," not its hapless godly magistracy or wider religious culture. "Democratic" Connecticut, meanwhile, was for a good part of her history *more* guilty than her northern neighbor, and was saved from further guilt not so much because of "popular enlightenment" but, again, by "the moderation and humanity of the magistrates." Yet New Haven alone had the right governmental instincts. Here, argued Levermore, the notion of trial by jury and other democratic secularisms had been overridden by both ministerial and magisterial wisdom combined. Here, nuisances like the rebel and (naturally) witch-accuser Roger Ludlow, sued for slandering the supposed "witch" Mary Staples in 1654, would be countered by solid men like John Davenport and his colleagues. "Magistrate [Samuel] Eaton," said Levermore of the trials of Elizabeth Godman at New Haven in 1653 and 1655, "was cool-headed and too good a lawyer to over-estimate 'the verdict of the vicinage,'" and Godman was released on both occasions. Surprisingly, then, theocracy was the best guardian of individual life and liberty, with the government of oligarchs coming second and — Levermore's most important conclusion — democracy, even in its limited early modern form, a poor third. What really mattered, once again, was whether *democ-*

*racy* was dangerous or not: a restatement of the old conservative position after half a century of the liberal indictment of repressive elites, and one grounded in localized American history.

Yet, as we have seen from the records, there was in reality little observable distinction between the social class and moral fiber of the witch accusers and magistrates of New Haven, Connecticut, and those of Massachusetts, despite Levermore's mythmaking rhetoric. In fact, the records of Elizabeth Godman's 1655 trial suggest that Samuel Eaton or members of his household were among her *accusers*: "other passages Ther were aboute Goodwife Hodgkins churning, and at Mr Samuell Eatons also, who after some discontent with her [Godman], or some thing spoke of her, have mett with many hinderances in there way."[73] But, for Levermore — regardless of the records (as usual) — men who were educated, socially aware *and* good churchmen were those most likely to make good judgments on witchcraft, as on other matters. The local populace could not be trusted. Colonial aristocracy, although it was not to blame for the outbreaks of injustice occurring in its jurisdiction, was still unsound, with its rivalries and mutinies based on personal aggrandizement (as the Ludlow incident showed) and conducive to oppressive tendencies. Like others, Levermore was inclined to see Cotton Mather as a demagogue: "there was in Connecticut no Cotton Mather to pester the community with distorted learning and hidden ambitions."[74] Individual ministers, therefore, might be corrupt and ambitious. Only the combination of proper magisterial training with ministerial responsibility, government strengthened and tempered by Christianity, where godly elites worked together, democracy was inclusive but limited in its authority and "gaps between social classes were small," was the proper one. As Levermore wrote about the witch-hunting past state by state and polity by polity, he thus articulated precisely, as others had done before him, his vision for Gilded Age America and the world.[75]

*Civil War and a Changing America*

Americans' anxiety about popular politics and interstate differences was exacerbated by the nation's having almost torn itself into two different countries in the Civil War. To the anxiety expressed about popular revolt in the witchcraft debate — identified by Gould in the first half of the nineteenth century and resurgent by the 1880s — and the interstate comparisons that accompanied that anxiety, the north-south divide thus added a further political meaning, which found its way into witchcraft history. In 1869 Samuel Gardner Drake rebuked "a south-western Head of the Church" for twitting New England with its witch-hanging past and speculating that Satan "took so remarkable a Fancy to the early Yankees" because of "some secret Congeniality of Feeling between the two."[76] In *Putnam's Magazine*, also in 1869, W. C. Elam launched a vitriolic attack on Virginia, based in part — and this was his opening argument — on her historians' perceived refusal to acknowledge that their ancestors, like the Massachusetts Puritans, had persecuted witches.

> Old Virginia has self-complacently held herself guiltless of those crimes and follies which she has attributed to New England. When a Virginian is in his most unwholesome frame of mind against the "Yankees," he is apt to refer, in terms either derisive or denunciatory, to the New England trials and executions for witchcraft. In vain have the descendants of the Puritans endeavoured to palliate the errors of their ancestors, by proving the witchcraft delusion to have been rather the malady of the age than the crime of the individuals who labored under it. The Virginian was not to be propitiated nor silenced by any such process of confession and avoidance. *His* forefathers had escaped the contagion, and he triumphed in the boast, too easily credited, that the "sacred soil of Old Virginia" had never been desecrated by a trial for witchcraft. Yet this boast is not warranted by facts . . .[77]

Elam went on to describe and examine the case of Grace Sherwood. He asserted gleefully, moreover, that Sherwood was "a negress" or "at least a mulatto of the despised 'free nigger' order." Although he did not elaborate on the meaning of this, there was no need: in the context of his article,

Sherwood was already positioned clearly as a victim of proto-Confeder-ate pro-slavery prejudice. Elam's reproof continued with an account of an attempt made at Abingdon, Virginia, by "a poor white" to murder a man he suspected of bewitching him — in 1838. It was concluded with five pages demonstrating to his northern reader that early modern Virginia was just as guilty as Massachusetts of ignorance, religious intolerance, and the devising of cruel, illiberal law codes.

Elam had some grounds for attempting to rewrite the history of Ameri-can witchcraft, as we have seen. The notoriety of the Essex County cases from the Mather-Calef dispute to the present distorted (and distorts) that history, and there was no account of southern colonial witchcraft to coun-ter this. When Elam wrote, the publication of Upham's *Salem Witchcraft* had just focused attention even more securely on Massachusetts. In con-trast, it was not until the 1880s, and especially the 1894–95 series of articles in the *William and Mary Quarterly Historical Magazine*, that historians brought Grace Sherwood's trial records in full to the attention of scholarly Virginians. In answer to Elam's polemic on Sherwood's race, the author of the *WMQ* articles, Edward W. James, provided evidence that "she was, in fact, the daughter of a substantial mechanic and small landowner" whom records suggested was white, adding acidly that "a great many fanciful things have been written about Sherwood's origin and position in life by ingenious authors, who, instead of searching the records for facts, have tortured their imaginations for theories."[78] As Elam might have known, had Sherwood been black, she would almost certainly have been clearly described as such, although he may be right when he suggests that she was a darker-skinned woman.[79] Either way, he made full use of the witchcraft trial record to portray the South as backward and racist. Impoverished and dislocated, the southern historical establishment was unable to reply for over two decades. Meanwhile, the stick was taken up by, among oth-ers, John Gorham Palfrey, who likened the apologists for witch-hangings to those northerners who supported the southern case for the return of fugitive slaves.[80]

All these undercurrents of interstate, north-south, and liberal-conservative tension bubbled under the surface of writing about American witchcraft from 1700 to well after 1900. The cases of conscience of the witch-accusing colonists had become matters of vicious polemic for their descendants, where a strong opinion for or against democracy or oligarchy mattered far more than a thoughtful reading of actual court records. And in the years before the First World War, the debate developed further to focus on the issues of most concern to modern Americans: immigration, its relationship to America's Anglophile, Anglophone identity, and America's role in Europe, which was moving toward and into war. In 1907 to '11, a set-piece battle was fought between Cornell's George Lincoln Burr and Harvard's George Lyman Kittredge on the subject. Professor Kittredge spoke first, in 1907, and continued to hold his views more or less unchanged until and beyond the publication of his magisterial *Witchcraft in Old and New England* in 1929. Kittredge was sensitive to the smallest nuance of localized feeling about witchcraft. He made this clear from the first, restating it in the preface of the book: "My Salem friends will expect me to remind the reader that the great outbreak of 1692 occurred in Salem *Village*, now Danvers, though the trials were held at Salem." Kittredge then proceeded logically to exonerate Massachusetts, New England, and finally the New World in general. The Salem trials were "not . . . an abnormal outbreak of fanaticism," but "a mere incident, a brief and transitory episode" in the wider world history of "a terrible, but perfectly natural, superstition." New Englanders did not invent belief in witchcraft, or spectral evidence, and nor did Puritans — and it was not only Puritans who believed in it. In fact, in the seventeenth century it was almost impossible to disprove either the specifics of witchcraft accusations or a general belief in its existence, and everyone from Bacon to Boyle, Tory and nonconformist alike, agreed. The colonists of Massachusetts, Kittredge argued, therefore brought their beliefs in witchcraft with them from Old England, and it was no surprise that with their perception of the new world's "heathen population" as "devil-worshipping neighbors" that they thought that Satan was among them. Any Londoner, Yorkshireman, or

Devonian would have thought the same. "Our forefathers," said Kittredge "believed in witchcraft not because they were Puritans, not because they were Colonials, not because they were New Englanders, but because they were men of their time."[81]

At first sight, this argument was simply a further needful corrective to the strictures of Upham on Mather, or the jibes of non–New Englanders noted by Levermore. Kittredge was quite right to point out that it was abnormal in the early modern period not to believe in *malefic* witchcraft, although by the 1690s this consensus had broken down in England into a highly politicized dissension that *could* accommodate the denial of witches' existence, or at the least their criminality. He was also right to note that demonology was an inevitable extension of other early modern discourses, a stance taken up most recently by historians of linguistics.[82] But as Kittredge's case builds, one can see why despite its intellectual merits Professor Burr found it troubling. Kittredge seemed to assume that all his readers would have Puritan "forefathers" in New England, which was no longer the case for many Americans, never mind readers in other countries. If, however, he was speaking simply to the New England elite and especially to his fellow-historians, he was certainly correct — even Burr had forebears in Springfield, Massachusetts, and Fairfield, Connecticut, and the little world of American academe was as exclusive as that anywhere in Europe. But what were readers outside this brahmin circle to make of Kittredge's assertions that "the immediate responsibility for actual prosecution rests frequently, if not in the majority of cases . . . on the rank and file of the community" or that "the belief in witchcraft is still pervasive among the peasantry of Europe, and to a considerable extent among the foreign-born population of this country"? If the ordinary American (yet again) and especially the newly immigrant hyphenated American from witch-hunting Europe were to blame for witch trials, Kittredge seemed to suggest, then "it is not permissible to blame our ancestors." He went further: it could even be said that "the facts are distinctly creditable to our ancestors" for stopping the prosecutions when they did. Kittredge, of course, was descended from the magistracy and clergy of which he spoke, and his heartfelt defense of his own class, ethnicity, and culture caused Burr great discomfort, falling as it did into the conservative tradition of blaming anyone other than the New England elite.

Burr's troubled reply was delivered in the same forum where Kittredge's original paper was given, a meeting of the American Antiquarian Society at Worcester, Massachusetts, in 1911. And, interestingly, he was keen to display his own colonial credentials to engage the sympathy of his august audience:

> If to any here it seem treason to those who made New England to dissent from aught that can be urged in their praise, bear with me while I plead that, despite my birth and home in the wilds beyond the Hudson, there flows in my veins none but New England blood.[83]

Burr spoke of his Puritan forebears, and he used the same language as Kittredge: "our ancestors." But perhaps his family's remove from Fairfield to Oramel, New York, and with it a defection to the Baptist church, did influence his thinking, for he stated immediately and flatly his opinion that Kittredge had been "much more generous to our ancestors than I can find it in my conscience to deem fair." "To urge in defense of those who — in New England or elsewhere — hung women as witches that the belief in witchcraft is universal seems a juggling with words," said Burr, for witchcraft "has widely different meanings." Many peoples certainly engaged in magic and non-Christian religion, but many observers recognized (and had recognized in the past) that these were not witchcraft. The paganism of the ancient Europeans, the folk magics of seventeenth-century emigrants, and the religious beliefs of Native Americans could not all be described as "witchcraft," and most definitely not in the sense that demonologists such as Increase and Cotton Mather used the word. Yet "this was precisely the attitude of Christianity," which defined everything non-Christian as demonic and so created and criminalized the specific notion of witchcraft with which Burr and Kittredge were dealing. Moreover, the Puritans clung more tightly to this belief than any other Christians and ought to bear more responsibility for the consequence, Burr argued.[84]

Burr had long been interested in the libertarian, tolerant aspects of the thought of European Anabaptists like Sebastian Franck and Sebastian Castellio, and from them he derived his view that when the Catholic Church in Europe decided during the early Renaissance period to reclassify as "witchcraft" those beliefs it had previously tolerated or derided as superstition, others faced no obligation to follow suit. But Calvinists and especially the English and colonial godly, upper and lower classes, did so with enthusiasm. This was a choice that could not be explained away by a supposedly consensual pan-European view imported to America. Therefore, Burr concluded, "I cannot acquit our ancestors on the ground that their belief in witchcraft was universal or was not discreditable or was more logical than disbelief." In fact, "I am forced to admit that it was superstitious and bigoted and cruel, even by the standards of their own time." Burr was motivated to make these claims not simply out of a dislike of Kittredge's reading of history but because:

> if I would have History unflinching, it is not because I think we are better than our fathers. It is because deep in ourselves, I feel stirring the impulses which led to their mistakes. It is because I fear that they who begin by excusing their ancestors may end by excusing themselves.[85]

Burr gave the debate about witchcraft history an overtly moralistic and presentist focus, and it was no accident that he and Kittredge differed not just over their response to the political culture, class, and ethnicity of witchcraft accusers in the past, but over modern American politics, too. Their most obvious difference was over the European war of 1914–18: Burr supported intervention; Kittredge did not.

An international dimension had thus been added to the habitual debates played out in discussion of America's witchcraft history. Was it right to combat injustice wherever it occurred, to become the world's policeman? Burr, while in no sense a warmonger, believed that America belonged in a war that was being fought for liberties that had been outraged by the German invasion of neutral Belgium. Consistent with his historical theories, he could not "excuse" himself. He undertook military training and offered his support when friends and students volunteered. Kittredge, meanwhile, despite his much-prized English descent, opposed entry to both the First and Second World Wars. He was unwilling to differentiate between European factions, in his own lifetime as in the early modern period. Americans were different, having moved away from European delusions into anti-imperial isolation. They should not be expected to sort out political problems in the countries from which their most recent immigrants had fled. And Kittredge and Burr were not the only witchcraft historians to extend their historiographical stance into contemporary international politics. In 1924 Charles H. Levermore won the Bok Peace Prize with a vision of firm, ethically driven governance that bore a remarkable resemblance to that which he had imagined in early modern New Haven. Now it was expressed primarily in a plan to participate in the League of Nations and a World Court. The Levermore plan would rein in European demagogues and fetter American isolationists alike by removing key decisions from the parochial national electorates whom he had so denigrated as witch-accusers in 1885.[86]

***

The adversarial debate of 1700 to 1930, for all its shifting ground and contemporary resonances, had proved unable to determine which class, political group, or sect of Americans was responsible for witchcraft accusation — unsurprisingly, since it tended to attribute malice to whichever accusers, ministers, or judges were selected as uniquely blameworthy, and to ignore the written records almost completely. In fact, as we have seen, malice was strikingly rare in the records: accusations were not obviously made for cynical political reasons or personal gain. They show clearly, too, that a consensual approach was adopted in American courts: it was not possible for a Cotton Mather, a John Gibson, an Anthony Morse, or a Bethiah Carter to "get up" an accusation unaided, however much they wrote or had written for them about the matter. A witchcraft accusation had to be widely supported and sustained by conscientious agreement across social groups. Burr was right: it was time to stop excusing one group at the expense of accusing another, and to move on from a focus on accusation generally. In Chapter 3 we shall explore how the literature of American witchcraft moved from accusing to understanding, and from accusers to witches as its primary focus.

Meanwhile, however, eighteenth-, nineteenth-, and early-twentieth-century political historians cast long shadows over America's understanding of her witchcraft history. Upham is still the favorite authority on "Salem" witchcraft, and his and Burr's view — a summation of liberal-Christian impulses expressed in the medium of witchcraft history — is dominant in liberal American culture. But something of Levermore's and especially Kittredge's stance — highly protective of the ruling forefathers of the nation — remains too. And the historians of particular states have also enjoyed a remarkable longevity. So, struggling to tell their own version of the truth, both to honor their "strong and heroic" ancestors and to promote inclusive and democratic American beliefs, scholars, genealogists, local historians, and museum curators have, essentially, to choose between or synthesize two mythic versions of the past: the deluded, persecuting patriarchs and the wise, if not infallible, fathers of the nation, both expressed frequently in highly localized terms.[87] They have done so with more or less success from Colonial Williamsburg to the Salem Witch Museum, and the next chapter explores their endeavors.

## 2

## "OUR WITCH": LOCAL HISTORIES

## OF AMERICA'S WITCHES

Witches . . . were rare in the extreme South. Warm weather or something else discouraged immigration.

Voice of Giles Cory: "More weight! More weight!"
Senator Yokell: "Mr. McDee, have you ever been a member of the Communist Party?"
Mac stands mute.[1]

### Danvers and "Witch City": The World Redeemed from Superstition's Sway?

On 17 December 1875 a remarkable meeting took place in the New England Genealogical Rooms in Boston. It marked a turning point in the historiography of American witchcraft, and the transformation of the most famous of the books dealing specifically with the American witchcraft trials into an icon of modernity, literally setting it in stone. The meeting was a gathering of some of the descendants of Rebecca Nurse, the elderly godly woman hanged for witchcraft at Salem in 1692, and their purpose was to establish an association and raise funds to build a monument to her memory. The association took its understanding of what had happened to Rebecca and her fellow accused directly from Charles W. Upham's account of the Salem witch trials, and to emphasize his continued ghostly dominance of the proceedings his son William P. Upham began to document the proceedings of the association with as much care as Charles had used in reconstructing the events of 1692. William was married to one of Rebecca Nurse's descendants, and from his account we can follow the thinking and actions of the association as they moved toward the triumphant completion of their project ten years later. The most significant events were a series of set-piece fund-raisers, including a "Basket Picnic" that became an annual event. The culmination of the process was a lengthy and solemn series of dedicatory events on the afternoon of 30 July 1885.

The Nourse Monument Association — its title using the spelling of the family name that was current among Rebecca's nineteenth-century descendants — symbolized the change in attitude toward the witches of American history that had taken place since around 1700 and continued through the histories of the nineteenth century. The game of mutual blame and self-accusation continued unabated, and the witches were seen as the victims of either a malign ministry or magistracy or of popular ignorance. But feeling about how the guilt of their executions should be reflected in the material world beyond the historical journal altered decisively. For over a century no one had wished to remember the terrible events of 1692. But in "Alice Doane's Appeal" in 1835 Nathaniel Hawthorne had regretted that on "Gallows Hill" at Salem there was "no relic of old, nor lettered stone of later days" to help remember the witches.[2] In 1868 Henry Wadsworth Longfellow's play *Giles Corey of the Salem Farms* had made a hero out of the most prominent male victim of the trials, suggesting that "this poor man . . . will be counted as a martyr."[3] And in the period after the Civil War the country was being dotted with memorials to a more recent sacrifice. In this climate of sorrowful pride, William P. Upham echoed the words of his father:

in some coming day, a sense of justice, appreciation of moral firmness, sympathy for suffering innocence, a diffusion of refined sensibility, a discriminating discernment of what is really worthy of commemoration among men, a rectified taste, a generous public spirit and a gratitude for the light that surrounds and protects us against error, folly and fanaticism, shall demand the rearing of a suitable monument to the memory of those who in 1692 preferred death to a falsehood.

After half a century of wishing, it was now time to *do something* about America's witchcraft history. It should be something that could be seen and felt by everyone in American society, and could symbolize in such lofty terms a change in attitude, America's coming of age, an atonement for past sins. Salem could now move beyond apologic into commemoration.[4]

The form of commemoration chosen in 1875 and built in 1885 was interestingly symptomatic of the ways in which the mythic aspects of the Salem witchcraft case were developing. First, the proposed monument commemorated only Rebecca Nurse, and not the nineteen other people who had been killed or the many people who suffered loss of goods and reputation and were imprisoned as a result of the decisions of the court in 1692. Rebecca was emerging as the paradigmatic example of the injustice of the "delusion." She had been self-evidently good and godly, a church member who had protested her innocence and piety strongly in answers that were available for inspection in Salem's records and had been publicized not just by Upham but in William Elliot Woodward's edition of the records in 1864. The court's jury had found her not guilty until it had been suggested to them by the magistrates that they might wish to reconsider their verdict, so some had doubts about the legality of her execution, as well as its justice. Her neighbors had signed a statement attesting her good character, also still extant. She was aged, frail, and partially deaf, an eminently respectable wife, mother, and grandmother, and from the earliest sympathetic accounts of the Salem trials historians had advanced her as the shining example of a transparently guiltless person unjustly condemned. Now she was almost canonized, as the Reverend Fielder Israel referred to her in his commemorative address in Miltonic terms as a "slaughtered saint."[5] She was the ideal candidate for uncontroversial commemoration: not cantankerous, criminal, or overly assertive; not morally suspect; and not problematic in racial, sexual, or any other terms.[6]

Second, her commemorators were members of her own family. Although nearly two hundred people became involved in the funding and erection of the Rebecca Nurse monument, the inspiration for its building and its actual design came from her lineal descendants. Walter B. Nourse of Worcester, Massachusetts, contributed the resources of his architectural practice to the campaign and designed the simple obelisk himself. The family kept tight control over the project, dominating the board of the association under its President Benjamin F. Nourse and Vice Presidents Benjamin B. Nourse and Francis Nourse, and the monument was erected on land belonging to the Nourses at their old family home in Danvers. They made no call for public funding from taxes: private subscription raised the whole sum of $527.52 needed for the monument, with an extra $80.17 going to endow the monument lot so that it should be fenced and maintained in perpetuity. Many of the contributors who were not Nourses were members of the churches of Danvers and Salem, so that, third, the project was carried on under the auspices of the church community, with not only its blessing but also its active promotion. This became especially clear at the dedicatory events in 1885. They began with what amounted to a Puritan exercise, a series of sermonic lectures in the First Church of Danvers, interspersed with hymn singing. The congregation was addressed first by Fielder Israel, pastor of Danvers (once Salem Village, scene of the first accusations), and then by the Reverend Charles B. Rice, pastor of Salem's First Church. Rebecca Nurse had been a member of the Danvers congregation, and it was evident that her commemoration was an opportunity for the church to purge itself of guilt and distance its modern incarnation from its past errors.[7]

Fielder Israel told his six hundred assembled listeners that the ancestral belief in witchcraft "had corrupted the minds of the people and permeated the life of the Christian Church with its malevolent spirit" — now it was time to heed Charles W. Upham's words and acknowledge "what is really

worthy of commemoration among men." But Charles B. Rice of Salem
went much further. His church had been at the heart of the revision of
American beliefs about the Puritan past, not only because of Upham's pas-
torate, which had preceded his own there and had produced *Salem Witchcraft*, but because of its highly controversial conversion to Unitarianism,
of which Upham had been a part and which Rice now embodied. Salem's
First Church had embraced what to William F. Poole had been pernicious
"liberal Christianity," and to its founders would have been heresy.[8] For
Rice, then, it was not enough simply to note the wider changes in church
beliefs: a radical statement of personal responsibility was needed, in keeping with his own religious revisionism and the determinedly material
focus of the Nourses' campaign. Accordingly, he offered a striking testament, which contrasted uncomfortably with Israel's gentle platitudes:

> As our predecessors the pastors of both these churches sinned in the for-
> mer evil days, it was judged that we ought both to make confession and
> explanation. . . . The children of any of those who have suffered grievous
> injury in the former generations may properly take redress from man-
> kind in the following ages . . . there is a public interest also with every
> man demanding that public errors of the past should stand in the light
> and be reproved. . . . [O]ur Puritan fathers . . . should not have failed . . .
> we cannot read the record without sorrow and shame. . . . We mean to be
> warned by their errors, and to do better than they wherever we can.[9]

It was Rice's extraordinarily pointed speech that set the tone of the day
and embodied the association's endeavors over the previous decade. For
the Nourses and their fellow campaigners, it was not enough that a history of the belief in witchcraft be offered and deplored in general terms.
What mattered was that political change and conversion take place here
and now, and be symbolized in a concrete, material way — in practice and
not just words, in works and not just faith. By the act of erecting a monument, and offering public penance for past wrongs, a general Whiggish
sense of the progress of human history was in fact being transformed into
the righting of specific wrongs in a way that had the potential to become
highly symbolic, especially in religious terms.

This potential was emphasized by two elements of the dedication ceremonies that William P. Upham was careful to mention in his account of
the proceedings. The first was the invitation of a representative of the Society of Friends, Miss Elizabeth T. Larkin. Miss Larkin was unable to attend,
but Upham thought her inclusion so vital to his *Account* that he printed
in full her letter apologetically declining the invitation. Why should he
do so? Because when Americans thought of the persecution of witches by
their Puritan forebears, they also thought of their persecution of Quakers (as Charles H. Levermore noted when he spoke of his Southern and
Western friends in Chapter 1). Miss Larkin's invitation by the committee
was another way of marking the advances of modern society in denomi-
national tolerance, and reminding modern Americans of its importance.
And a small change made to the inscription on the Rebecca Nurse monument itself also indicated that its creators were thinking as much of the
edification of their contemporaries as of the sins of their fathers. The eminent New England poet John Greenleaf Whittier had been asked to write
four lines for the monument, and his first draft had been as follows:

> Rest Christian martyr who for Truth could die
> When all about thee owned the hideous Lie!
> By souls like thine from Superstition's sway
> Redeemed at last, the world breathes free to-day.

But the lines proved to be slightly too long to fit in the allocated space, and
Whittier was informed that they would have to be broken up. The correspondence on this matter prompted a rethink and in conjunction with the
committee, he suggested a new version:

> O Christian Martyr! who for Truth could die
> When all about thee owned the hideous Lie!
> The world, redeemed from Superstition's sway,
> Is breathing freer for thy sake to-day.[10]

Gone in the second draft is the presumption of total present freedom,
replaced instead by the qualified "freer." And there is no mention of "rest"
in the new inscription, no closing "at last." Instead it is an impassioned

apostrophe to Rebecca Nurse, with the implication that only by emulating her example can the freedom of the world be enlarged further — the battle is emphatically not yet over.[11]

It was a message emphasized over a century later when, alongside the human rights advocate Elie Wiesel, Danvers chose to invite the New York playwright Arthur Miller to the dedication of its 1992 tercentennial memorial to all the "Salem witches." In the early 1950s, Miller had begun to think that the Salem witchcraft trials offered a useful parallel with current political events, as had the poet William Carlos Williams in the late 1940s.[12] As Cold War suspicion of the Soviet Union deepened in America, a drive to find Communists and spies had begun, led on Capitol Hill by the House Un-American Activities Committee (HUAC) and its chairman, Senator Joseph McCarthy. Writers, activists, artists, filmmakers, and other supposedly leftist subversives were called before the committee and examined. Simultaneously, a Jewish couple, Julius and Ethel Rosenberg, were convicted of treason and eventually executed. The House Un-American Activities Committee's interrogations, and even the mere fact of having been called before it, ended careers and plunged suspects into financial and social ruin. To be accused of being un-American was a terrible fate. In Miller's justly famous 1953 play *The Crucible* (revised with additional commentary in 1958), the witches therefore came to represent those accused of Communist sympathies by HUAC. As Miller said in his 1958 additions to the play:

> in America any man who is not reactionary in his views is open to the charge of alliance with the Red hell. . . . A political policy is equated with moral right, and opposition to it with diabolical malevolence.

With Miller's invitation to the 1992 ceremonies, once again the commemorative activities at Danvers, and also this time at Salem (which dedicated its own memorial), focused on the continuing political and social relevance of the events of 1692, from a liberal, now left-wing, perspective. The supposed common sense of the old Dutch New Yorkers was imported to modern Massachusetts in the form of two modern Jewish campaigners.

The Auschwitz survivor Wiesel's presence reminded everyone of prejudice and genocide against Jews and the possibilities of heroic resistance to persecution, while Miller's play celebrated in his troubled hero John Proctor precisely the virtues that Whittier saw in Rebecca Nurse a century before: a commitment to truth and freedom and an unwillingness to compromise personal integrity, even when refusal meant death.

But Miller's play was not just about national politics. It also contained a surprising strand of conservatism: a condemnation of feminine wiles that had been expressed before in witchcraft fiction. In 1903 Marvin Dana's novel *A Puritan Witch* told the story of the deranged and jealous Anna, who tried to get her rival for the love of John Wicker executed as a witch.[13] Similarly, Miller's Abigail Williams attempts to dispose of John Proctor's wife Elizabeth after beginning an affair with John. The literary critic James J. Martine ascribed this misogynistic sexualization of the story to Miller's increasingly strained relationship with his first wife and Marilyn Monroe, whom he would marry in 1956. Miller confirmed this reading himself in 1996 as he reflected on his new film adaptation of the play: "My own marriage of twelve years was teetering and I knew more than I wished to know about where the blame lay . . . [John Proctor] demonstrated that a clear moral outcry could still spring even from an ambiguously blemished soul."[14] In developing his ideas from the records at Salem, then, Miller spun from his own troubles a love triangle consisting of John and Elizabeth Proctor and Abigail Williams, who in reality was only eleven or twelve in 1692, while John was in his sixties.[15] It is Proctor's guilt that drives much of the action, as well as Abigail's malevolence and Elizabeth's chilly dutifulness. Despite Miller's heroic reputation for resisting persecution, this was curiously at odds with the way that many Salem citizens wished to remember the witch trials. For some Americans they were classic examples of male violence against women rather than a tragedy of American masculinity.

By the 1990s Salem society contained a strong feminist element, with many practicing Wiccans and Witches keen to ascribe at least some of the trials to precisely the male fears about women's sexual power that fuel

Miller's play. As we shall see in Chapters 3 and 4, their belief that what happened at Salem and elsewhere when witches were accused was a kind of patriarchal violence has long roots in the American women's suffrage movement and in the fiction and historiography of Salem since about 1930. One of the ways in which witches are unofficially memorialized at Salem, as distinct from Danvers, is therefore as women. In fact, along with John Proctor, four other men were executed: George Jacobs, John Willard, Samuel Wardwell, and the minister George Burroughs. One, Giles Corey, was pressed to death because he refused to enter a plea at his trial, and Roger Toothaker died in prison. Many other men were arrested and questioned, and many of their accusers, and the accusers of the women who were condemned, were women themselves. The museums and visitor attractions at Salem, then, walk a difficult line. Some are keen to offer a balanced and factual representation of what happened, while others prefer a simpler story that sometimes bears little relation to actual events in 1692. Almost all the items on sale show a female witch, usually on a broomstick (some of the witches of 1692 were said to ride on poles, but not brooms), sometimes as a goddess or hag. From the 1880s, when — at the time of the Rebecca Nurse commemoration — Salem first began to print guidebooks and postcards for tourists, the flying female witch gradually became the city's emblem, appearing on spoons, plates, tins, pipe bowls, coasters, mugs, posters, bottles, and even the police department's badge. In shops and attractions, some of the information offered both formally and informally suggests that women were the primary focus of "persecution" because "men are afraid of women's power to give birth," "male physicians wanted to stamp out women's herbal medicine," or, more simply, "men just felt threatened by women."[16]

Salem's approach is very different to that at Salem Village itself. Danvers is a sleepy, pretty, suburban village, where quaint old signs direct the visitor to the sites of significant witchcraft-related events: the old training ground, the old meetinghouse, the Witches Memorial, Ingersoll's ordinary, the Rebecca Nurse house. It is easy to get lost, and even easier to worry that you might be trespassing on quiet private lives. Is this the site of

Samuel Parris's house or someone's garden? Is it really fair to bother these nice people with the embarrassing events of three centuries ago? Danvers wears its history with dignified reserve. For the 1992 commemoration, the Danvers archivist Richard B. Trask produced a modest and accurate little volume that allowed the accused and accusers to speak for themselves in careful transcripts of original documents.[17] Salem, meanwhile, proclaims its witchcraft history from the rooftops. Marilynne K. Roach suggests that the town has found itself with a "huckster reputation," and that some people involved in the commemorations in 1992 felt that this overshadowed the serious political points they were trying to make about freedom and justice.[18] Yet Salem is a lively community that has made an astonishing success out of a dreadful tragedy, overcoming the loss of traditional industries in a way that contrasts sharply with other communities in the state. The town bustles with witchcraft museums and souvenir shops, magic supply stores, bookstores, and witch-themed events. There are guided tours and books of self-guided ones, and video documentaries and full-length films for sale, including *Three Sovereigns for Sarah*, the 1985 dramatization of the story of Sarah Cloyce that was filmed in a reconstruction of the Salem Village meetinghouse built on the Nurse homestead. The rebuilt meetinghouse itself is now part of the tourist trail.[19] Goths, alternative therapists, and Wiccans run businesses and workshops. The town has a much-discussed "Official Witch," Laurie Cabot.[20] While the people of Danvers were the main participants in the witchcraft-related events of their community, it was to Salem that they turned for leadership and resolution — and it is now in Salem where the most persistent myths of witchcraft were and are made, remade, and sold.

But actually what the visitor experiences at Salem and Danvers is an important unity in its own right, as a concrete continuation of the mythic significance of the Salem witch trials in American liberal life. No matter how apparently inappropriate, commemoration and at least a gesture toward social and political liberalism is the theme everywhere. In Salem's Witch Museum, which has a *son et lumière* show with mannequins and an interpretive exhibition, the witch trials are likened to the internment of

Japanese Americans during World War II, discrimination against women and gay people, and even the ignorant maltreatment of AIDS sufferers.[21] Meanwhile at Danvers, Trask spoke of the phrase "a Salem Witch Hunt" as meaning "a scapegoating position taken by people or groups emphasizing hysterical, blindly illogical and intolerant actions or expressions."[22] The august liberal gentlemen of 1885 have their direct intellectual descendants in the historians, feminists, former hippies, and political activists who have made Salem town their home today. Legislators and ministers, too, have continued to feel the weight of their responsibility, in a way that reflects the notoriously liberal and Democratic nature of Massachusetts politics. In 1957, 1992, and 2001, resolves and acts of the state legislature cleared and honored the names of those accused. In 1992 bones found on the old Jacobs farm, and believed to be those of George Jacobs, were interred at the Nurse family burial ground beside the Rebecca Nurse memorial. And in 2002 an ecumenical service was held at the First Church, just as in 1885, to commemorate the "Salem witches."[23] Witchcraft is taken seriously here, and its lessons are many and often repeated in a penitent echo of the soul-searching that we saw in the records of Massachusetts witchcraft in the seventeenth century.

*Trouble in Paradise: Fairfield, Widow Hardy, and Mercy Disborough*[24]

The witchcraft memorials at Danvers and Salem are now famous, items on every tour itinerary. But elsewhere in America witches are also remembered, in ways that reflect both the differing colonial cultures of prosecution and the localized nature of witchcraft historiography. Fairfield, now in Connecticut but originally in New Haven colony, is an excellent example of a small town with a strong sense of its witchcraft past. It has no witchcraft memorial, but there are several witchcraft events to be remembered there. The first was the execution of a woman known only as Goodwife Knapp in about 1653. This incident has left no surviving documentation, but it was recalled by witnesses in the slander suit brought by Mary Staples of

Fairfield against Roger Ludlow a year later, of which we have already heard briefly in Chapter 1. Charles H. Levermore praised the New Haven colony, where this case was brought, for the discernment of its magistrates in punishing Ludlow and clearing Staples's name. But Fairfield itself did not come out of the trial well: its inhabitants, not satisfied with the death of Knapp, had questioned her at length before her execution, and she had allegedly conceded under this intolerable pressure that there was another witch in the town yet to be discovered. That woman was, Fairfield thought and Ludlow said, Knapp's friend Mary Staples. Staples had tried to prove during Knapp's trial, and even after her death, that her friend had been innocent, arguing that the witches' teats found on her body were natural growths. But no one would listen to her, and they found her arguments self-incriminating. Her Fairfield neighbors soon charged her with having "Indian gods" and of appearing as a specter to her own sister. Staples was a well-connected woman whose defensive accusations of slander against Ludlow were supported by New Haven's powerful governing family the Davenports — in whose house Ludlow had made his charges — but nevertheless she was lucky to escape trial. Allegations about her resurfaced in Fairfield's next bout of witch-hunting in 1692.[25]

As the Salem witchcraft trials were continuing farther north in 1692, the inhabitants of Stamford and Fairfield, now in Connecticut, became embroiled in a witchcraft controversy of their own. A young servant named Katherine Branch began to be ill, with fits that seemed like a classic possession or obsession — either way, a demonic attack by witches. Katherine came into her employer's house one day crying and falling down in peculiar fits, and two days later began to claim that she was seeing visions of demonic cats. They tempted her with fine goods and society, and she seemed in her visions to be attending a kind of witches' Sabbath, in the rather tame form of a meat supper. Soon Branch claimed to be able to see the specters of witches: she named Elizabeth Clawson of Stamford, Mercy Disbrow or Disborough (who was from the area of Fairfield known as Compo, now Westport), and a third woman whom she nicknamed "hooke back" or "Goody hipshod." Branch's employer, Daniel Westcott, decided to take the matter to the magistrates, and on May 27 they began to investigate the matter. Mercy Disborough asked to undergo the water trial — like Grace Sherwood in Virginia thirteen years later — and the test was carried out. A special court was appointed to investigate the matter, and between 2 and 30 June further evidence was heard, with more testimonies offered on 12 July, and throughout August and early September. On 14 September Clawson and Disborough were at last tried by a Court of Assistants held at Fairfield by order of the general court, by which time other women had also been accused, so that Mary Staples, her daughter and granddaughter Mary Harvey and Hannah Harvey were brought to court with them.[26]

But the case against the witches was already beginning to collapse, just as in Essex County, Massachusetts, doubts were beginning to derail the witch trials there. Several people gave sworn statements accusing Katherine Branch of lying, and protesting the innocence of Clawson and Disborough. Although the grand jury approved the indictment of Staples and the Harveys, only two witnesses wished to testify against them, and the testimony was thought by the magistrates to be inadequate. Their cases were dismissed, and the three women cleared by proclamation of the court. Meanwhile, in the way that we saw so often in the last chapter, the petty jury could not agree on verdicts on Clawson and Disborough. The court was adjourned, and the jury asked to reach a verdict before it met again. At the next meeting of the General Court, local ministers were consulted — as in the case of Katherine Harrison thirty years before — and their advice pointed strongly toward the innocence of the accused, noting that the water trial was suspect on religious grounds, that the "witches' marks" found on the suspects ought to be confirmed by physicians, that Branch might well be lying or deluded by sickness or Satan, and that the rest of the evidence against the women was minor and unconvincing. So when the Court of Assistants reconvened on 28 October, the bench of magistrates must have hoped for a straightforward acquittal. But instead, the jury found Clawson not guilty and Disborough guilty, and even when they were asked to reconsider they refused to alter their verdict. The magistrates then sentenced Disborough to death but reprieved her until the next meeting of the General Court, and it looks very much as if an officially encouraged campaign began to challenge the unwanted guilty verdict and save her life.[27]

A document dated 12 May 1693 explains what happened next. In a letter to the General Court, the magistrates Samuel Wyllys, William Pitkin, and Nathaniel Stanley stated why they had reprieved Disborough. They felt that they had satisfying reasons that the sentence of death passed against her ought not to be executed. They asked the General Court to concur with them. There were reasons of evidence, as expressed in the ministers' advice. But the most important reason was a legal technicality: one of the members of the jury that had returned the guilty verdict had not been a member of the original jury charged with determining Disborough's case. The original jury member had been in New York when the court reconvened and another man had been sworn in his place. The magistrates argued in the strongest possible terms that when the prisoner "put herself on the country," as it was termed, she was entrusting her fate to the specific countrymen of the jury assembled in court that day. If one of these men was changed, the whole jury was changed, and it might even be argued that two juries had power to determine the same case — a legal nonsense, which might lead to charges being brought against those who sanctioned an execution based on such a flawed process. But more than legal technicality was at stake in this case, and the three magistrates also offered a passionate defense of the rights of English and American defendants to a fair trial: "Tis the Birthright of the Kings Subjects so and no otherwise to be tried and they must not be despoyled of it. . . . Blood is a great thing and we cannot but open our mouths for the dumb in the Cause of one appointed to die by such a verdict." Finally the magistrates reminded their brethren and deputies that there was a political and humanitarian context to their decision that should give pause to anyone wishing to execute Mercy Disborough on the faulty evidence presented: "the miserable toyl they are in in the [Massachusetts] Bay . . . is warning enof, those that wil make witchcraft of such things wil make hanging work apace." Although no record of the assembly's decision survives, Disborough was apparently released, giving Connecticut and the town of Fairfield reason to congratulate themselves, on this occasion, on their treatment of witches.[28]

But the earlier case of Goody Knapp continued to trouble the town. And just like Salem and Danvers, Fairfield was forcefully reminded of its heritage in the late nineteenth century by its clergyman. Pastor Frank Samuel Child faced a dilemma, however. His town was not in guilty Massachusetts, where the public was very well informed about whose ancestors had accused and been accused in the seventeenth century. Instead, he was in Connecticut: here, tradition had enshrined an upright smugness about the colony's witchcraft record that owed something commendable to historical fact but also something less commendable to willful ignorance, as we saw in Chapter 1. So Child was torn between his desire to write about witches such as Knapp and his love for his community and its good people, many of whose ancestors, he well knew, were named in the documents as having accused witches. What to do? He did not wish to follow the author of *The Witches: A Tale of New England*, who had solved his or her problem about representing Fairfield's witchcraft in 1837 by anonymity. His solution was to invent a witchcraft case, set among Fairfield's inhabitants — Golds, Burrs, Ludlows — but entirely fictional, and located moreover in the pseudonymous town of Paradise. Paradise was obviously Fairfield, but no one need be upset by Child's fiction. Instead of naming the accusers of the "Widow Anne Hardy," he numbered them: Number One saw her muttering curses, Number Three believed she had caused a storm, and so on. Child reused phrases from the accounts he had read of Mary Johnson of Wethersfield, Goody Knapp and Mary Staples of Fairfield, and some of the Salem witches, but he named no names. He had been both bold and politic: he could look his parishioners, both the good and the powerful, in the face and still tell his tale of superstition without offense.[29]

Child did not really blame Fairfield's or Paradise's seventeenth-century inhabitants for their mistakes, however. His fictional witch was a woman who attracted suspicion, and it was by no means clear at the end of his novel, *A Colonial Witch*, that she had not actually covenanted with the devil. His character Anne Hardy is a poor parent and a peculiar woman. She has christened her children Ananias and Sapphira — after the bible's most notorious liar and his wife — to mark her defiance of Puritan culture. She disciplines them erratically, shaking and beating them, and spoils them with indulgence at other times. As a result, they are completely out of control. It is Sapphira's laughing during meeting that begins the suspicion about her mother, and ultimately it will be Sapphira's evidence that hangs her mother. Widow Hardy is without a husband, and that excuses some of her inadequacy as a parent, but she is also a woman of independent mind and income, practicing as a herbalist, hypnotist, and nurse and speaking her mind to her enemies. Worst of all, she is a woman who reads Shakespeare instead of scripture. Without a shred of irony, Child's hero, Pastor Johnes, debates with Mrs. Hardy the weakness of the female mind when it overstresses itself with reading and writing. She puts up a minimal defense and is forced to concede that her "mind is often in great straits." Widow Hardy is a victim of her own passions, therefore, indulging her unrequited love for Johnes by putting love potions in his food, reading demonologies, wandering about alone at night, and even considering whether to accuse her rival in love, Lady Stanley, of witchcraft simply in order to revenge herself on Johnes. She considers herself a "lost soul" and in her "madness" comes to deny the existence of God and confirm that she has signed the devil's book and renounced her faith. *A Colonial Witch* implies that Connecticut witches brought their fate upon themselves, as much as being victims of their neighbors' error.[30]

Child presented his version of witchcraft in Fairfield so persuasively that it effectively replaced the unhappy reality of Goody Knapp and her friend Mary Staples. At the Roger Ludlowe High School — named, of course, for Staples's accuser — at the commencement exercise in June 1932, one of the students delivered a stirring address in which she innocently described how "the peace and happiness of domestic life in Fairfield was disturbed in 1653," not by the death of Knapp but by the trial of Widow Hardy. "The evidence given by her neighbors was voluminous and convincing," she explained, "so Widow Hardy was condemned to die on the gibbet. On a dismal, rainy morn, she was dispatched to a happier abode." Apparently no one objected that this was untrue, and the students' speeches were printed in a celebratory book later deposited at the Historical Society. More accurately, the speaker, Mary Wilson, also told the story of the trial, condemnation, and reprieve of Mercy Disborough. "And thus," she concluded,

> passed the only two instances of witchcraft in Fairfield. Although these cases disclose a prevalent superstition, they also reveal the prevailing common sense of the community. These forefathers did their work well in obeying the Almighty and in keeping His laws. The recompenses of their labor may be seen in our proud, energetic town, in her stately elms and beautiful buildings and particularly the genial warmth of heart which prevails here.

It was indeed a heartwarming sentiment, worthy of Child himself.[31] Staples had disappeared entirely from history and Ludlow's blushes were spared, while Knapp had been replaced by Hardy. Only Mercy Disborough's story bore any relationship to the truth. The witches of Fairfield had thus become a subject of a selective mythologizing, and it is significant that Mercy Disborough has become the central figure in the town's collective memory. Her status probably comes from her connection with the famous "Salem" trials, since she was tried in 1692, but also from her escape from death. Disborough's story reinforces the central comedic myth of Connecticut and New Haven witchcraft — in this case that the good-hearted and sensible citizens of Fairfield learned from their earlier mistake, and in 1692 stepped back from the brink of disaster, whereas the people of Salem pressed on into infamy.

Some people identifiy with "their" witch Mercy Disborough through family ties. They are either demonstrably descended from her, or claim descent in indirect and speculative ways. Two articles in the *Fairfield Minuteman* in 1995 explore the relationship of Mercy's descendant Stephen Taylor Squires with his witch forebear, and his sense of pride and wonder at his ancestor's story is typical. During the 1990s Squires lived in Hartford, and had become interested in his family history. He researched it back to his great-grandfather, whom his obituary revealed to be a descendant of Thomas and Mercy Disbrow of Compo. But he had not realized that the name Mercy Disborough had any particular resonance in Fairfield until he visited the Historical Society on the Old Post Road to ask about her. When he was presented with a printed handout featuring his ancestor, as well as John M. Taylor's book *The Witchcraft Delusion in Colonial Connecticut*, he was astonished. "Far from being embarrassed at discovering an ancestor accused of a crime," he wrote, "I was instead fascinated and delighted. For this was not some horse theft, it was the crime of witchcraft, a hanging offense. . . . " If Mercy had been an offender, at least she had been an interesting one, and — perhaps because of the nature of her supposed crime — Squires began to feel an almost supernatural connection with her. He was drawn to look at particular tombstones that contained the names of members of his own immediate family, stumbled on useful books, and found unexpected coincidences. He felt that Mercy Disborough was "leading" him, and was relieved to discover that she was "reprieved by excellent Connecticut leaders" whose "writings read today as among the finest examples of Yankee good sense."[32] The tension in his story between romance and that "good sense" realism is a recurrent one in the history of Mercy Disborough's memorialization at Fairfield.

That tension can cause sharp disagreement about the ownership of her story. Michael S. Disbrow, organizer of the Disbrow Family Association, angrily wrote in his account of the family history that two articles about Mercy by the creative writer Lawrence Cortesi "are sensationalized accounts and contain much questionable material and some outright falsehoods."[33] He was right to note that Cortesi had used considerable poetic license, which he had not distinguished from documented fact.[34] However, Disbrow's own account of Mercy's life, despite being based on careful research, can also be questioned. His belief that Mercy was once the stepdaughter of Fairfield's pastor John Jones is based on an acceptance that a Mary Holsworth mentioned by John Winthrop is Mercy Holbridge (later Disborough), which cannot be proven. The identification of Mercy Holbridge as a divorcée, Mercy Nichols/Nicholson, is also problematic. But Disbrow is scrupulous in presenting his evidence, and another family

member, Susann Disbro-Davis, has used it as the basis of a fictionalized
journal of Mercy Disborough's imprisonment and trial.[35] In footnotes, Disbro-Davis acknowledges her debt to Disbrow's account, to Taylor's book,
and to a number of general histories of the Salem trials and of American
witchcraft events. But she also used Elizabeth George Speare's children's
book *The Witch of Blackbird Pond* as a source. In Speare's cheerful tale,
with its typical Connecticut ending, the witch survives and the community remains unstained, *unlike Salem*. Likewise, Disbro-Davis imagines
with delight Mercy's last journal entry: "Justice and sanity have prevailed.
I'm going home!"[36] Her first-person rendering of her ancestor is an extension of the identification with Mercy also felt by Squires and Disbrow.
Each writer has his or her own version of the witch ancestor, in which is
invested considerable emotional capital.[37] Her escape is to be celebrated,
with appropriate credit to Connecticut's sensible judiciary.

All these documents have been carefully preserved at Fairfield Historical
Society, along with stories from other nearby communities and anything
thought to be relevant to witchcraft. When in 1996 a Bridgeport Wiccan
was accused of seducing a fourteen-year-old boy who was a passenger on
the school bus that she drove, and the *Connecticut Post* covered her trial,
the Fairfield Historical Society kept copies of the story. Anxious not to
appear reactionary and biased, the *Post* wrote up a feature about the anger
that pagans felt at the misrepresentation of their religion in other coverage
of the case. The paper had previously provided positive coverage of several
groups of Massachusetts Witches, including the Earthspirit organization
and the Salem-based Witches' League for Public Awareness, and the Historical Society kept those too, along with the *Fairfield Citizen-News*'s article
on the theory that witchcraft accusations were prompted by the delusions
victims experienced from ergot poisoning. When local poet Julie Swanson
won an award for a poem about the hanging of Goody Knapp at Fairfield,
the Historical Society helped her research the event and kept a copy of the
story in the Sunday *Post* celebrating her achievement.[38] Here was and is a
community sensitized to its witchcraft history, but regarding it as a source

of proper community spirit and creative inspiration rather than a matter of either polemical campaigning or shame and expiation.

## *Wethersfield and The Witch of Blackbird Pond*

It is a much more politically pointed story at Wethersfield, the hometown of five of Connecticut's accused witches. Here the Historical Society actively promotes community study of Mary Johnson, John and Joan Carrington, Katherine Palmer, and Katherine Harrison. An exhibition in the 1990s, titled "Hearts Against Hearts: The Wethersfield Witchcraft Accusations," made accessible the sociological theories of John Demos and the feminist argument of Carol Karlsen about witchcraft and the motives and status of accusers and accused.[39] It included an explanation of the decline of local interest in witchcraft prosecutions, which drew on Mary Jeanne Anderson Jones's reading of the gradual collapse of godly culture in the face of capitalism. "Growing materialism challenged their Puritan world view," explained the interpretive panels at the exhibition, while "new immigrants, many of them non-Puritans, helped foster the values of tolerance and personal and religious freedom that became hallmarks of our democracy after the American Revolution."[40] The Historical Society's narration, however, gave Jones's theory a more Whiggish spin: the loss of a culture of covenanted mutual responsibility and charity was transformed into the welcome dilution of fundamentalist zeal, which permitted and even encouraged the evolution of modern American values. This positive reading also prevails in a folder of high school students' essays, collected by the Historical Society after the students had completed their research there in the early 1990s. The young women who wrote the essays — and the essays were all by girls — were interested in their town's history and also in modern Wicca and Witchcraft, especially their feminist aspects.[41] The society has also amassed a substantial collection of scholarly articles on Connecticut's witchcraft history. The study of Wethersfield's witches, then, goes beyond the reiteration of Connecticut's relative innocence into a careful engagement with scholarship that sometimes cuts across received myth.

Most interesting is the teachers' pack prepared by the Historical Society in response to requests for material that might serve as background information in classes on Elizabeth George Speare's classic children's novel *The Witch of Blackbird Pond*, which is set in Wethersfield. The plump pack contains maps of the early colonies, and of places in the town Speare mentions in her book, illustrations of early buildings and ships, excerpts from demonological works and histories, a general history of the town, and information on each witchcraft case.[42] It reinforces the explicitly liberal approach of the town and the Historical Society to Wethersfield's past, differentiating fact from fiction and concluding with a rousing attack on "modern intolerance . . . preconceived notions, lack of awareness and general ignorance." When this flourishes, "race, ethnicity, sexual orientation, beliefs or other differing characteristics become targets for others." The pack compares witch-hunting with "many such scenes in America, from the Japanese internment camps of WW II to the Communist blacklisting of the 1950s McCarthy hearings to today's Skin Heads and Neo-Nazis," and recommends a Web site called teachingtolerance.org. This emphasis is very much in keeping with the attitudes expressed in Speare's novel, and both are a reflection of the cast of mind of the historians of Connecticut's oldest inhabited town. They may not march in the streets at Halloween, as Salem's Witches do, but there is a strong concern for liberal values and a commitment to inoculating American youth against scapegoating behavior.

It is my argument in this book, however, that despite such efforts to separate fact and fiction, myth has shaped perception at least as much as, and in some cases more than, the many factual records, books, and essays on American witchcraft or any of the actual events of the period of the witch trials. Speare's novel is an excellent example. It is an appealing and powerful tale, which won the Newbery Medal for children's fiction. Because it is vividly imagined, sharply written, and broadly historically accurate, with several love stories and a political plot running through its fast-paced narrative, it can be read with pleasure by children, teenaged readers, and adults. Most visitors to the Wethersfield Historical Society can, it seems, be assumed to have encountered the book, so no introduction or explanation of its contents is offered there. It is less familiar to non-American readers, however. *The Witch of Blackbird Pond* tells the story of Katherine (Kit) Tyler, a girl who travels from Barbados to Wethersfield to start a new life with her aunt and uncle there. An outsider herself, Kit secretly makes friends with an old woman who is suspected of witchcraft by some of the townspeople, and has been twice accused already. This woman, Hannah Tupper, is a Quaker and thus automatically regarded as suspect. She suffers from occasional delusive fantasies that her dead husband is still alive, she is a wise and insightful person whose words are sometimes prophetic, and she has a suspicious-looking cat. So when some children fall ill in the town, a mob descends on Hannah's house and burns it. Kit helps Hannah to escape arrest with her "familiar," and is then accused of witchcraft herself. A good deal of inconclusive evidence is offered, but then the finding of a book in which Kit has been teaching the child of her chief accusers to write is discovered and thought to be a spell book. The magistrate commits Kit for trial at Hartford. The story ends happily, however, when the child comes forward to explain the evidence, and the accusations are then laughed out of court.

Kit Tyler perhaps most resembles Katherine Harrison, the Wethersfield "witch" who is mentioned in the book along with Mary Johnson. Kit's temper and her unconventional boldness, as well as other people's envy of her fine clothes and proud manner, get her into trouble. Anxieties surround her status and her proposed marriage to one of the town's most eligible bachelors: likewise, Harrison was a servant before her marriage to the wealthy John Harrison. Kit may also resemble Katherine Harrison in her association with female literacy: Harrison was said to have read the works of the astrologer William Lilly, and *The Witch of Blackbird Pond* repeatedly associates Kit with the reading of books disapproved of in Puritan culture.[43] But this element of her character is greatly expanded from anything that might have been drawn from Harrison's life. Kit Tyler becomes a dame school teacher, and the resolution of the plot hangs on the rightful understanding of educative processes of reading and writing. Her accuser Adam Cruff's realization that "this is a new country over here, and who says it may not be just as needful for a woman to read as a man?" is pivotal to ensuring that Kit is released, and is given wider significance by Cruff's additional remark that reading "might give" his own daughter ". . . summat to think about besides witches and foolishness." Literacy and education are thus inseparably linked with the decline of witchcraft belief and its prosecution by Speare's modifications to the story of a real American witch.[44] The character of Hannah Tupper is also unlike the "real" Wethersfield witches in a number of ways. Her Quakerism sets her apart for reasons of conscience. She is also deliberately positioned at the margins of society by her choice to live outside the village and her unusual mental world. She is much more like the stereotypical English witch — old, frail, and economically impotent — than the American one, who was often, like the real Wethersfield "witches" John and Joan Carrington or Mary Johnson, a younger person economically and socially active in their community — and, indeed, singled out by their neighbors precisely because of their transgressive activities.[45]

The Wethersfield Historical Society's teacher's pack and their exhibition about the Wethersfield witches thus seem to owe to Kit and Hannah at least some of their emphasis on the "differing characteristics" of liberal beliefs and behaviors as being a target for witch-hunters. The characters' attitudes of tolerance and progressiveness make them suspects: the real-life argumentativeness and illegal fortune-telling of the real Katherine Harrison or the gun-trading of John Carrington are far less attractive traits of which no political use can be made. It is instead through the sympathetic and open-minded characters of the novel that the lessons of Connecticut witchcraft prosecutions are to be carried into the modern classroom by the teachers' pack. Wethersfield's witches have thus become, through their fictional representatives, icons of liberalism and tolerance. Yet even with this clearly stated polemical aim, the Historical Society's representation of Wethersfield's past is remarkably clear and scholarly. It does not blur the boundaries between fact and fiction, appealing though the opportunity must have been. In fact, the careful discrimination between record and re-creation echoes Elizabeth George Speare's flat revelation in the Author's Note that ends her novel: "the story of Kit Tyler is entirely fictitious."[46] Here, then, fact and fiction complement one another in the service of a liberal message.

### *Springfield, The Bay Path, and an Untold Story*

Sometimes, however, witches are not remembered at all in the town where they were accused. A good example is the case of the Springfield "witches" of 1650 to '52, Mary and Hugh Parsons, who are almost entirely forgotten in their Massachusetts hometown despite its excellent archive and museum service.

Their obscurity contrasts interestingly with the memorialization of the case of Mary Bliss Parsons, who came from the same community. She was one of the accusers of Hugh and Mary Parsons and was herself accused of witchcraft when she and her husband moved to Northampton as one of its founding families in 1654. Her commemoration at Northampton is discussed below. But the outbreak of witchcraft at Springfield in which she, Hugh, and Mary Parsons were involved is almost unknown there. It is mentioned in passing in a number of the novels discussed in Chapter 3, and most notably a version of it is part of the plot of Catharine Maria Sedgwick's *Hope Leslie* (1827). But here, instead of Hugh or Mary Parsons, the suspected witch is a Native American women, Nelema, in a fictitious episode designed to illustrate ill-feeling between settlers and "Indians." In fact, while the godly were perfectly capable of the insensitivity to religious difference necessary to allow them to indict Native Americans for Sabbath breaking, and certainly associated them with devil-worship, they did not formally accuse them of witchcraft and proceeded cautiously where "Indians" accused one another of religious crimes.[47] So in Sedgwick's Springfield a witchcraft accusation that would not have occurred in reality is a metaphor for general hostility. It is not even certain that she knew of the Parsons's indictments: she makes no reference to them.

Yet in Springfield in 1650 at least four white people were suspected of witchcraft. A brickmaker's wife, Mary Parsons, was tried and acquitted, although she was probably executed for another offense (the murder of her own child, which she confessed) or died in prison before she could be hanged. Her husband Hugh was tried and convicted by the jury of the Court of Assistants, but was, as we have seen, discharged after an appeal to the General Court. One other woman may have been tried, although no record now remains of the case, and one woman may not have been tried at all, although she had been accused. So how do we know these things? What are the texts that remain and might allow a reconstruction of the events of one of the best-documented New England witch trials of its time? We have Mary Parsons's indictment of May 1651, and a record of two verdicts, the sentence for infanticide, and a short reprieve because of her illness. We also know from the records of the Court of Assistants that by October 1651 several people ("those . . . accused of witchcraft") were being held in prison, awaiting a trial to be held in May 1652. One of these was Hugh Parsons, of whose supposed crimes and trial we have records, both from the Court of Assistants and from the personal papers of the Springfield magistrate William Pynchon. The other person, or persons, may have been Sarah Merrick and/or Besse Sewell, who had been accused by Mary Parsons in evidence recorded by Pynchon. Or there may have been other accused persons. John Hale's *Modest Enquiry into the Nature of Witchcraft*, written after the Salem trials, certainly asserts that "two or three of Springfield [were accused], one of which confessed."[48]

Even with important details missing, a mass of documentation about the case still remains. The testimonies taken before Pynchon, now in the New York Public Library, are supplemented by his and his son John's account books, which feature the accused as well as many of the accusers and witnesses prominently, and the records of Hampshire County Court at the Connecticut Valley Historical Museum at Springfield. There are also documents about the case in the archives of Suffolk County Court, and at

Harvard.[49] Perhaps it is partly this scattering of records that has kept the case comparatively little known for so long. Samuel G. Drake published an edited transcript of the Pynchon notebook material in 1869, adding to the sense of confusion and mystery surrounding the case by his claim that it had been bound in the wrong order in the late eighteenth century, and thus that there was something unreliable about it. In fact, all that he meant was that some of the testimony had been placed in the book before testimony that must have preceded it in date. As Drake himself surmised, however, the collection of depositions is a copy of lost originals, probably made for the purpose of Hugh Parsons's trial. This took place over a year after his original examination, during which time new accusations had emerged. So although we know the order in which some of the accusations were made, there is no indication of the order in which Pynchon wrote them up when he made the copies, or of their relative importance in the trial itself. We can make what we like of the texts supplied. It is because of this openness and the reluctance of historians to write a definitive account, I think, that Hugh and Mary Parsons remain uncommemorated in Springfield. No account has been given of them that is both accessible and reasonably truthful. They have not been placed in the wider context of Massachusetts's "guilt," or differentiated from that tradition. The novel that tells part of their story is based on patchy consultation of records and has its own agenda to promote. Where there is no seed — a good popular history, an engaging and reasonably durable fiction — knowledge is lost and no usable myth can grow.[50]

The novel that does refer to Hugh and Mary Parsons is Josiah Gilbert Holland's *The Bay Path* of 1857.[51] Even this is a more wide-ranging story, as its title (and subtitle, *A Tale of New England Colonial Life*) suggests. Its focus is on the troubles of Hugh and Mary's marriage, but it also deals with the founding of Springfield on the "bay path" from the coast, a deliciously syrupy romance between William Pynchon's daughter Mary and Elizur Holyoke, and with Pynchon's own philosophical standpoint, which got him into trouble with the general court and probably persuaded him to return to England in 1652. As Lawrence Buell shows, the novel sprang out of Holland's reading for his *History of Western Massachusetts*.[52] But Dr. Holland also had a moral and political agenda. In some ways, he intended to provoke his readers in much the same way that John Greenleaf Whittier intended to inspire those who read his poem on the Rebecca Nurse monument. In his preface to *The Bay Path*, Holland wrote:

> Fiction . . . has always been a favorite mode of communicating truth. . . . The author of the Christian system spake evermore in parables . . . the necessity was to exhibit truth in its relations to the feeling, thinking, acting soul. . . . In the birth of new questions, in the revolution of opinions, and in the shifting aspect of affairs, this great necessity becomes perpetual.

His aim in writing was to illustrate the perils of "dim forests of superstition" and "barren hills of bigotry" and to extol the "mountain-tops of high resolution and noble action" through his hero, William Pynchon, and his "beautiful, lovely, noble" daughter Mary.[53] Mary is the Dorothea Brooke of Agawam, while William, "much less bigoted and intolerant than most," is a prototypical Unitarian, half-convinced that Christ was simply a good man, and wholly depressed by the union of church and state, which he cannot challenge without losing his own position. Through the debates and actions of the Pynchons and Holyoke, Holland explores whether "unimportant errors wear out" or if, distracted by a desire to preserve the *status quo* and their own interests, those who could best instruct others and advance the causes of enlightenment are "endangering truth by . . . compromises with error." The novel is thus an extension of his many years of journalism for the opinionated and moralistic daily newspaper the *Springfield Republican*, and it is dedicated to its editor, Samuel Bowles.

Yet for all his apparently progressive rhetoric of tolerance, Holland was also intensely conservative. He was one of a number of New England novelists who, Buell notes, answered the Unitarian challenge and produced novels that "came out sounding strangely liberal" but were not.[54] In 1872, he summed up his political philosophy in a sonnet:

> God, give us men! A time like this demands
> Strong minds, great hearts, true faith and ready hands;

Men whom the lust of office does not kill;
Men whom the spoils of office cannot buy;
Men who possess opinions and a will;
Men who have honor; men who will not lie;
Men who can stand before a demagogue
And damn his treacherous flatteries without winking!
Tall men, sun-crowned, who live above the fog
In public duty, and in private thinking;
For while the rabble, with their thumb-worn creeds,
Their large professions and their little deeds,
Mingle in selfish strife, lo! Freedom weeps,
Wrong rules the land and waiting Justice sleeps.[55]

Here is the democratic mob again, and *The Bay Path* shows the rise and fall of one such leader, William Pynchon, dragged down into "the fog." The book's unlikely antihero, the would-be revolutionary John Woodcock, is also a problematic figure. In the novel, Woodcock is the father of Mary Parsons, although in actuality she was the divorced wife of a long-absent man named Lewis when she married Hugh Parsons. Woodcock did exist, and was regarded as a troublemaker in Springfield's courts, but he had no known connection with her. Holland's character Woodcock is much more important and articulate than his real-life counterpart. He cannot bear it that "it's 'Mister' and 'Goodman' — Misters get cream, the rest skimmed milk." "Here," he tells the minister George Moxon and the magistrate Pynchon, "are you a' rulin' on us, and I don't see the justice on it." He complains that he cannot become a freeman or vote, because he is not a church member. Accordingly Moxon comes to suspect him of witchcraft, and when he flees to live with the "Indians" this reputation descends to his unfortunate daughter. Despite Holland's sympathy for John and Mary Woodcock, one can see in his and his daughter's tragic lives the insistent fear of the dispossessed, the "treacherous flatteries" of the "demagogue," that also marked the writings of other nineteenth-century writings on witchcraft. In this case the witches as well as their ignorant accusers personify the ungovernable "rabble" and their downfall is their own fault.[56]

There is also a heavily gendered polemical purpose behind Holland's retelling of the Springfield witchcraft story, which militates against its usefulness to the modern reader: not only the rabble but also women may be a threat to the "tall men, sun-crowned" and their ordered, rational world. As she blooms into a "self-reliant, courageous" woman, Mary Woodcock, like her father before her, spurns all "restraint and control." But her rebellion leads her "even to masculineness," and she completes her identification as a misfit by choosing to woo Hugh Parsons, "an effeminate man." Hugh will not "bend her will," she feels, and so she "did all the courting," struck by Hugh's "meekness and modesty" and the fact that even in his own estimation he is "not in will and purpose, in thought and feeling, in strength and determination, a man." It is not clear where Holland got this idea: although Hugh was portrayed by his contemporaries as a man reviled and accused by his wife, he was also described as an aggressive businessman and sometimes a tyrannical husband. Helplessly, however, the womanlike Hugh of the novel marries Mary Woodcock, who then slips into insanity under the pressure of the contradictions within her and their exaggeration by the community's suspicion and hatred, like the later Widow Hardy but with less excuse. She does indeed smother her baby at the book's close and Holland's interest in women's health surfaces in his description of Mary's illness. He trained and qualified as a physician, and practiced medicine in Springfield before turning to journalism. His special interest was in female ailments, and his portrayal of Mary Woodcock's decline inspires genuine horror. The novel implies that had she been properly governed by the men of Holland's sonnet she might have lived happily. Despite Holland's sense that women *and* men who have a "not . . . unnatural, but . . . unusual" approach to each other, and to gendered behavior in general, shamefully have no place in a censorious, dogmatic world, the book endorses the belief that most women are biologically predisposed to modesty, nurturing, and subservience.[57]

*The Bay Path*, then, is no proto-*Crucible* or *Witch of Blackbird Pond*, and offers no explanation of witchcraft prosecution that is readily acceptable to the modern mind. It is even further removed from modernity than the later *A Colonial Witch*. In addition, Holland's novel has at best a strained relationship to the world of seventeenth-century Springfield. *The Bay Path* is really about the world of his hero Lincoln, of his friend Emily Dickinson, of secessionists and suffragists. Although Holland includes in his text some of the names of actual deponents who spoke against Mary Parsons during a slander case in 1649 — such as John and "Goodwife" Matthews, and the plaintiff "Widow" Marshfield — he embroiders their testimony to suit his own themes. He has John Matthews say Mary Parsons only spoke ill of Widow Marshfield after an insulting joke about her husband's small, feminine stature was made to her. Goody Matthews meanwhile is made to discuss with Mary some missing veal, which may be Holland's misreading for "wool" in the original manuscript, and to allege that when Mary visited her house she was unable to continue carding with any success. It was a common complaint that witches affected household processes like wool spinning and carding, or the churning of butter, but it was not made by Goodwife Matthews in this case: she was simply describing her daily work, an essential part of the town's economy, rather then pettily excusing her incompetence. Mary had come to her house while she was carding, she said, and alleged that there was a witch in town. Mary had also reported the gossip of her neighbor Ann Stebbins that the Widow Marshfield had been previously suspected of witchcraft, and since her arrival in Springfield strange lights had been seen in the meadows. Mary had added that Widow Marshfield had envied other women their children, that her own (Mary's) child had died and her cow had died, too, apparently as a result of Marshfield's "grudging." John Matthews's testimony matched that of his wife. But in keeping with his unease about women's speech and their power to influence events, Holland has changed Ann Stebbins into Mr. Stebbins, and has reattributed "his" conversation with Goodwife Matthews to her husband.[58] History comes a poor second in *The Bay Path* to social and sexual politics of a conservative kind.

In fact, we now know quite a lot about John and Pentecost Matthews, and their support for the Marshfields' slander suit, as well as their role in the witchcraft accusation made against Mary and Hugh Parsons, and later against Mary Bliss Parsons. John, a cooper, had a skilled and profitable job that involved making barrels for all the many kinds of commodities shipped from Springfield downriver from the 1640s to the 1670s. One of his best customers must have been Samuel Marshfield, son of the slandered widow. Marshfield was an up-and-coming merchant, tailor, and later the keeper of an ordinary, so that he needed beer barrels and containers for various kinds of supplies, and he also worked from time to time as a smith, teamster, a canoe man for the Pynchons, a drover, and so on. In the 1640s, when his mother was slandered, he was beginning to be ubiquitous in local life. But he was also becoming a wealthy and prominent citizen, a selectman for thirteen years and later the representative to Massachusetts's General Court. In 1652, after the witch trials were over, he married Esther Wright, whose family similarly provided the town with representation in the latter half of the seventeenth century. Marshfield's single-minded pursuit of his aims can be seen in a complaint made against him in Hampshire's county court in 1665, that he "hath gotten the land of ye Indians into his hands by vertue of a deed of morgage" [*sic*]. The Native Americans now "haveinge little or nothing left to plant on" were desperate, and Marshfield was told to give them some of the land back.[59] We know something of what John Matthews's reaction to this powerful man's slander suit might have been from his actions in 1656 in another court case involving witchcraft.

In 1656, Mary Bliss Parsons (who was not related to Hugh and Mary Parsons, but was the wife of the wealthy businessman Joseph Parsons) was slandered by her former neighbor Sarah Bridgeman, whom we met in Chapter 1. Sarah said that Mary was a witch. Both women by then lived in Northampton, but they called witnesses from Springfield to testify to past events. John Matthews gave evidence supporting Sarah Bridgeman's accusation: he had, he said, been at Joseph Parsons's house in 1652 making barrels when he heard him arguing with his wife. Joseph told Mary she was led by an evil spirit, and she countered that he had caused her trouble by locking her in the cellar, which was full of spirits, and leaving her there. Joseph also alleged that in a fit Mary had walked across the Great Swamp in her shift and emerged without getting wet. All this seemed good evidence that, as accusers put it, Mary Parsons was "not right" and might well be a witch. But later Matthews had suffered an abrupt change of heart.

He presented himself before the magistrate John Pynchon, son of William, to say that he actually had "no grounds of jealousy [suspicion] for himself of Mary Parsons . . . to be a witch." Then he added a humiliating, but conscientious, admission: "what he testified yesterday on oath was upon the earnest importuning of James Bridgeman and his brother." The brother is probably Richard Lyman, brother-in-law of James, who was wealthy and well connected and actively gathered evidence not only of the justice of his sister Sarah's accusation but (as we saw in Chapter 1) of the bias of local officials who took testimony, he said, in favor of Mary Parsons.[60] Matthews is thus portrayed in the surviving documents of the case as a man of some substance swayed by the powerful businessmen of the community around him. Neither he nor his wife, therefore, fit the template of the ignorant "rabble, with their thumb-worn creeds" forced on them by Holland. In fact, Matthews had a few ideas of his own, and in 1669 he was whipped for reviling the town's minister Peletiah Glover in a way that reminded his hearers of the Quakers. Pentecost Matthews, meanwhile, was a literate and educated woman, who worked as schoolmistress to John Pynchon's children.[61]

Holland's depiction of the case of Hugh and Mary Parsons, then, is a completely fictional one, bearing little relation to surviving contemporary texts. Unlike Child or Speare, he does not flag up his fiction in any clear way. In fact, he was keen to show in lengthy footnotes in the book that he had researched his history in the published records of the Bay colony and the "Pynchon Record Book" at Harvard, although he clearly did not know of the other texts still in existence. The book became a piece of political propaganda, tailored to Holland's Republican agenda and based only on four or five documents, rather than the usable social history of Springfield witchcraft it might have become after the publication of Drake's transcript of the New York Pynchon notebook. Holland also omits the details of the witch trial that ended Mary's and her husband's lives in Springfield. "The tale of her trial for this offence would be a disgusting record," he opines, "weary to write and sickening to read."[62] The book is thus neither one thing nor the other: a pure fiction appealing to modern readers or a sound history. It was not until the later twentieth century with the work of the historian Stephen Innes that a truer picture of life in the Connecticut Valley river towns in the seventeenth century emerged, but, being an economic history, it hardly mentioned the witches. There is thus no coherent story of witchcraft to be told at Springfield — nothing usable for exhibition or narration — because creative writers and historians have taken widely divergent and in some cases badly dated approaches to the Parsons case, where they have noticed it at all.

### Northampton, John Demos, and an Unmade Myth

Things are very different at Northampton, and that is almost entirely and unintentionally the work of John Demos, who discussed the case of Mary Bliss Parsons at length in his book *Entertaining Satan* in 1982. *Entertaining Satan* is the kind of work that is eminently usable by curators and librarians. It offers a detailed narration built on thorough research, with a clear interpretation of events and a strong sense of the historical and personal context of the story to be told. Demos explains the accusation and vigorous self-defense of Mary Bliss Parsons in a number of ways. Economically and socially, she may have been a dominant and much-envied woman, unlike her chief accuser Sarah Bridgeman, who was no more than middlingly successful. Mary's husband Joseph Parsons had a special relationship with the Pynchons, who dominated the Connecticut Valley's trade, and he had a share in their monopoly in the fur trade that was making him rich quickly. On the domestic front, too, Mary Bliss Parsons's female accusers may have envied her her large family and relatively healthy babies. As Demos discovered, she bore the first settler child in Northampton and had an additional eight children who reached maturity, while her accuser Sarah Bridgeman had only one surviving (and sickly) child and lost her new baby in circumstances that she blamed on Parsons. Mary was not afraid to speak out about other people's failings, and she had herself an unusual mental and spiritual history that she was not shy of discussing, as John Matthews's testimony about her fits and visions suggests. Finally, as his evidence also shows, her marriage was turbulent despite its economic success, and her husband himself thought her possessed of peculiar powers of self-assertion. In summary, Demos suggested, Mary Bliss Parsons was anomalous in a number of economic, social, and gendered ways, making her a likely target of gossip, speculation, and suspicion, what Demos calls "a thick trail of *talk*." When she moved from Springfield to Northampton, she left anger and dislike in her wake, and citizens of the two towns were soon engaged in a battle over her reputation.[63]

Demos thus offers a brilliantly readable re-creation of the world of seventeenth-century Northampton, and his arguments are extremely convincing. This is good history, but it is also good mythmaking: Demos chose one of a number of stories that might have been told of Mary Bliss Parsons, and sometimes, especially to the twenty-first century eye, his less central conclusions seem more debatable than they might have thirty years ago. Perhaps most problematic to a more skeptical world is Demos's attempt to reconstruct a lost psychological state, with the attendant dangers of anachronism. Although Demos's research into the background of the Parsons and Bridgeman families yielded much that is incontrovertibly of psychological importance — that, for example, Sarah Bridgeman was a member of the successful Lyman family, and had lost a number of children in the period before her accusation of Mary Bliss Parsons — some of his deductions made are from slenderer evidence. The romantic story of Mary Bliss Parsons's immediate ancestry is a good example:

> Thomas Bliss [Mary's father] . . . was by this account the son and namesake of a well-to-do, locally influential citizen in the village of Belstone, county Devon. In the opening decades of the seventeenth century the father had become a determined advocate of the Puritan cause. . . . On one particular occasion he and three of his sons . . . had accompanied a party, led by the local member of Parliament, in riding up to London to engage both king and archbishop in direct confrontation. The upshot was their imprisonment and the levying of heavy fines (said to have been in excess of £1000) in lieu of their freedom. Payment of the fines required the virtual liquidation of the family estate. . . . Impoverished and broken . . . Thomas Sr. subsequently returned to Belstone and lived in the

> household of his daughter, Lady Elizabeth Calcliffe . . . the father sum-
> moned his sons, divided among them what patrimony he still retained,
> and advised them to remove to New England.

The problem here is what seems to be a confusion by the genealogists who compiled this account between the histories of Devon and Northampton-shire, as Demos admits in his notes. In fact, the parish records of Belstone do not record the Bliss or Calcliffe families, which would be odd if they had lived there and even odder if they had indeed been wealthy people. The latter at least seem to be from Northamptonshire. It also seems highly unlikely that the Blisses would be able to meet with the King and Arch-bishop on anything like equal terms to discuss the religious matters that James VI and I, Charles I, and their archbishops found deeply irritating — what might be the occasion? Then there is the titled but apparently impo-tent patron, the folktalelike dispatching of the sons to seek their fortune and the size of the fine, which would have bankrupted most Englishmen of the period many times over. Much of the story's detail is, then, fairly unlikely. But Demos, despite his reservations, uses it as the basis of part of a gestalt reading of Mary Bliss Parsons's psychological life, by "assuming the reality of all (or most) of this."[64] Yet, as he is careful to acknowledge, "tradition" is not a very reliable source of information.

As a source of *myth* it is invaluable, however. Here is the good and wealthy patriarch with his fine upstanding sons, ruined by the honest expression of his godly faith, and subjected to imprisonment and cruelty by the tyrannical and snobbish Royalist English. Somehow he has acquired a titled relative, however, and enough money to send his sons adventur-ing. His daughter, proud though unexpectedly impoverished, is subjected to a traumatic relocation to the new world and then accused of witchcraft as she tries to rebuild her family's status. The known facts do not square very well with what is known of Thomas Bliss junior, Mary's father, dur-ing his residence at Hartford, Connecticut, after he arrived in America. He held no public office, and his inventory, painstakingly researched by Demos, represents "the household of (at most) an average yeoman." It is valued at eighty-six pounds in total. But it sets up Demos's reading of Mary Bliss Parsons as a woman of "haughty manners," who "lived through a time when the family fortunes were much diminished and its prestige reduced." Although Demos regards the family's story in Old England as "a provisional *addendum* to the main threads" of his argument, he ends up emphasizing, just as other accounts of the family's history have emphasized, "the factor of *envy*" as important in the accusation of Mary Bliss Parsons as a witch, and blaming in part her status-conscious *hauteur*.[65] What Demos is doing here is creating a wonderfully coherent and usable myth, as well as a fine general history.

Demos's Mary Parsons is part of the great story of American migration — the story taught in schools of the persecuted Puritans who with stubborn self-confidence left England and made a wealthy and enviable future for themselves in the New World. His book was widely applauded for its pioneering exploration of the social, economic, and psychological aspects of this building of new communities, and why they might have led to witchcraft accusations. It became the standard history of New England witchcraft, and Wethersfield's Historical Society titled its witchcraft exhibition after one of his chapters, as readers might have noticed. So too it is Demos's Mary Bliss Parsons, who is commemorated in Northampton, at the town's museum "Historic Northampton," built on the old Parsons lot. When I visited in 2003, the staff were at work not only on an exhibit about Mary, but also on a project to digitize the documents of her two trials and take her story into local schools. And it was based on their reading of Demos's chapter "Hard Thoughts and Jealousies," which had suggested to them a bid to the Massachusetts Foundation for the Humanities for an internship to build a Web site. It would encourage children and young adults to consider the questions of gender, power, economic status, and other historical variables that might lead to accusations of witchcraft.[66] With an eminently usable story to tell, Northampton has had cause to remember its witch where Springfield has not, and Demos's book is thus one reason why Mary Bliss Parsons is commemorated where Mary and Hugh Parsons are forgotten.

But there is also a sense that Mary's putative history — of riches to rags and back again — fits with Northampton's self-image. In many ways, it is the story of the town itself. Northampton was a thriving agricultural and business community that fell on hard times in the mid-twentieth century and has only recently been reinvented as what local people call NoHo, a gentrified and bohemian community of art galleries, fine restaurants, tattoo artists, New Age healers, music clubs, bookstores, and antique fairs. Northampton has regenerated, and so has the money to tell its story where Springfield has not. Northampton is also the location of the famous women's university Smith College, and the town has a large and proud lesbian community with an interest in women's history. In fact, it seemed to me a town with a new witch-myth waiting to be made, one that complements the story of Bliss Parsons as a triumphant Cinderella. In the account given of Mary by John Matthews we learned that she was believed to have a troubled marriage, to be locked in the cellar by her husband and there to see visions and fall into fits. We also know from his and other statements that in which she was involved in about 1650 to '2 with a group of women and girls who appeared to be possessed and some of whom accused Hugh and Mary Parsons of bewitching them. When she was in these "fits," she would run from her house into the fields and swamps that surrounded Springfield, where she then lived. Later William Hannum testified that to his knowledge "Joseph Parsons had in a sort beaten his wife." Finally, William Branch said that Parsons himself had told him that "where ever he laid the key his wife could fynd it and would goe out in the night and that when she went out a woman went out with her and came in with her." All these circumstances led the people of Northampton to conclude that Mary Parsons was "not right" and a witch, and to a modern reader they suggest a woman determinedly, if undefinably, untamed by patriarchy. The idea that respectable women would go out together at night was disturbing to seventeenth-century minds, but lesbianism was unnamed.[67] We have no way of knowing what Mary Bliss Parsons thought or whether her husband's stories about her were true, but one interpretation of them open to the modern creator of witch myths would certainly be that she was at the least an unhappily married woman who sought the company of other women just as she sought the freedom of the marshes and meadows.

There is another incident that would fit into this mythos too. In 1960 Northampton was the scene of a disturbing prosecution, now seen as analogous to HUAC's attempt to uncover Communists in the 1950s, when three male professors at Smith College and twelve other men were arrested for possessing and distributing among themselves photographs of male models and nudes. These the police defined as gay pornography. All three professors were convicted and dismissed, and one, Newton Arvin, the friend and lover of Truman Capote, died three years later following a mental breakdown. The other two professors eventually overturned their convictions, on the grounds that the material seized should not be classed as obscene and that the searches were illegal. Now that the story of this "Great Pink Scare" is becoming more widely known, it is openly being referred to as a "witch-hunt."[68] The story of Mary Bliss Parsons's troubled life at Northampton seems to fit beautifully into this pattern of persecution and resistance, by people burdened and victimized either for their desire not to conform to gendered expectations, or for their sexual orientation. But Northampton is not Salem, despite its strong associations with feminism and gay pride, and this is a myth that remains unmade.

## *Virginia: Entertaining History*

Witchcraft stories both untold and fictionalized are especially common in the southerly states that have grown from English colonies. We have seen how little attention the witches of colonial Virginia had and have received, both before and after the discovery of the records of Grace Sherwood, Virginia's supposed "sole witch," and things are not greatly different in the early twenty-first century. The loss of records is a hindrance that cannot be overcome. One major scholarly article, one recent thesis, and a small number of popular articles — often in genealogical publications or general history magazines and books — represent the coverage of the subject.[69] But wider cultural factors also work against an interest in witch-craft. Even those Virginians engaged on a daily basis with history and archival work tend to shy away from the discussion of witches, so trans-parently unpopular is the subject in wider southern society. Some believe still that Virginia had no witches, while others know something of their existence but little of the detail of the records about them. Only a few sig-nificant fictional works on witches exist — nothing comparable with the outpouring of novels about Salem or the steady trickle of Connecticut. The enquirer is sometimes told that the Salem witch trials are the nation's only focus for research on the matter. Many of the Virginians that I met did not really want to talk about witchcraft, and I was told a number of stories of others who have been looked on with suspicion for their interest in the subject. Witches have become a part of the tradition of southern storytell-ing and folklore, as in S. E. Schlosser's *Spooky South*, but the study of real witches is another matter.[70] Grace Sherwood is best remembered from an innocuous children's book, *The Witch of Pungo*, which retells some local legends about her: for example, that she sailed to England in an eggshell and brought the herb rosemary to America. Throughout Virginia's history, writers have been unable to resist romanticizing her story, such as Beverly Campbell, who in 1934 inexplicably added to Grace's story an English-trained lawyer, who by "showing us the error of our ways" ensured that "Old Dominion's justice . . . narrowly escaped a blot on its escutcheon." She appears as a kind of superwoman in George Holbert Tucker's *Virginia Supernatural Tales*, carefully differentiated from the historical Grace Sherwood. Tucker lists further fictions about Sherwood — that she was ducked with a bible round her neck, that she called up a storm to soak and drown spectators at her ducking, that she flew with the aid of plates strapped to her arms. The entertaining fictions about her are much better known than fact.[71]

Two exceptions prove the rule. One is at Colonial Williamsburg, the reconstructed eighteenth-century town that was the colonial capital before Richmond. Here, a sensitively written and performed "reenact-ment" by Carson O. Hudson titled *Cry Witch!* plays several evenings a week at the Capitol building. Yet even here, reenactment in the strict sense is not attempted, and the performance neatly sidesteps the making of any judgment about the existence, nature, and punishment of witchcraft. *Cry Witch!* is the entertaining story of Grace Sherwood's trial for her life — the trial that may or may not have happened in the colony's General Court in about 1706. It is based on the surviving records from Princess Anne County Court, since, as we have seen, the General Court records were destroyed during the Civil War. We do not know whether, after the lengthy examination of her case by County Court magistrates, and the "verdicts" of a jury of matrons and a ducking, Sherwood was forwarded to the General Court for trial or not, and we do not know the outcome of any trial there. So, in an artistically brilliant and politically convenient finale, *Cry Witch*'s audience members are left to deliver for themselves the final verdict on Grace Sherwood at this part-fictional courtroom drama.

The interactive play opens with a short talk by an actor who is simultaneously speaking as a twenty-first-century tour guide and, as his costume makes clear, as one of the court's officials. He begins by telling the audience that American witchcraft is often seen as synonymous with the Salem witch trials, but that in fact the belief in witches was widespread. He discusses the coverage of the subject in the bible and King James VI and I's *Daemonologie* of 1597. God and the king are therefore identified with the trial of witches, and the audience is encouraged to think themselves back into the seventeenth and early eighteenth centuries with the aid of a brief explanation of court procedures and the introduction of several almost subconsciously operative hooks, including interpellation into the linguistic and bodily habits of the court. The audience must rise in deference to the actor playing the governor, and be obedient to his direction of the case, and all speakers including female and junior audience members are referred to as "sir," in keeping with the all-male composition of early modern courts. The theater is the actual, although reconstructed, courtroom of the capitol, lit only by candles, and without microphones or other modern technological aids. The actors speak in authentic-sounding eighteenth-century language, based very frequently on surviving documents

from the county court and the minutes of the council. They represent genuine historical figures: Luke Hill; another accuser, Elizabeth Barnes; the
prosecuting Attorney General, Stevens Thompson. As far as is possible in
the twenty-first century — with a T-shirted, cellphone-, and camera-tot-
ing crowd at least half-composed of educated and trouser-wearing females
— the audience suspends its disbelief to imagine itself back in 1706.

But they are not allowed to remain quietly in the dusk of the courtroom:
Salem's mannequins here come to life and the audience must respond.
While the action of the play is pushed forward and controlled by straightforward interaction between judge, prosecutor, witnesses, and accused,
audience members have opportunities to cross-question the participants
in the trial. Luke Hill and his wife Elizabeth were, on the night I saw the
performance, subjected to careful questioning about the miscarriage that
*Cry Witch*'s version of Mistress Hill attributed to Grace Sherwood's witchcraft. Elizabeth Barnes could not be questioned, as she fell into a "Salem"-
like fit under cross-examination by Sherwood, and was dismissed weeping
by the governor, protesting his suggestion that she might be committing
perjury. The audience's intervention is limited, but it establishes a right
to judge, which is reinforced by the careful representation of conflicting
interpretations by the actors themselves of Sherwood's state of guilt or
innocence. Although Barnes's evidence of Sherwood's spectral appearance to her with a devilish man, and as a cat, is questioned, as are some
of Luke Hill's statements that Sherwood dismisses as superstitious gossip,
the audience is also shown that Sherwood is a mean woman, shouting
insults after the departing witnesses, and that she cannot complete her
rendition of the Lord's Prayer, a common test for witchcraft but not one
administered to the real Grace. In pursuit of further balance, the presentation of spectral evidence leads to a brief argument on its admissibility
between the attorney and the governor, which is only partly resolved. In
his summary of the case before asking for a verdict, the governor notes
that there is little to plead Sherwood's innocence, and that her behavior
does her cause no good, but that the court met to judge her is not that of
the Inquisition. We are Englishmen, he reminds the audience, and Virgin-

ians. He himself is not sure what to think of the case. And so the verdict is put to the audience's vote.

What is astonishing is that Sherwood is very often found guilty, as she was by a majority of seventeen votes on the night that I attended *Cry Witch!* Enough evidence has been presented, and the audience sufficiently interpellated into seventeenth- and early eighteenth-century behavior that they are willing to send Grace Sherwood to the gallows for her supposed crimes.[72] Responding as they assume that contemporary jurors might have responded, they perhaps also reflect something of the experience around them at Williamsburg. In this atmosphere, where the past is venerated as a pious time of heroic struggle, the innate conservatism of much of Virginia and the deeper south is set in context, and it becomes perfectly possible to imagine a world where magistrates and ministers could honestly and conscientiously hang a woman for bewitching her neighbor. Why not? Although religion is barely mentioned in *Cry Witch!* it is omnipresent, and the audience is clearly prepared to take the word of God and the king above that of all the rationalist historians in America.

On 10 July 2006, after a campaign by a local reenactment volunteer Belinda Nash, the Virginia Governor Timothy M. Kaine pardoned Grace Sherwood at the second of the exceptions to Virginians' reluctance to encounter their witch-hunting past. A reenacted ducking of Sherwood has been held at Witchduck Point, near Virginia Beach, every year since 2003, to go with a reenactment at the Ferry Plantation House where she has her property restored to her, allegedly in recompense for her sufferings. Nash was delighted, she told *The Washington Post*, repeating a series of facts and myths about Sherwood that the newspaper managed to turn into a more or less total fiction. The governor named 10 July "Grace Sherwood Day," to celebrate "the fact that a woman's equality is constitutionally protected today, and women have the freedom to pursue their hopes and dreams."[73] At the first reenactment, local historian Stephen Mansfield had been quoted by *The Virginian-Pilot* as musing that "unlike the shame and embarrassment that Massachusetts residents feel about the witch trials in Salem, Sherwood has become somewhat of a celebrated figure in Virginia

Beach's history." "In this area, people have a certain affection for Grace Sherwood," he concluded.[74] But her ostentatious pardoning still feels like a gesture at odds with the verdict of the crowd at *Cry Witch!* It might be fun to celebrate Grace Sherwood in a carnivalesque or theatrical event, but Virginian witches are little known outside such fiction. Inside the old capitol's walls at Williamsburg something of a true attitude toward them in conservative America was clearly expressed. Grace Sherwood's pardon, together with a slowly growing body of scholarship on southern witches, might, however, indicate that things are changing. The southern English colonies have a history of witchcraft to rival anything in New England, and their witches deserve greater representation not just in folklore, theater, and oral culture, but in scholarly history, too.

### Maryland: Witches on the Battlefield

It is a similar, even starker story in Maryland. Here fiction and folktale have completely eclipsed the (at least) ten witches who appeared in court in the state's history, and who are barely known at all. Putting the terms "Maryland" and "witch" into a search engine is, in fact, almost certain to lead the researcher to a site about the fictional film *The Blair Witch Project*. The film, made in 1999, tells the story of three students who hike into the Maryland woods near Burkittsville to investigate the legend of the Blair Witch. She, the film tells us, was Elly Kedward, a woman condemned and banished for witchcraft — anachronistically — in the late eighteenth century. Despite Kedward having been tied to a tree, taunted by village children, lynched, or left to die of exposure, by the next winter all the children who had accused her and around half of the town's other children have disappeared. Blair (now Burkittsville, we are told) was abandoned for sixty years until it was rediscovered by property developers building the railroad in the 1820s. Almost immediately, a girl was drowned in the creek, pulled down by a ghostly female hand. Sixty years later, another girl was lured away from the town by a lady in the woods, to an old house with a cellar in which she was told to wait. She escaped from the cellar, only to find that the search party sent to look for her had been massacred, their bodies disemboweled and covered in ritualistic cuts. Sixty years later, a hermit named Rustin Parr announced that he had killed seven of the town's children because he had been prompted by a ghostly lady. One boy who had got away told police that he had been told to stand in the corner of the cellar while other children were disemboweled and killed behind him. Naturally enough, when the fictional student filmmakers of the *Blair Witch Project* arrived sixty years later and trekked determinedly to find the witch's haunts, they disappeared. Viewers were left to presume that they had been murdered by the witch, especially as the film's makers cunningly whipped up publicity for it by presenting the story as fact.[75] The Blair Witch is probably based partly on Moll Dyer, a woman suspected of witchcraft in St. Mary's County in the 1790s, who allegedly left her hand-print on a rock at Leonardtown.[76] But all the rest is fiction.

The area of Maryland where *The Blair Witch* was supposedly set is, how-ever, one where a number of American cultural fault lines intersect. It is on the boundary between north and south, in the contested hills beyond Frederick, near the battlefields of Antietam, Gettysburg, and Monocacy. If the woods of the fictional Blair are anywhere, they are somewhere on the battlefield of South Mountain, one of Maryland's most folklore-rich spots. Here among the soldier-ghosts live, in the storyteller's mind at least, the "snarly yow" (a ghostly black dog), the "dwayyo" (a hairy, bearlike mon-ster) and the "snallygaster" (a dragonish creature something like the Jersey Devil). Here also are witches, holding Sabbaths with the devil in deserted houses, bewitching neighbors who denied them milk, and riding their vic-tims in the shape of horses in the night. But they are not the witches who were prosecuted in Maryland's history.[77] The area is also the setting for other supernatural yarns. In an episode of *The Twilight Zone* from 1961, "Still Valley," a Confederate scout finds in a small front-line town a group of Yankee soldiers, frozen into immobility as they march down its main street. He discovers that they have been bewitched by an old man using "conjure" magic from a book called simply *Witchcraft*. The old man is a supporter of the southern cause and, knowing that he will die later that day, gives his book to the scout, urging him to become his successor and use the "black magic" to destroy the Union army. The scout takes the book back to his commanding officers, and a fierce argument ensues over the use of the witchcraft. Eventually the scout's view — that it is damnable — prevails. Recognizing that to use the magic would bind the Confederacy to the devil, he reasons that it is better to let "damned Yankees" win the war than for the southern forces to be literally damned themselves.[78] The supernatural is a political football between north and south in such fictions and in *The Blair Witch Project* it has also become a matter of bitter contention between those countercultural conspiracy-theorists who believe the film's fiction and the irritated residents of Burkittsville who are tired of being told that a murderer lurks in their woods.

Burkittsville is a pleasant hamlet that can be driven through in two minutes at its very low speed limit. Its residents were appalled at their portrayal in the film and its sequel. Far from embracing, as Salem has, the potential to attract visitors, they shrank from publicity. There is a studied refusal to link the place in any way with the film: no souvenirs, no signs, no attractions. The local Historical Society of Frederick County, likewise, offers no material on the Blair Witch. It has some good books on folklore, but nothing about historical witchcraft. Once again, this is because there is almost no work on witches in Maryland for the Historical Society to keep.[79] Even folklore has struggled to keep its place in a historical culture dominated by study of the Civil War. The State Folklorist George C. Carey wrote in 1970 that before 1968, when Governor Agnew established a commission to investigate folklore survivals, surprisingly little effort had been made to preserve them. "There is a harsh and unfounded rumor abroad," he warned, "that folklore in Maryland is dead." He helped to produce a special supplement for the *Baltimore Sun* in 1974 to demonstrate the contrary, with stories drawn from Maryland's diverse ethnic groups. Ironically, in view of the cultural impact of *The Blair Witch Project*, he also protested that "surely, time has shown that the traditions which have sprung from these cultural groups are truer and more durable than the disposable culture we confront every day . . . flickering across a 12/15-inch screen in our living rooms."[80] While folklore barely survived, then, and the television screen has triumphed, interest in "real" witchcraft has never really taken hold.[81]

This seems to be partly because, as we saw in Virginia, in Maryland witchcraft is still a live issue. Commemoration in the northern sense is inappropriate: the matter is not closed and consigned to history, buried under monuments with a simple statement about "the world redeemed from superstition's sway" inscribed on them. Folklore and fiction here both cloak and express metaphorically continuing anxieties about the past: superstition, satanism, state identity, and the ongoing tension between northern and southern, conservative and liberal cultures. The old southern colonies still see things differently from their northern neighbors, for all the pardoning of Grace Sherwood. Witchcraft, then, seems likely to remain a matter over which Americans differ from each other according to where they live, to accidents of historical preservation, and to how and why they write, read, and reenact their history. In the southern colonies in particular, more recent and difficult history seems to stand between the present and the early modern period, which has meant that mythic distinctions between the witchcraft histories of north and south have been preserved largely without question, while actual differences have been left unexplored. It is time to see America's colonial witchcraft history as a whole, asking awkward questions about the beguiling myths — that witches were rare in the south, that Massachusetts is especially guilty of shedding their blood, that Pennsylvanians and New Yorkers did not believe in witchcraft — in order to uncover the detailed local history of American witchcraft that still remains partly unexplored.

# "THERE'S A LITTLE WITCH IN EVERY WOMAN": PSYCHOLOGY AND THE SOCIAL HISTORY OF WITCHES

"Shall we never, never get rid of this Past? It lies upon the Present like a giant's dead body. . . Just think a moment, and it will startle you to see what slaves we are to bygone times"

Guardian of the Gate: "Good morning, my dears. What can I do for you?"
Jinjur: "Surrender instantly!"[1]

## Witches and the Opening of the American Mind

In the late nineteenth century, alongside the reading of American witchcraft that emphasized the hard political choices to be made by the nation's governors — one aspect of which was the negotiation between oligarchy and multiethnic democracy discussed in Chapter 1 — another construction was also gaining favor among scholars and general readers. It was a psychological one, and it began a trend of understanding witchcraft prosecution in terms of wider social-scientific and biological, rather than narrowly political, factors.

The first indication of this psychological turn was not especially promising. In 1882, George Miller Beard published his *Psychology of the Salem Witchcraft Excitement of 1692 and its Practical Application in our Own Time*. Beard was a controversial neurologist, and his specialty was the unexplained exhaustion and even insensibility apparently caused by the stresses of modern, particularly urban, life. In 1869 he named this condition *neurasthenia*. By the time that he wrote his book on witchcraft, he had published extensively on — as the title of one of his books calls it — "American Nervousness," and he felt that he could explain the fits of the "witchcraft" victims at Salem quite simply as neurasthenic in nature. In some ways his attraction to the subject was inevitable, since he had theorized that "no other enlightened nation has expended so much cerebral force in the emotion of fear as America" (67) and, to his severe rationalist mind, the witchcraft episode seemed to epitomize this fear of nothing. But the immediate cause of his writing was the assassination of President James A. Garfield (who died of his gunshot wounds in 1882), and the insanity defense offered by his assassin Charles Guiteau. Beard had been called to give evidence for Guiteau at the trial, but his contribution had been disallowed for technical reasons. The case had become a test of American notions of insanity and their relationship to law, and although there was strong evidence that Guiteau was not in his right mind when he shot Garfield, he was convicted and executed. Deprived of his day in court, Beard determined that there were obvious parallels between the Guiteau trial and the witchcraft trials of 1692, and that it was his duty to publicize them. The "Salem" trials thus were obliged to take second place to hotly debated modern issues in a book that was a hybrid of history, contemporary political analysis, and medical treatise.

Beard based his understanding of the Essex County trials primarily on a reading of Upham's *Salem Witchcraft*, and added to Upham's explanation of the events his own diagnosis. He made a comparison — which was by now conventional — between the supposed "circle" of girls at Salem experimenting with magic and a contemporary case usually believed to be fakery, "the spirit-rapping excitement at Rochester."[2] But more sympathetically than any previous writer, he then argued that under the stress of transgression against their society — practicing divination, shrieking during prayers — the Salem girls had become genuinely sick. They were not frauds, but mentally ill. Beard went further. He also suspected that some "witches" at least had used artificial trance states — a kind of hypnosis — to cure people suffering from mental afflictions, and he offered Margaret Jones, hanged at Boston in 1648, as an example of this. His evidence seems to have been John Winthrop's report in his journal that when she stroked or touched anyone, they might be taken with deafness, vomiting, or violent pain — not exactly therapeutic.[3] But Beard chose to read the record differently, and explained that because such matters were not understood in the seventeenth century, persons in prostrate or insensible states induced by others or by their own medical infirmity were thought to be bewitched by the help of the devil. In the mass panic that followed, the suspects were tried overhastily, in circumstances of high political tension, and condemned on the basis of evidence that a few months later would seem laughable. This could explain all witchcraft trials, not just the Essex County ones of 1692. And in this process, "the penalty of our ancestors' non-expertness in psychology," Beard saw a parallel with the case of Guiteau. He brought to bear some of the political theories about witchcraft that we have already encountered in Chapter 1, in particular that "the outside mob influenced the trial . . . by interruptions in court, and by threatening the judges and prosecutors" (of which there is no evidence) but concluded that the "leaders of the three great professions," theologians, doctors, and lawyers, had also erred greatly in conducting the cases as they did. His main argument, then, was that the Puritans, like the Americans of 1882, had not known insanity when they saw it and that was why they had both killed innocent people in a form of judicial murder. Guiteau was thus "in one sense the successor of the victims of witchcraft" for whom "this country has been on its knees in repentance" for two centuries, Beard concluded.

Beard was at the forefront of a movement to examine the past in terms of the psychological theories of the moment. He wished to "lift the general subject of witchcraft . . . out of narrative and tradition into the science of psychology," and was joined by others. In Britain, David Nicholson published a series of articles on witchcraft in the *Journal of Mental Science* in 1882, while an editorial in the pharmaceutical periodical *Merck's Bulletin* in 1892 titled "Modern Witchcraft" described some Parisian experiments on subjects who could enter trance states at will.[4] A small but newly significant branch of medical science believed that it had found the answer to the "delusion" that it held belief in witchcraft to be. Cultural, religious, and historical differences were minimized in the service of the idea that all America's and the world's witches were part of an epidemic of variously misunderstood insanity. Practical lessons could thus be drawn from the events at Salem that might wash off American guilt.[5] Beard in particular gained considerable fame with his popular psychological explanation, and gave public lectures on the topic, including a particularly successful demonstration at the New York Academy of Sciences, which he recounted in his book. Here, two subjects in a trance state were induced to experience convulsions and claim that they saw spectral visions of the kind familiar to Abigail Williams and her fellow-afflicted. Beard was delighted. He pointed out that even if his audience did not accept his own belief that the trance states were genuine and not pretended, they could still see how seventeenth-century magistrates might have credited the testimony as evidence of witchcraft.[6]

But Beard's work drew not only on the work of physicians and researchers, but also on literary sources. He quoted repeatedly from Longfellow's drama *Giles Corey*, which portrayed Corey as precisely the victim of ignorance and judicial haste that Beard saw also in Guiteau. Like other psychologists — notably Freud and Jung — Beard made no distinction between the abilities of poets and historians to tell truths about the "witchcraft days," and he was right to believe that his interest in psychological explanations was shared by the public and its favorite authors alike. Alongside the strong trend in literary works about American witchcraft to dramatize the historians' debate about good governance, there had been for over half a century another that meditated on the relationship of that history to the inner life of Americans. It had become commonplace to suggest, as D. R. Castleton (Caroline Derby) did in *Salem: A Tale of the Seventeenth Century*, a novel of 1874, that the girls and young women who accused witches were "at the most nervous and impressible period of life — a period when a too-rapid growth, over-study, over-exertion, or various other predisposing causes, are often productive of hysteria, hypochondria and nervous debility."[7] In a great number of novels witches were also accused by people who were themselves salving some inner torment. The first was *Salem: An Eastern Tale*, published in parts in 1820, and Dana's *A Puritan Witch* was another, but in many others witchcraft accusations were the revenge of a rejected suitor: J. W. de Forest's *Witching Times*, in which Reverend Noyes accuses his former loves Martha Carrier and Rachel More; Henry Peterson's 1907 *Dulcibel*; and the Englishman Henry William Herbert's *The Fair Puritan* of 1856, to name but three.[8] And as the nineteenth century clattered on into a rational industrialized future, the more intangible aspects of the modern American psyche found expression in tales of psychological terror, gothic romance, ghosts, and witches. Into these fed the latest interests among American intellectuals, mesmerism (or animal magnetism) and spiritualism, as well as modern theories of mental disorder like Beard's.

Two common threads in this essentially Romantic view of witchcraft history were an interest in delusion and mental instability and a belief that there might be states of mind and biological energies in the world — the latter often in the form of "electric fluid" or spiritual emanation — unknown or unexplained by mainstream science. We have already seen the first strand of thinking, a linkage of witchcraft prosecution with mental illness, in Holland's realist novel *The Bay Path*, but the best-known exponent of witchcraft romance was one of America's foremost creative writers, and a man very unlike Josiah Holland. He was Nathaniel Hawthorne.

*Romance versus History: Hawthorne, Curses, and Mesmerism*

In a sense, the choice of how to write about witchcraft was one that reflected the most important literary debate of the nineteenth century: that between realists and romancers. To modern readers this distinction often seems hopelessly confused and confusing — and so it is. But to those who used the terms *realism* and *romance* in the nineteenth century, the two *R*s embodied entirely different conceptions of the world. Realists tended to emphasize deterministic readings of human life that focused on rational choices, philosophy and politics, the great movements of history, and their relationship with the individual. Writers of romance, meanwhile, often stressed the importance of chance, irrational and inexplicable impulses, supernatural events, and the individual as the subjective center of his or her own mental world, detached from wider social processes. America's witchcraft history could be read in both ways, but a writer's attitude toward it is often something of a touchstone, helping to place him or her on the spectrum between realism and romance, history and fiction. For Holland, despite his interest in mental health and superstition, witchcraft prosecutions were about sociopolitical status and a bad system of government. Witchcraft was firmly located in a specific moment of cultural history, with identifiable persons and documents wheeled in as evidence, and an attempt made to imagine the world of the seventeenth-century colonist and its political workings. The idea of the supernatural was to be condemned as folly, and alienated mental states as tragic aberrations. For Nathaniel Hawthorne, however, witchcraft was as much alive in 1850 as it had been in 1650. Nothing had changed in the human "heart" — and Romantic writers used the word "heart" rather than "mind" as a matter of course. The heart felt while the mind thought, and so it was the seat of pity, terror, and all the emotions normally conjured up during a witch trial. Why should these cease to exist when witches were no longer prosecuted? Although it was a fine thing that they were no longer hanged, the possibilities of their supposed powers and the fears and visions of their "victims" remained as matters of endless speculation, partly painful, partly pleasurable. The past was never quite dead and in Hawthorne's books and short stories, America was very much haunted by her witches.

The Romantic conception of the dark yet delicious influence of the past on the imaginative mind is best demonstrated in Hawthorne's *The House of the Seven Gables*. The first quotation that heads this chapter is spoken by Holgrave, Hawthorne's representation of himself in the book. In many of his other works — *The Scarlet Letter*, "Young Goodman Brown" — Hawthorne set his stories in the past itself, with witches as a part of the colonial experience.[9] But in *The House of the Seven Gables* he wrote about modern America, the Salem of 1850, which he had just left to move to Lenox. Here were steam engines, cent shops, political meetings, and insurance offices, but here too were witches, ghosts, and the killing power of an unbroken curse haunting the Pyncheon family since 1692. The name Pyncheon recalls, as it was meant to, William Pynchon of Springfield, and it was based on the story told of the condemned Salem "witch" Sarah Good who was said to have told her accusers that God would give them blood to drink for their sins; but in reality the family about which Hawthorne wrote was his own. Descended from the Salem trial judge John Hathorne, Hawthorne wrote the book in part to explore his own feelings of guilt and anxiety about his family's past. These went wider than witchcraft, and the familial guilt for having taken part in the condemnation of innocents.

To begin with, Hawthorne sounds almost like Josiah Holland in his fretful concern with the rights and wrongs of social status and differential wealth. The branch of the Pyncheons with whom the novel is chiefly concerned have fallen on hard times and the spinster Hepzibah Pyncheon decides to open a shop in the seven-gabled house where the Pyncheons/ Hawthornes lived. But, describing herself as now a mere woman rather than a lady, she is snobbishly reluctant to do so: "I never can go through with it! Never, never, never! I wish I were dead, and in the family tomb, with all my forefathers!" Hawthorne makes his own feelings on this distinction between "new Plebeianism and old Gentility" very clear. In the person of the writer and photographer Holgrave, he tells Hepzibah:

hitherto, your life-blood has been gradually chilling in your veins, as you sat aloof, within your circle of gentility, while the rest of the world was fighting out its battle with one kind of necessity or another. Henceforth you will at least have the sense of healthy and natural effort for a purpose, and of lending your strength . . . to the united struggle of mankind.

"In this republican country . . .," adds Hawthorne bitterly, "somebody is always at the drowning-point." Even Hepzibah is led to meditate, from her new position of subjection, on why "ladies" exist: "Must the whole world toil, that the palms of her hands may be kept white and delicate?"[10] In the Pyncheons, Hawthorne explores his own sense of unease at belonging to a family and thus a class traditionally protected from the vulgar striving of capitalism. His own engagement with that world and his financial problems, when set alongside the experience of such people, only made his reflections more pointed.

But as the story unfolds, such realist considerations slip from view behind the brooding contemplation of the family curse. True, the curse is related to the family's insatiable seeking of wealth and land, at the expense of other and better men, but its power goes well beyond that material origin. It was laid on the Pyncheons by Matthew Maule, a "wizard" condemned to death for witchcraft at the insistence of the family, who coveted his plot and later built their mansion upon it. The house's inhabitants meet with one disaster after another so long as they cling to their inheritance. We hear not only of the death of the founding Pyncheon, choking on his own blood at his housewarming party, but of the strange enthrallment of Alice Pyncheon to Matthew Maule's descendant by apparent bewitchment, the false conviction of Clifford Pyncheon for the supposed murder of his uncle and the resultant emptiness of his sister Hepzibah's life, and, at the heart of the book, the eerie, lonely death of the real culprit, Judge Pyncheon. Ironically, while Hawthorne based his understanding of the Salem witch trials on his former friend Charles Wentworth Upham's reconstruction of quarrels over land preceding the accusations, he then based Judge Pyncheon's less attractive characteristics on Upham, with whom he had fallen out over political office. The book is most memorable for the author's spine-chilling gloating over Pyncheon as instead of attending a dinner that will secure him the nomination for state governor, he lies dead in the house of the seven gables. It is the keynote passage in a text haunted by bitterness, regret, and the fantasy of magical revenge. Almost every character in the book and a good number of animals, objects, and inanimate substances are at some time described in the language of spell, magic, and bewitchment — tea, the shop doorbell, a scissor-grinder's wheel — but the reader is left with the unpleasant sensation at the book's end that it is the author who most relishes his witchlike power to snuff out a privileged life when he gives Judge Pyncheon "blood to drink."[11]

The "magic" of Hawthorne's romance and his own status as a witch — unexpected for the descendant of a witch-trying judge — are part of his sense that for all her modernity America is a bewitched land where reason and the dry histories of economics and politics can never truly triumph. Although, rational and Upham-like, he blames the Pyncheons for accusing Maule of witchcraft in their anxiety to seize his land, he also states repeatedly that Maule and his descendants do actually have inexplicable psychological powers. Their skill is not witchcraft as such, but a power just as magical and sinister in its operation: "animal magnetism," which nineteenth-century opinion believed gave its possessor the ability to hypnotize victims and compel them toward their doom. It is this power that Matthew Maule, grandson of the wizard Matthew Maule, deploys against Alice Pyncheon. She falls into a trance in which she sees visions like a medium, and for the rest of her life is

> Maule's slave . . . [S]eated by his humble fireside, Maule had but to wave his hand; and wherever the proud lady chanced to be . . . her spirit passed from beneath her own control. . . . "Alice, laugh!" the carpenter, beside his hearth, would say; or perhaps intensely will it, without a spoken word. And even were it prayer-time, or at a funeral, Alice must break into wild laughter.

This is an "explanation" for supposed demonic possession or obsession, but it goes beyond the explicable in that the wizard can command his victim even from remote distances, by telepathic, mesmeric means.

He has power over Alice's very soul, asserts Hawthorne, and since such malign witchcraft usually carries its own punishment Maule is justly mortified when his playful tormenting leads inadvertently to Alice's death.[12] And when Holgrave (who at the tale's close is revealed also to be Maule's descendant) reads to Phoebe Pyncheon a short story he has written, his words have a similar, though unintended, effect on her. Making the same gestures and "incantations" during the reading of his work as its subject Matthew Maule, Holgave almost hypnotizes Phoebe and is forced to take action to release her at the end of his story. Holgrave is Hawthorne's representative, and in this passage his creator plays half-seriously with the idea that his own story is bewitching his listener.

Thus complex psychological and metafictional patterns are being worked out in the interplay between witchcraft's history and its transformed retelling in romance. In *The House of the Seven Gables*, Hawthorne symbolically kills the witchcraft historian Charles W. Upham, and substitutes his own re-empowered witchcraft for Upham's rational explanations. For Hawthorne, the drama of the individual psyche is the focus of the tale, rather than the mundane life of the wider community as it was for Upham. It was just such a focus that Beard adopted in his examination of the psychological forces at work in Essex County in 1692, and by the 1890s this paradoxically romantic yet scientific reading of witchcraft was poised to work its way into mainstream historical writing. It did so via a long and little-traveled road that began with the late-nineteenth-century connection between some kinds of radical "feminism," the biology of "animal magnetism," and the exploration of the occult.

### A Witch's Brew: Romance, Science, and Feminism

In the 1880s, a New York campaigner for women's suffrage, Matilda Joslyn Gage, became interested in witches. She had investigated spiritualism, the teachings of theosophy, and animal magnetism and been convinced by their claims, so in one sense her discovery of witchcraft was an extension of her existing beliefs. But her understanding of the nature of witchcraft was in another way quite different from that of Beard and Hawthorne, and was summed up in a phrase from her 1893 history *Women, Church and State*: "for 'witches' we read 'women.'"[13] Although this is a sweeping generalization, it now seems obvious that a focus on the sex of suspects was necessary to understanding anything about witchcraft prosecutions, since in most jurisdictions women were much more likely to be accused of witchcraft than men. As David D. Hall put it in 1985, "gender is the most reliable of all predictors of who would be singled out and labeled 'witch.'"[14] But in the mid-nineteenth century, as we have seen, scholars and creative writers had not made any significant issue of that information, in as far as they perceived it at all. Gage leapt to remedy that omission — not out of an interest in the crime per se, but by incorporating a section on witch-craft in a pioneering history of what she saw starkly as women's age-old oppression by men. Her purpose in the book was firmly rational, to force her readers to "Think for Themselves" (Dedication). Yet she approached her subject from a position familiar to Beard and Hawthorne and other romancers, in the belief that witchcraft prosecutions might be explained by two kinds of biological phenomenon: paranoid fear and what we might now call psychopathic cruelty on the part of inquisitors, and genuine psy-chic and physical abilities on the part of the suspects.

Matilda Joslyn was an unusual woman, brought up by parents who believed strongly in female education. They schooled their young daugh-ter themselves to as a high a standard as was possible in the upstate town of Cicero, impressing her with the beliefs that through learning a woman could achieve anything, that her skills were many and not to be slighted, and above all that she must think for herself. These were ideas she was later to apply in radical fashion to the history of witchcraft. Because her parents were committed temperance activists and abolitionists she developed a strong social conscience, strengthened by further education in liberal cir-cles. And even though she married a dry goods merchant, Henry Gage, at eighteen, and bore four children, Matilda Joslyn Gage never stopped read-ing and working for the many causes in which she believed. During the

Civil War, she pushed for the Union to adopt the abolition of slavery as the moral basis of its military struggle. She campaigned for better treatment of Native Americans, and "hyphenated" Irish- and German-Americans. She was a founding member of the National Woman Suffrage Association, taking part in attempts by women to vote, researching legal arguments in test cases, organizing conventions and protests. Any movement toward the equality of all people attracted her energetic support.

But because of her interest in multiple types of discrimination, Joslyn Gage had a rather different view of the female suffrage campaign than did many other campaigners. She became increasingly convinced that the oppression of women was linked to and inextricable from that of other disadvantaged groups by their representation in Christian texts and practices. Christianity had been used by some to denigrate women, justify slavery, and promote ruthless western expansion, she believed. So, like the Unitarians and Universalists but in a more extreme form, she became increasingly impatient with orthodox piety and turned to alternative spiritualities. In 1878 she made her first public speech at a free thought convention, stating that, "the Christian Church is based upon the fact of woman servitude." The Church's attitude toward Eve, she argued, was clear evidence of this. Christianity's own story about its origins was a tale of a woman who had sinned in seeking knowledge and been punished by inferiority to her man. How, then, could suffragists accept modern Christianity as an ally, even when its intentions seemed good? Many suffragists, however, were conventionally religious women, and Joslyn Gage failed to convince the N.W.S.A. of the importance of freethinking to their struggle. She did not abandon the association but she did found a sister organization, the Women's National Liberal League, so as to be able to put her case alongside theirs. And by the late 1880s the difference in emphasis in the women's suffrage movement between religious women and radicals had become a chasm. As it widened, Joslyn Gage was pushed further to the margin, into a more extreme denunciation of orthodox religion and a stronger commitment to unorthodox ideas. In an effort to strengthen her case, she concentrated her research increasingly on the history of medieval Christianity in Europe — especially the persecutions that the church had undertaken and the abuses it had tolerated — and on the occult forces that she believed might help explain witches' prosecution.

In 1890 came the decisive event that shaped her major work, *Woman, Church and State.* It was a merger between the N.W.S.A. and the American Woman Suffrage Association, overseen by the N.W.S.A.'s leader Susan B. Anthony in an attempt to unite women of all religious and political persuasions behind the shared demand for the vote. The A.W.S.A., however, included the Women's Christian Temperance League. And although they argued for equality as part of the Christian ethic, they often combined this with a demand for a Christian constitution for the United States, and the incorporation of biblical codes of behavior into law. Many women in the N.W.S.A., including Joslyn Gage and her friends, believed therefore not only that organized religion was implicated in oppression, but that the conservative women threatened American liberty. It looked as though moves to Christianize the constitution might be successful, and radical women could not countenance this even if it meant gaining the vote. When the merger took place, therefore, freethinkers, anarchists, and pro-secularization moderates from the N.W.S.A. decided to separate and form the Women's National Liberal Union. Although it would work — uneasily — alongside the merged suffrage organizations, it would promote its members' wider reading of the need for political, religious, and social reform, as against the narrow focus on votes for women. At its inaugural meeting in 1890 a number of speakers denounced the Christian church as an enemy of progress, and Joslyn Gage found enthusiastic encouragement for her views. She was the Women's National Liberal Union's president until her death in 1898, and *Woman, Church and State*, which numbered witches among the victims of male tyranny, thus grew out of the W.N.L.U. and the support she found there from fellow radicals. It was part of a stand against the union of church and state that many feared in the early 1890s.[15] And so in her book Joslyn Gage argued that the "witches" who were killed in large numbers by church courts in the medieval and early modern periods were actually liberal protosuffragists: forward-looking, skilled, and wise, with special biological and mental powers linked to their femininity. They were militant feminist versions of Beard's Margaret Jones, and they were persecuted for precisely these qualities, which the reactionary church could not accommodate. It went without saying that a church with such a history ought not to be given power in a modern and liberty-loving nation like the United States.

The basic arguments of *Woman, Church and State* were shaped by two texts in particular, which Joslyn Gage had encountered in her reading on medieval Christianity. The first was the Dominican Inquisitors Heinrich Kramer and Jacob Sprenger's notoriously misogynistic demonology *Malleus Maleficarum (The Witch Hammer)*, written in the 1480s.[16] The second was more recent and less authentic: the French historian Jules Michelet's *La Sorcière*, a work on witches as early modern female revolutionaries, published in 1862. Michelet blamed the medieval Catholic Church for beginning the witch hunts, and consequently so did Gage. Chronologically, this was broadly correct, but she and Michelet both made Inquisitors sound cynical and conspiratorial — using the old Protestant insult "priestcraft" — which was not demonstrable. There is every indication that Kramer, Sprenger, and other demonologists believed what they wrote, no matter how far-fetched and inaccurate it may seem to the modern mind. They were also expressing some widely held beliefs about the way the universe worked: good versus evil, God versus Satan, clerics (therefore) versus witches. Many of the same beliefs were held by secular authorities and in Protestant jurisdictions where witch-hunting could also be found. Finally, it must be said that *Malleus Maleficarum* is rather untypical of medieval and early modern demonologies in its relentless focus on women. Michelet based a fantasy of empowered revolutionary priestesses on its more extreme claims — with his own anticlerical twist — but it was more or less alone in making them. So while Gage responded with justifiable horror to Kramer and Sprenger's words, and exulted in the negative image that they presented of witches as independent women, she missed the more balanced understanding of cultural history, theology, and demonology that might have come if Michelet had not been her primary guide.

She did, however, make a number of important assertions that have sustained feminist writers on witchcraft to this day. First, she argued that unlike its pagan forebears, "the church degraded woman by destroying her self-respect." Second, she asserted that the women accused of witchcraft had in fact been early scientists, mesmerists, and workers with plant extracts, elemental spirits, and psychic forces not yet understood. "The so-called 'witch' was among the most profoundly scientific persons of the age," she said, resorting to explanations of her powers that included astral light and the special "Pacinian" corpuscles recently postulated by an Italian physician. With these abilities, women who were "psychic sensitives of high powers" could really heal others, levitate, and fall into cataleptic states at will. While modern feminists have discarded such theories, they have often echoed Joslyn Gage's basic argument: that the church suspected and suppressed women's scientific knowledge by accusing them of witchcraft. For Joslyn Gage, such repression was an attack on "human rights," a "bondage ... over free thought" springing from "patriarchism" — an early formation of the word *patriarchy*. Finally, she said, the witchcraft prosecutions of New England had taken place because the "Puritan Fathers" had "adopted all the unjust previsions of European christianity [*sic*] as parts of their own religion and government." She based her account of the Salem prosecutions on Upham, and his assault on Cotton Mather. For Joslyn Gage, then, the American demand for female suffrage was an extension of the revolt against the persecutors of the Salem witches: women's "rebellion ... against the tyranny of Church and State" had its beginnings in early times and "its progress will overthrow every existing form of these institutions." The road from Salem, she thought, would lead eventually to "a regenerated world."[17]

This hotchpotch argument, partly derivative and partly highly original, is strikingly coherent. Yet it is questionable in a number of important ways, just as the parallel mythmaking of nineteenth-century political historians can be questioned. Essentially, Gage suggested that the church degraded women, disposed of knowledgeable and powerful women as "witches," and imported this evil to America in the seventeenth century. We have already examined the third point in discussing Charles W. Upham's belief that ministers were primarily responsible for the Essex County trials, and the arguments advanced against this view by Poole and others. The first point is also debatable, since little evidence has been found of the widespread pagan matriarchies that Joslyn Gage and later feminists thought could be found in the pre-Christian world. Goddesses were venerated in many societies, but their status was not necessarily reflected in a concern for the equality and well-being of most of the actual women who worshipped them. Both Michelet and Gage made it seem that Christianity invented sexism, but European churchmen based their understanding of women on Classical, pagan sources. As we shall see in the next chapter, however, Gage was not alone in her belief that paganism was a more woman-friendly spiritual path than Christianity. It is, therefore, her second point that is the most original and interesting, and it was taken up in various forms not just by activists but by professional historians in the late twentieth century. Were the women accused of witchcraft in some way different to their fellow females? Were they rebellious? Were they particularly learned or skilled or transgressive or ambitious or freethinking? Did their female minds and bodies attract prosecutors to them in some way hitherto unexplored?

To suggest such a thing was radical stuff even in late nineteenth-century Washington and New York. Joslyn Gage had ignored most of the accepted scholarly parameters of the debate about American witchcraft and the Mathers, the one being conducted by men like Trumbull and Goodell. Although she built on Upham's reading, it was not important to her whether a particular minister, the magisterial class, or a demagogue-led mob should be blamed for hanging witches. The social standing of the prosecuting group and the kind of polity that they represented did not matter. What did matter was that they were all of them Christians and men, and that most of the hanged (and, elsewhere, burned) were women. To make this important point, Joslyn Gage had to discount some evidence and privilege a simple interpretation over a complex one. She either bypassed or was not aware of the evidence that many women accused other women of witchcraft, and she minimized both consideration of the Christianity of many of the accused and the place of male witches in history and demonology. Her argument was based on a limited acquaintance with relevant scholarship, and she referred primarily to sometimes questionable secondary sources — not that that was unusual among historians of her time. But Joslyn Gage was very different from Levermore, Taylor, Drake, or Poole. Despite her public speaking and organizational role, she was primarily a homemaker and small businesswoman who in 1893 was trying to run a struggling dry goods store in Fayetteville, New York, after her husband's death. She had to mortgage her house to help pay for publication activity, travel expenses, and fees for suffrage conventions. She had no academic standing, no salary, and no private money, so she also had no access to the European and most of the American trial records and library collections that would have formed the basis of a more nuanced argument.[18] Few original documents were in print, and those few were in expensive and rare volumes. There are errors and overstatements in her work, and it has been used to underpin a number of oversimplified polemics. Yet a clear century ahead of the historians of the 1980s, Joslyn Gage, informed largely by romantic notions and pseudoscience, articulated a basic truth and asked a basic question about witchcraft prosecutions that no one else seemed to care about: most of the accused and executed were women — why?

### Teenage Witches and The Devil in Massachusetts

Matilda Joslyn Gage's views fell on deaf ears during her lifetime, as did those of her fellow pioneer George M. Beard. The prevailing historical account of American witchcraft was still Upham's, in which the accused men and women were innocent victims of delusion, and their accusers were malicious and lying girls. But in 1949, the journalist Marion Starkey published what was to be one of the most popular books on the "Salem" witchcraft trials, second only to Upham's in its longevity and still in print. Starkey approached the witches and their accusers from two different viewpoints. The first was the traditionally New England–historical, since she was herself descended from a *Mayflower* immigrant. The second, however, had elements of both Beard's and Joslyn Gage's work — now reworked into the modern and fashionable science of psychoanalysis, with its emphasis on the unconscious, hypnotism, and the importance of childhood fantasy. Her book *The Devil in Massachusetts* caught the public mood of the mid-twentieth century, where psychoanalytic notions were becoming well known in a popular form, and in the Time Books edition of 1963 two prefaces help explain why. The first was by "the Editors" of *Time*, and echoing Starkey's work it related the Essex County witchcraft trials directly to the modern American phenomenon of the teenager — dissatisfied, oppositional, and threatening to traditional American norms. The Editors told the story of a recent court case, in which a young woman had set fire to the Stars and Stripes in a church, saying that it felt right to her, "like I burned God." In 1692, such a "girl" might, they argued, "have been deemed a witch, or perhaps more likely, she could have become an accuser and identifier of witches." Early modern witches and their accusers were conflated here in the contemporary image of the disorderly female and the disorderly youth, who were both so far from the expected standard of behavior as to seem both criminal and mentally ill to those who sat in judgment on them. Some seventeenth-century Salem people, the Editors summed up, seemed also to have had "a thoroughly irreverent and skeptical attitude" and may well have been "power-mad unbelievers intent upon 'burning God.'" If such problematic people still existed in Truman's or Johnson's America, how much more extreme must their alienated behavior have seemed to the Puritans of the seventeenth century?

Having given a contemporary relevance to the figures of the witches and the afflicted girls of Salem, the Editors also found in Starkey's book a disturbing parallel between those who arrested, tried, and executed witches and the more recent "rounding up of the 'the enemies of the people'" in Nazi Germany and Stalin's Russia. Presumably drawing on Arthur Miller's reading of Salem as analogous to the McCarthy "witch hunt" against American Communists (a reading that drew in turn on Starkey's book when it was first published), they suggested to readers that "the gas chambers and other efficient horrors of twentieth century concentration camps" were not so far from the American imagination as had complacently been thought. Thus, by choosing Starkey's book for republication in their prestigious series, *Time's* editors set the seal of approval on her attempt to make the history of American witchcraft accessible to a new generation by ignoring the traditional arguments about democracy and good government and foregrounding instead modern preoccupations with sociology, biology, and psychology: the "problem" of teenage rebellion, the potential for scapegoating in troubled times, and finally sex and gender issues that seemed new to the debate. Everyone had forgotten Joslyn Gage, although Starkey had read Beard's *Psychology of the Salem Witchcraft Excitement*. The eminent novelist and commentator Aldous Huxley wrote an introduction for the book, adding his weight to the notion that Starkey's work somehow solved the problem of witchcraft for a modern readership, explaining what was really going in the minds of accusers and accused.[19]

With the more polemical political issues pushed into the background a new consensus had emerged by 1949, which endured until the 1990s. In this view, witchcraft prosecutions were "about" interpersonal social tensions, primarily between ages and genders, "deviant" and mainstream people, which had exploded into a community tragedy because of mistaken thinking by a few powerful people. They were no longer the fault of the "mob" or the mass of governing oligarchs, and thus theories about them ceased to have a straightforward political application, a revolutionary or repressive charge. Nor could they be blamed on demagogues who traded on popular ignorance, just as the Holocaust could not be blamed solely on Adolf Hitler. Instead the generality of people — people like us — were to blame for bowing their common sense and humanity to hysteria and seeking a scapegoat when their lives were pressurized by unrelated circumstance.[20] This hysteria might, in the right conditions, empower demagogues and dictators — but Starkey's book seemed to suggest that it was up to the ordinary American to act in ways that would make this a nonissue in the United States. As we know, and as William Carlos Williams's *Tituba's Children* and Miller's *The Crucible* dramatized, her warnings went unheeded as the House Un-American Activities Committee's hearings came to dominate the political climate of the 1950s. But as the detailed and personalized biographical studies of her book show, Starkey's main interest was not political in the narrow sense. Instead, her reading of the "Salem" trials sprang from her own experience as a female student and journalist. If there was a lesson of Salem for Starkey, it was perhaps most genuinely the suggestion that it behooved American men to behave better toward girls and women, affording them opportunities for education and self-expression that in the aftermath of the Second World War seemed under pressure from social conservatism. Starkey's book made it seem that witchcraft was relevant to everyone. But for Starkey it was especially relevant to the plight of women in a repressive society, and to the mental ills that came from their condition.

Starkey insisted that modern American girls must not lead lives like those of the girls and women who accused witches: "their activity was the same monotonous round . . . [of] unrelieved drudgery" with "matrons made pregnant nearly as often as milch cows" and unmarried girls "without a sense of direction, and worse, without dignity . . . instinct with repressed vitality."[21] Bored, anxious, and frustrated, these girls and young women, Starkey suggested following Upham, turned to Samuel Parris's slave Tituba for compassion and entertainment and were led astray by her into magical practices in her supposed idle hours. Ironically for a work that deliberately paralleled witch-hunting with genocide based on concepts of race and nation, Starkey's reading was not liberal in its thinking about Tituba or other nonwhite people accused of witchcraft in Essex County in 1692. She represented Tituba as "half-savage," "tricksy," and idle, blaming her for starting the witchcraft accusations by her conjuring and lack of moral fiber.[22] But Starkey was indulgent toward the accusers, the young white girls and women of her story. She called Ann Putnam, Elizabeth Hubbard, and their friends "a pack of 'bobby-soxers'" who were "inflamed by the terrors of Calvinism" and "depressed by the lack of any legitimate outlet for their natural high spirits."[23] No wonder, Starkey implied, they began to cause trouble, partly consciously but also partly driven by genuine mental torment. They were almost justifiably rebels without a cause, long before their time.

But despite Starkey's lead — and the many questions that were begged and remained unanswered in her popular account — the history of American witches or their accusers as *women* received surprisingly little attention in the years that followed *The Devil in Massachusetts*. As we have seen, suffragists and radical feminist activists had been writing about the connections between women's power and witchcraft persecution since about 1880. Meanwhile, as discussed in Chapter 5, Hollywood and the television industry were also busy, equating female sexuality with witchcraft, and feminism with witchcraft. But very few scholars related these unscholarly yet suggestive explorations back to the seventeenth century. The two readings of witches did not seem to belong in the same world — and one still finds resistance to the idea that they do. One is popular and practical, prone to sweeping statement in the service of polemic or entertainment. The other is scholarly and reticent, reluctant to ask questions that seem to lie outside traditional disciplines or might upset the status quo. The most daring attempt to connect the popular view of witches with new scholarly directions came in John Demos's *Entertaining Satan*, which discussed women's lives as part of its focus on sociological history. As we saw in Chapter 2, Demos also added to the literature on female psychology in witchcraft cases, striving to reconstruct the emotional worlds of women like Mary Bliss Parsons and Sarah Bridgeman from the stories and statistics that were available. But a book-length study of American women and witchcraft per se remained unwritten for four decades after 1949.

*Woman, Church, and State Revisited*

In its place, some activists' works were taken to be all that scholarly feminism had to say on the subject of witchcraft. One such was Barbara Ehrenreich and Deirdre English's *Witches, Midwives and Nurses: A History of Women Healers*. When historians cite this work (usually in condemnatory terms), it often seems as though it must be a full-length, scholarly history, although one that comes to unusual conclusions about the history of witchcraft. In fact, it is nothing of the kind. Although they published with a press based at the City University of New York, Ehrenreich and English admitted freely that they were "in no sense 'professional' historians" — and their "book" is only a forty-five-page pamphlet. As a history it is inaccurate and incomplete: it abruptly dismisses all American witch trials as "small scale, very late ... and in an entirely different social context than the earlier European witch-craze," but does not explain what the differences are. It blames witch-hunting exclusively on the Catholic Church and states that witches were burned, without qualifying either of these statements. It asserts that "thousands upon thousands," even "millions" of women were executed for witchcraft crimes. Like Joslyn Gage, Ehrenreich and English follow Michelet in claiming that witches may have been part of "a female-led peasant rebellion." And their central thesis is that witches were pretty much always healers or midwives, skilled and compassionate herbalists who knew their business, and that their demonization was due to their medical skills threatening the emergence of a male-dominated medical profession. Unfortunately, little evidence supports these claims. Michelet's linkage of women with peasant revolutions was a fantasy. He offered no medieval or early modern evidence of what he suggested, and none has been found. Furthermore, most European witches were not described as midwives or healers. A minority do seem to have been people of both sexes who prescribed herbal and/or magical remedies, and it may be assumed that some of the women at least assisted in childbirth along with other women present. But there is no evidence that their remedies were any better than those of the physicians, and where accounts do survive some of the methods seem unlikely to help the patient in any measurable way.

For example, Ursley Kempe, a woman executed for witchcraft in Essex, England, in 1582 described to her examiner a method for curing lameness caused by bewitchment. Her instructor had told her to:

> take hogges dunge and charvell [chervil] and put them together and holde them in her left hand, and to take in the other hande a knife, and to pricke the medicine three times, & then to cast the same into the fire, and to take the said knife & to make three pricks under a table, and to let the knife sticke there: & after that to take three leves of sage, and as much of herbe John (alias herbe grace) and put them into ale: and drinke it last at night and first in the morning.

Ursley said that "shee taking the same had ease of her lamenesse," and she had advised others to take similar steps to cure their own ills.[24] Ursley's remedy is a fascinating piece of folk wisdom, which seems to involve some kind of sympathetic magic: the ball of dung and chervil is pricked and burned as if to symbolize an attack on the disease. Ale with herbs might cheer and relax the patient, but would be unlikely to have any particular or lasting effect on lameness. Handling dung would be actively unhealthy. So while Ehrenreich and English conjured up an image of European "peasant women" deploying an arsenal of "pain-killers, digestive aids and anti-inflammatory agents," they adduced no actual evidence to support their claims. They also unwittingly ignored a substantial amount of scholarly work that showed efficacious remedies as only part of a wider spectrum of everything from spoken charms to downright harmful practices, which were prescribed by both men and women on the basis of oral tradition.[25]

But, in fact, Ehrenreich and English were not trying to provide a full, referenced, or scholarly account of witchcraft's history. What they were trying to write was a polemical pamphlet about masculine discrimination against female health workers, which they saw continuing to their own time. Undoubtedly they believed that they were offering a fair interpretation of history, but their main purpose was not historical, despite their pamphlet's title. They concluded their booklet with a summary of their real concern: a strong analysis of the "institutional sexism" of the modern American health system that called for an alliance of nurses and other female health workers with the female consumers of healthcare. They wanted to end hierarchies within medicine, in which only doctors were regarded as professional and professionalism had come, they thought, to mean expensive and exclusive training and little else. Their ultimate aim was to unite women, nonwhite and working-class health workers, and patients to build an inclusive system where expertise was recognized and valued wherever it occurred, and nurses in particular were no longer "a uniformed maid service to the dominant male professionals."[26] *Witches, Midwives and Nurses* was not really the American feminist historians' comment on the witch trials of the seventeenth century and before. Instead, it was a polemical and incidentally ill-informed intervention in a dispute about the roles of twentieth-century health workers. It committed all the same errors that accounts such as Levermore's or Upham's committed: overstatement, limited consultation of relevant sources, a focus on presentist concerns at the expense of understanding past ones. But because it was written in the 1970s and not the 1870s, and written by women on the margins of a traditionally male preserve, it was especially vulnerable to attack.[27]

Ironically, if Ehrenreich and English had concentrated their attention on American witchcraft trials, they would have found a surprising amount of evidence to support their claims. While, again, most witches were not in any way identifiable as midwives, some certainly were the kind of magical, herbal, or religious healers that Ehrenreich and English had imagined to be the forebears of modern physicians. Ann Burt of Lynn was such a woman: in Chapter 1 we saw Bethiah Carter telling a magistrate of her sick sister Sara Townsend's complaint that "my father carryed me to boston But carryed her too Lin too an owld wich" to seek medical help. Burt had, according to Carter, told her patient that if she would believe in her God (just which God was left unspecified) she would be cured. Previously she had cured believers, but could not help her own husband because he had refused to believe. Other witnesses against her said that she had tried to cure them with a variety of methods. Jacob Knight had drunk a bottle of liquid that Burt gave him, because she said that it would help his headache, while Sarah Pearson had been given a pipe to smoke when she had a sore throat. The physician Phillip Read gave evidence against Burt, accusing her of bewitching Sara Townsend, in a manner that would have gladdened Ehrenreich and English's hearts.[28] Similarly, at Boston in 1641 Jane Hawkins, described by John Winthrop as a midwife suspected of witchcraft, was banished from the Bay Colony and ordered not to practice surgery or physic, or dispense any drinks, plasters, or oils.[29] Winifred Holman of Cambridge, so strongly suspected by John Gibson, had offered to cure his grandchild when it was sick, and alleged that she had cured rickets in another patient.[30] And so on — there are clearer and more numerous records of female medical practitioners in America than in most other contemporary jurisdictions, per head of population. Ehrenreich and English's study, then, is not without merit, flawed as its premises might be.[31]

It was not the scholarly feminist history of American witchcraft that was needed, however, and neither (although better informed) was Selma Williams and Pamela Williams Adelman's *Riding the Nightmare* (1978), which explored witchcraft prosecutions as an "uncoordinated, though murderous, war on women" from Lilith to Sarah Good and Rebecca Nurse.[32] It was not until 1987, with academic feminism rising, that such an account, nuanced and fully researched in archives, was at last produced. In that year Carol F. Karlsen published *The Devil in the Shape of a Woman*. It was a book that began as a doctoral dissertation at Yale, and it blended scholarship with an unconcealed indignation that the witchcraft history of American women had received so little attention. Most accounts of women's history in general, Karlsen said, "leave readers with the impression that sustained historical investigation of the realities of women's position in their communities is either impossible or unnecessary." She felt very differently: "only by understanding that the history of witchcraft is primarily a history of women . . . can we confront the deeply embedded feelings about women — and the intricate patterns of interest underlying those feelings — among our witch-ridden ancestors." Karlsen was also motivated — as were and are many feminist historians — by a belief that her research on the early modern period might also illuminate the present. "We still live with witches in our culture," she said, "however much their shape might have changed." For her, contemporary activist and popular cultural readings of witchcraft *did* connect with the early modern world. But Karlsen's book was not simply a feminist rant against early modern men. She saw that because women often accused women of witchcraft, there was a problem with the simple binary reading that blamed patriarchy for everything. Witchcraft prosecutions, she argued, were about "a deeply ambivalent but violent struggle *within* women as well as an equally ambivalent and violent struggle *against* them."[33]

Karlsen's basic contention — that biological sex and gendered behavior was an important factor in witchcraft prosecutions — was irrefutable. She calculated that between 1620 and 1725, 78 percent of those accused of witchcraft were female. It was not as big a percentage as in England, where the figure was around 90 percent, but nevertheless it proved beyond doubt that the stereotype of the witch as a woman was more than just a myth. Having made this overarching case, Karlsen then proceeded to examine all the cases that she could find that involved female witches, identifying as she searched the records several that were previously unknown. Karlsen concluded that at least some of the women who were accused of witchcraft seemed to have been targeted not because they were old, poor, and economically and socially dependent — the classic reading of English witchcraft cases by scholars like Keith Thomas and Alan Macfarlane — but because they were sexually and socially independent and wealthy. It was an unexpected statement: the idea that witches were downtrodden female victims might have been predicted, but Karlsen was suggesting that some early modern women were in fact more powerful than had been thought. In her reading, which in some respects strikingly echoed Joslyn Gage's now-forgotten conclusions, they were persecuted precisely because they were so successful. It was an argument that had a profound resonance for many women of the 1970s and 1980s, who felt under constant attack precisely because of their success in careers outside the domestic sphere and were angry about the response to their prominence, both politically and in personal terms. Karlsen thus touched a raw nerve in American society, making her book another landmark in the ongoing story of how the supposedly obscure study of witches by scholars interacted with mainstream political culture.[34]

It was a connection that Karlsen made explicit in her "Afterword" to the 1998 edition of *The Devil in the Shape of a Woman*. "Politicians and their supporters," she said, "have created their own witches . . . most obviously Anita Hill, whose alleged discontent, anger, envy, malice, sexual fantasies, lying, and pride, was matched only by her supposedly unbridled ambition, plagiarism of *The Exorcist*, and determination to destroy 'a good man.'" Hill is a law professor who in 1991 accused Judge Clarence Thomas of sexual harassment, almost preventing his elevation to the Supreme Court. Karlsen linked the abuse heaped on Hill to the argument she had made in *The Devil in the Shape of a Woman* in 1987 that in portraying witches as "difficult, turbulent, contentious, opinionated, unreasonable, unpleasant, shrewish, envious, easily offended, or malicious," and female accusers as "lying, manipulative, twisted, hysterical, merciless, mentally ill, childish, whorish or demonic," historians had participated in an inherently sexist discourse, based on "past and present assumptions about how women ought to behave." She said that she suspected the persistence of this stereotype, which suggested that the witch in some way deserved her fate and her accusers their afflictions, was "related to the deeply embodied tendency in our society to hold women ultimately responsible for the violence committed against them."[35] Karlsen also launched an attack on American academia for its attempt to, as she saw it, "avoid according gender the place it deserves in the history of witchcraft." She suggested that both "overt and covert strategies" had been deployed to this end, including the "misrepresentations or gross oversimplifications of feminist analyses . . . reductions of arguments to one or more of its parts, and in challenges to interpretations that are barely acknowledged, if at all." "Another approach," she suggested, "has been to lump together all feminist treatments of witchcraft," equating work such as her own with accounts based only on secondary sources or with older and less accurate texts.[36] The debate is ongoing. In 2002 Mary Beth Norton remarked in her new history of "Salem," *In the Devil's Snare*, that a number of important historians had denied "the significance of women's prominence as both accused and accuser" in 1692. In her "Acknowledgements" she then blandly described how she and a single female colleague had been the only two women in the History Department at Cornell University for a staggering fifteen years. Readers were left to draw their own conclusions about why women's histories of witchcraft had remained rare and undervalued.[37]

## Witchcraft, Gender, and Race

Norton's book did not just redirect the attention of scholars to the gender of most of the accusers and accused, and their psychological state. It also summed up in a comprehensive and original form a concern that had been growing quietly in the scholarly community for about thirty years: that the place of the Essex County witch trials in the history of race had been neglected, and in some cases misrepresented in racist terms. To begin with, why was Tituba Indian, one of the first three women to be accused of witchcraft at Salem, usually portrayed as a half-Native-American, half-black, or wholly black woman, even though all the seventeenth-century texts referred to her flatly as "Indian"? There were a few black people who were accused of witchcraft — Mary Black and a woman known only as Candy at Salem, for example. Mary Black would not confess anything, while Candy spoke in apparently broken English to accuse her mistress, Margaret Hawkes, of making her a witch, saying that she had not been a witch in her own country (which she did not name). She also produced some knotted rags, which she said she had used to bewitch people.[38] But why was Tituba numbered among these black "witches"? The first expression of this unease came in an article of 1974. Chadwick Hansen stated in "The Metamorphosis of Tituba, or Why American Intellectuals Can't Tell an Indian Witch from a Negro" that Tituba had only become wholly black in Miller's *The Crucible* in the early 1950s. Until then, he said, she had been portrayed as being of mixed Native American and black race ever since Upham's *Salem Witchcraft* in 1867, and before that as wholly Native American — which was clearly the nearest approach to her true identity available to those who knew her. Hansen, and the literary scholar Bernard Rosenthal (who followed his lead in examining Tituba's representation in fiction in 1993), both concluded that Tituba had begun to be portrayed as half- and then fully black because the stereotypes of African Americans as superstitious and morally lax encouraged even the most upright and liberal Americans to see her as such. Hansen was wrong about Miller, however: Tituba had been portrayed as black in a variety of much earlier texts, such as Peterson's *Dulcibel* (1907), where she is a "negro."[39] In *The Crucible*'s immediate precursor, William Carlos Williams's *Tituba's Children* (1948), she was called a "black slave," despite the description of her in the *dramatis personae* as "half-Carib, half-Negro."[40] Miller was not alone in his involuntary lapse into racism.

One portrayal that casts Miller's Tituba into a far better light is the poet Shirley Barker's assault on her in *Peace, My Daughters* (1947), where she is a "Negro" who speaks a stereotypical pidgin, practices African magic ("Tituba *obi* woman in own country"), drugs the girls, beats a drum, and sends them deliberately into fits. Her witches' Sabbath is an African trance ritual, made malign by her racially charged evil, which she practices with Satan himself in the person of a man named John Horne.[41] Tituba, such writers seemed to think, was a deceitful and superstitious woman, the first confessor of what must have been either a straight lie that harmed her white co-accused, or an admission that she — though not her white fellow-prisoners, surely — had been practicing some kind of "voodoo." Her confession was thus either believed implicitly — as far as its details were realistically possible, which was a very debatable point — or doubted as a wicked attempt to deceive her master, Samuel Parris, and spread panic through the white community that had enslaved her. She was a "dark Eve," as Rosenthal explained, bringing death and destruction to her New England Eden. Few stopped to ask important questions about this easy scapegoat: even Hansen missed some of these. Was it definitely true that Tituba had confessed with great celerity, or confessed first or first accused others? No — the precise circumstances of her confession are, in fact, unclear and accounts differ on important details. Tituba seems to have accused only those already named by others; her confession as recorded is not in any way unlike that of the other (Indian, black, or white) "witches," and she began by protesting her innocence. Had she confessed under intolerable pressure? Hale, Mather, and others suggest not, but Calef said that Parris beat her. Did Tituba's ethnic origin make her exceptionally likely to practice magic, or did white people also tell fortunes and use divination? Yes they did, in large numbers. Why, then, blame Tituba for the terrible events that overtook Essex County?

Whatever the truth, the oft-told story that Tituba was a partly or wholly black woman, one, moreover, who practiced magic in her kitchen and drew in a "circle" of girls and young women to have their fortunes told has no foundation in the historical record whatever. Rosenthal took Hansen's contentions about Tituba's race further and demonstrated that the myth of her as a "real" witch was based primarily on a few lines in John Hale's *Modest Enquiry.* Here he says very circumspectly that "I knew one of the Afflicted persons, whom (as I was credibly informed) did try with an egg and a glass to find her future Husband's Calling" (i.e., she probably broke an egg into water and looked for a shape in the white, which might indicate the profession of her husband-to-be). He also said that he knew another person who tried the same charm and later had fits. Hale's secondhand report of one girl and knowledge of another, both as far as we know from his account unconnected with Tituba, and both trying a common European divinatory practice, was transformed by Upham and later writers into a group of girls clustered around Tituba to learn magic. Upham wrote that "a circle of young girls" had got into "the habit of meeting at Mr. Parris' house for the purpose of practising palmistry, and other arts of fortune-telling, and of becoming experts in the wonders of necromancy, magic and spiritualism." The "Indian" servants, he stated, were part of this group, but it was mere speculation. As Hansen pointed out, Upham was also responsible for introducing blackness into Tituba's racial make-up: true, he most often represented her as "Indian" but once he spoke of her as "of mixed African and Indian blood."[42] Here, then, is the origin of the black Tituba, who led astray the little white girls of Salem Village. It suited the prevailing climate of racial tension in the twentieth century that Tituba be black, and the myth was repeated ad nauseam until it seemed to be the truth.[43]

As confirmation that the "dark Eve" Tituba and her husband John Indian could easily and with a transparent racism be made to represent any disliked race or ethnic group, they have also appeared in fiction as Spaniards in an astonishing episode in D. R. Castleton's *Salem: A Tale of the Seventeenth Century*. Written in 1874 at a time of ongoing tension between north and central American states, following the Mexican War and predating the Spanish-American War, the novel portrays Parris's servants in the act of devil-worship itself, dwelling on their "fierce Spanish blood" in apparently free misreading of Upham's statement that the couple came from New Spain. Deliberately, if paradoxically, denying that they were "Indians" or Africans, Castleton has Tituba and John dig a hole in the ground to which they bring "a hideous wooden figure, an idol, probably — bearing a mocking and frightful resemblance to a human being . . . of ghastly ugliness and coarsely bedaubed with red and blue paint." The idol is set up by a fire, and John sacrifices a newborn puppy to it, "coolly severing the head of the blind and unresisting little victim." As blood drips for the idol, "the woman (forgive me, oh! ye of the softer sex) drew from the folds of her dress some rough wooden puppets, or effigies," and she burns them, with John appearing to recognize or name each one as it is destroyed. Then the two fall on their knees, with heads touching the ground and hands extended, just, says Castleton, as in "the Syrian deserts we see pilgrims prostrating themselves before the terrible sirocco." John and Tituba are stereotypically cruel Spaniards, with all the viler adjectives associated with Mediterranean and South American peoples: "swarthy . . . sensuous . . . coarse . . . the ferocity of the beast of prey, united to the low cunning of the monkey." Clearly they are American "pagans," but for all practical purposes they are also Catholic conquistadors, the perpetrators of Mexican atrocities and the besiegers of the Alamo. Castleton's imagination runs riot and at last the Spanish stereotype even turns Moorish in an apparent, if confused, reference to Islamic prayer.[44] But while Castleton pursued her own racial agenda and was followed by M.V.B. Perley in 1911, most Americans were — as Hansen showed — reimagining Tituba as black.[45]

As is often the way with myths, no matter how utterly untrue, this outcome was not all bad. Although Tituba was portrayed before and after Hansen wrote as a partly or wholly black woman who might well have had knowledge of Native American or African magics, the more liberal portrayals of her as such served an antiracist cause. They were adopted by publishers, museums, and schools in part because of these institutions' commitment to reclaiming lost black history. Tituba appeared to be a rare find: a well-known black female American from the colonial period, whose experience could be used to explore and interrogate racism. Her story introduced readers to the tragedies of slavery, which could lead on to an understanding of the Civil Rights movement and its aftermath in affirmative action. In her landmark children's history, Shirley Jackson portrayed Tituba in 1956 as a Christian who meant no harm by her storytelling and palm reading.[46] Ann Petry's 1964 Tituba is a kind, self-aware woman, who speaks her mind in good English, belongs to the Church of England, and shows her intelligence and the pain she feels at her enslavement very clearly. She knows how to tell fortunes and can experience visions if she looks into oil or water, an ability that Betty Parris also has. But Tituba is pushed into revealing her visions and interpreting the tarot pack by the manipulative girls of Salem rather than offering to do so out of vanity or a desire for power, motives often attributed to her. She tells a few stories of Barbadian life and folklore, but it is Abigail Williams who transforms these innocent conversations into something more. What Petry's reader remembers is Tituba's dignity despite her powerlessness.[47] For Ann Rinaldi, too, writing in 1992, Tituba is a strong woman: "No one tells Tituba what to do." She tells fortunes and stories willingly, but does so as a kind of Christian protest against the hatred she finds all around her. In Salem are girls who need love and attention, and Tituba provides it. "Tituba only wakes the magic in the heart," she says.[48]

Most notably, an antiracist Tituba became the heroine of the 1986 novel *Moi, Tituba, Sorcière Noire de Salem* by Guadeloupean writer Maryse Condé, translated as *I Tituba, Black Witch of Salem* in 1992. Condé's novel portrayed Tituba and her family as victims of white oppression at every turn: raped, beaten, hanged, accused of witchcraft, driven to suicide, tortured. Shocking as it is, it also has a compelling beauty and optimism, for Tituba — like the other black slaves in the story — can escape into dreams, and finally into death and an otherworld. The novel is haunted by spirits and ghosts, which are more real to the slaves than all the barbarity to which they are subjected. Empowered by this otherworld, Tituba learns herbalism and witchcraft, bewitching her vicious mistress only to be sold to Samuel Parris, who reminds her of Satan himself. Once in Massachusetts she befriends the girls of the village and the villagers discover her magical powers. Other slaves and white people — even Rebecca Nurse — ask her to get rid of their enemies, but she will not be tempted to do evil. Eventually, of course, Tituba is accused of witchcraft and takes her revenge on her oppressors by denouncing them. Although she survives the trials, she is later returned to the Caribbean and hanged during a slave revolt. Condé was quite well aware that her Tituba was a fantasy, as fictional as Hawthorne's Hester Prynne — whom Condé has Tituba meet in prison. Her book even parodied historical novels and stories of black women reclaiming their foremothers' stories. "I decided I was going to write her story out of my own dreams," Condé told an interviewer, and "offer her her revenge by inventing a life such as she might perhaps have wished it to be told . . . the opposite of a historical novel." *I Tituba* is as much about Condé's anger that in "present-day America . . . in terms of narrow-mindedness, hypocrisy, and racism, little has changed since the days of the Puritans" as it is about the historical "witch" who inspired it. Tituba did not have to be black, however, to perform the recuperative function Condé imagined for her. In a foreword to the book, Angela Y. Davis argued that "should a Native American Tituba be recreated, in scholarly or fictional terms, this would be true to the spirit of Condé's Tituba . . . Tituba's revenge consists in reminding us all that the doors to our suppressed cultural histories are still ajar."[49]

In the mid-1990s came some further evidence about the possible origin of the real Tituba. A history professor at Morgan State University in Baltimore became interested in finding out more about her because of the questions that her students repeatedly asked. Instead of assuming — and answering — that nothing was discoverable about the obscure slave and her life before coming to the attention of history in America, Elaine G. Breslaw resolved to investigate the records of the early modern Caribbean. It was a bold step: all she had to go on was the speculation by scholars in the 1860s that Tituba probably came from "New Spain" and beyond that the South American mainland. This could mean anywhere in the Spanish West Indies, and anywhere in the region known as Guiana. Breslaw decided insouciantly that "Barbados seemed to be a reasonable place to begin a search," and applied for and was granted research leave by two international exchange bodies to go there. And in Barbados's records, she made the discovery of a slave with the unique name of Tattuba, whose name and placing in the inventories on which in 1676 she appeared as property suggested that she was young and of South American origin. The Arawak tribes from the Orinoco and Amacuro river regions were sometimes raided by traders looking for native people to kidnap and enslave, and their tribal and place names had several elements reminiscent of Tattuba/Tituba's name: Tetebetana, Tibetibe. Women and female children were particular targets for slavers because Native Americans were thought to make good house-servants. Tattuba "belonged" to Samuel Thompson, a plantation owner from St. Thomas parish in Barbados, and she was listed because he planned to sell her along with his land. Her name did not recur in any other records, but in 1679 Samuel Parris was recorded on a Barbadian census as possessing one slave of unspecified sex and race. By the time Parris had returned to Massachusetts, in the early 1680s, he had two slaves and in 1692 Tituba and her husband John were living with him in the parsonage in Salem Village where the witchcraft accusations would begin. Breslaw concluded on this limited but plausible evidence that she had found Tituba in Barbados and had substantiated what was said of her in the records of the witch trials: that she was "Indian" and not black.[50]

Breslaw's book is not, however, a definitive account of Tituba's contribution to the Essex County witch trials. Despite its convincing arguments for her origin, it proceeds to make less plausible claims about her knowledge of witchcraft and its impact on the course of the trials. For example, Breslaw suggests that Tituba's insistence that the witches at Salem were joined by a man from Boston and other strangers was linked to the Arawak concept of the "*kenaima*," a human attacker from outside the Arawak community who was thought to be responsible for bringing disease and magical harm to them, like a witch. If Tattuba is Tituba, and her origins are as Breslaw suggests, this may well be true. It might help explain why Tituba took the unusual step of implicating a complete stranger, a white gentleman from another community, in her evidence, instead of naming ordinary local people as witches. But it seems less likely to be the sole or primary reason for the spread of witchcraft accusations across Massachusetts, a story that "sent the Salem magistrates all over the province to find the co-conspirators." It was not unheard-of for accusers or accused to name people from other communities. It was unusual to accuse an unnameable stranger, but it was not unknown in English or European practice. Often a name would later be supplied, as a way of fulfilling the vaguely prophetic words of the accuser. Wealthy and respectable people were accused, too, in other cases: Ann Hibbins, the wife of a former governor, at Boston; Mary Bliss Parsons; Katherine Harrison. So it was not just "Tituba's story [that] made it possible for the magistrates to believe that a man like George Burroughs, a minister, could be responsible for the Satanic presence in their community . . ." or "opened the way to the accusation of women of respectable sainthood."[51] Her confession cannot be said to have been "a model of resistance rather than a confirmation of Puritan values" or to have "initiated a modifying process" in which confession was less prized as evidence, a trend that Breslaw says laid "the groundwork for the rationalism of the eighteenth-century Englightenment." Tituba may well have brought to her confession "the folklore of the American Indian," but she also reproduced in her stories a lot of material familiar to English and American magistrates for over a century.

Breslaw's thought-provoking reading of Tituba was, however, the right reading at the right moment and it was swiftly incorporated into scholarly argument and made headway in educational literature.[52] It offered new, imaginative ways of thinking about Tituba, and suggested new questions. How did her "Indian"-ness, and the backgrounds of other Native Americans caught up in the witchcraft events, contribute to the development of the Essex County accusations? Was there a relationship between the choice of Tituba as one of the first three suspects and the "Indian wars" that had threatened Massachusetts and Maine communities in the past and were about to do so again? Mary Beth Norton answered these questions in *In the Devil's Snare*, demonstrating that fears of Native American attacks resurfaced in both the imagery and the precise targets of accusers in 1692. Many of the accusers had experienced "Indian" attacks at Falmouth, Salmon Falls, and York, and clearly associated the Maine settlements from which they had fled with the devil and his agents. The accusation of the minister George Burroughs, who was brought to Salem from Maine and accused by a number of neighbors and members of his congregation there, was thus given added significance, as was the choice of Tituba Indian as one of the first suspects. For the girls who accused her, Tituba represented "the people who were then 'tormenting' New England as a whole," the Native American Wabanakis who had killed their families and friends.[53]

*Wonderful Witches: From the Bay Path to the Yellow Brick Road*

By 1900, four stereotypes of witches as women were competing in American thought, some of which would not achieve prominence until the later twentieth century. One was the exemplary feminist guru. Another was the powerful, if inexplicable, animal magnetist. A third was the deluded victim popularized by writers like Josiah G. Holland and Frank Samuel Child. And the last was the original seventeenth-century image: the satanic conspirator, who survived most obviously in portrayals of Tituba Indian. But at the turn of the old century a new synthesis came from a surprising quarter and ignored the negative images altogether. The man who married Matilda Joslyn Gage's daughter Maud published a children's story largely populated by witches, many of whom were women both powerful and good.[54] Almost certainly, Gage's work influenced her son-in-law Lyman Frank Baum, when he wrote his satirical fantasy *The Wonderful Wizard of Oz*. Witches are everywhere in the Land of Oz. When Dorothy's house is swept there by a cyclone, the little girl is immediately hailed as a "Sorceress" herself by the Good Witch of the North, for she has accidentally killed "the Wicked Witch of the East." Dorothy, "half frightened at facing a real witch," points out, "I thought all witches were wicked." But the Good Witch of the North retorts, "Oh, no, that is a great mistake." Later Dorothy meets another witch, Glinda, who is "as good as [she is] beautiful," and in subsequent books of the Oz series marches with her army of "girls" and those of the Queen of Oz, Ozma — a girl who was a boy when the reader met her, but who becomes a person of power and dignity as soon as she is refeminized. The rest of the original book details not just a mission to kill the land's sole remaining Wicked Witch, but a satirical examination of the power of self-delusion. The Wicked Witch dissolves at once when doused in water, but it is the power of the Wizard of Oz himself that is the book's biggest surprise. "Oz, the Great and Terrible," the male mastermind who rules over the witches and their countries, in fact, turns out to be governing by a series of stage tricks. Pretending to be a ball of fire or a monster, he is just a little old "humbug" from Omaha. Masculine power, in *The Wizard of Oz*, is the art of "make-believe" and "humbug," and when Oz leaves the city the people choose a scarecrow as his successor, for "there is not another city in all the world that is ruled by a stuffed man." In fact, Baum seems to agree with his mother-in-law that much of the world is indeed ruled by stuffed men.[55]

In this comic world of powerful women and witch-women — which Sally Roesch Wagner calls a "church-free, female-led utopia" — the only person powerful enough to send Dorothy home is the good witch Glinda.[56] And the witch does so in a significant way: she simply makes Dorothy aware that she has always had the power she needed, for she is wearing witch slippers.[57] The good sense, innate power, and kindness of at least some witches and the witchlike heroine are celebrated, while the book's male characters are the brainless (Scarecrow), heartless (Tin Woodman), and cowardly (Lion). Unlike the potent and emancipated witches, they are held in thrall by a fraud and induced to believe many things that are "a great mistake." Baum's witches had almost overnight become liberal metaphors for political dissent and female self-empowerment. This was a part of the psychologizing discourse that we have examined in this chapter, from *The Bay Path* to Joslyn Gage and George M. Beard, since it assumed that delusion and a misreading of female power were at the root of witchcraft persecution, and the resulting portrayal of witches as monstrous. But on top of that, Baum's fiction pointed the way to a distinctively antihistorical future in which the imaginative mind was free to reimagine witches as it liked, without reference to records, histories, or demonologies. And by 1938, when *The Wizard of Oz* was famously filmed — incarnating Dorothy in Judy Garland, the Wicked Witch in Margaret Hamilton, and Glinda in Billie Burke — the battle over the significance of witchcraft in American life had decisively shifted from the contested facts of history to the realm of the imagination.[58] It was not so important to understand what had really happened at Salem in 1692 as it was to grasp the possibilities that witchcraft might offer to modern women.

# 4

## "WE WILL NOT FLY SILENTLY INTO THE NIGHT"[1]: WICCA AND AMERICAN WITCHCRAFT

There is nothing healing or spiritual about the Salem story.[2]

In the nineteenth and twentieth centuries a few hardy American historians had pioneered the notion that witch-hunting had been a sexist activity
aimed at crushing the power of women. Some had also asserted that it had
been intended to exterminate a goddess religion that predated Christianity across the world. As has been discussed, the idea that "in these earliest
days woman is all in all" was not a view that originated in America, since
it had its roots in European writings, especially the work of Jules Michelet.[3] But it appealed peculiarly to the American mind, perhaps because
America had a strong attachment to the role of the revolutionary underdog. The new American nation also had its own melancholy experience
of the extermination of an indigenous culture. So the belief in the past
existence and the present possibilities of a pagan, goddess religion was
refined and made orthodoxy in the United States. And through the writ-

ings of a few highly effective Americans it became an accepted truth for many people worldwide. What was unexpected was that these American writers on women as witches were not usually or primarily historians, actually presenting what they said as "truth." Instead, they were creative writers, activists, and mystics. Not for them the dry survey of dates: these people were more interested in recapturing the ecstasies that they believed witches must once have experienced. Through their writings, from the 1890s to the present, these Americans gave the world the new (or, as they argued, revived) religion of goddess worship. If, as Ronald Hutton put it, "pagan witchcraft . . . is the only religion which England has ever given the world," then feminist Witchcraft is an American religion.[4] And in a sweet irony of history, it began in Pennsylvania, once touted as the most skeptical of American jurisdictions.

### The Witches' Messiah

In the years after the Civil War, the Philadelphian scholar and journalist Charles Godfrey Leland brought out a number of books on magical themes, including in a curious little book called *Aradia, or the Gospel of the Witches* in 1899. Leland had made his name with his war reportage and Irving-like reworkings of traditional tales and German-American jokes in the form of ballads.[5] He had long been fascinated by Native Americans, gypsies, and British, German, and Italian folklore.[6] He visited and talked with tribal and gypsy people, and wrote on Algonquin legends, gypsy magic, and Etruscan paganism. Excitedly, he noted similarities between Chippewa, Algonquin, Italian, Indian, gypsy, and "Black Voodoo" traditions.[7] His interest in European folk beliefs had been sparked on a Grand Tour in the 1840s, and he pursued it during subsequent residences in London and Florence. And in addition to his published work, for his own amusement he handwrote and bound for his own library several books on magical tales and folk traditions.

"The Witchcraft of Dame Darrel of York" is one of the most interesting. It is a pastiche of a medieval or early modern English illuminated book, and purports to be a collection of the wisdom of a Yorkshire "wise woman" or "white witch" written by her nephew. In fact, it was by Leland, who wrote a work that was part novel, part dictionary. He examined all the magical terms that he could find in British folkore — *hellwain, pixy, pooka, bullbeggar, spoorn, Robin Goodfellow,* and so on. He wrote in "olde Englishe" in a gothicised script, and he illustrated and colored his book so that to the inexperienced eye it would look like a genuine ancient memoir — or *grimoire.* Magic and fiction, and their romantic interrelationship, clearly stimulated his creativity and he threw himself into his task of making the reader shiver. Here he is on the subject of witches' "puppets":

> Dols are but the Poupets wherewith litel Maides do playe, howbeit of these are a strange Kind and such doe Witches make of Dead Man's Bones and these are Devills Dols. The which they give to their children and these Toyes walk and live.[8]

He also wrote poems about witches, conflating his own authorial persona with theirs, imagining a kind of haunting in poems such as "The Voice":

> . . . In my own voice
> Another voice seems known
> The witch who is calling to me.
> Somewhere indeed she lives
> But where can that somewhere be?
> To others her life she gives
> Yet no-one in her believes
> The witch who is meant for me.[9]

By the 1890s, he was a prolific author, perhaps best known to the outside world for his book on the remains of ancient traditions in Etruscan legend, and for work on gypsies and their language.[10] But *Aradia* was not exactly in his public, published tradition. Rather, it was like its unpublished siblings, a work of collected wisdoms and original writing. It was the poetic scrapbook of a late American Romantic, a onetime Transcendentalist.[11]

*Aradia* brought together a number of magical stories and rituals that Leland believed had survived in Italy from pagan, classical times. Transcribed side-by-side, they formed a semicoherent whole focusing on the worship of Diana. Leland explained how he had learned of this "Old Religion" from Maddalena, a practicing Florentine witch, and her colleagues and friends. She had told him of a text setting out "the doctrines of Italian witchcraft" as early as 1886. In 1897 she had at last brought him a copy, in her handwriting.[12] In this text — which Leland reproduced with other fragments — stories, rites, and poems jostled each other in an unstructured flow that suggested piecemeal collection, and translation from Italian. The stories were of Diana, as the goddess of the witches, and her messianic daughter Aradia (or Herodias), who had brought Diana's religion to the world. She had brought in particular the "Charge of the Goddess," spoken by Aradia to her followers:

> When I shall have departed from this world,
> Whenever ye have need of anything,
> Once in the month, and when the moon is full,
> Ye shall assemble in some desert place,
> Or in a forest all together join
> To adore the potent spirit of your queen,
> My mother, great Diana . . .
> And ye shall all be freed from slavery,
> And so ye shall be free in everything . . .[13]

This goddess religion, said Leland, had survived among the oppressed, those to whom the Catholic Church forbade freedom in life and love. Diana was the goddess of the underdog and the freethinker. She was thus particularly well suited to late-nineteenth-century America, where liberal and suffragist campaigners were in pitched battle with conservative forces, as we saw in the last chapter. Leland believed with Matilda Joslyn Gage that "with every new rebellion . . . humanity and woman gain something, that is to say, their just dues or rights."[14] He was delighted to have rescued for modern times the obscure revolutionary traditions of witchcraft, which "like the truffle, grows best and has its raciest flavour when most deeply hidden."[15]

But, as this picturesque phrase suggests, Leland was not thinking like a modern historian when he published *Aradia*. He loved poetry and mystery, and pagan rituals spoke to the "dreamer" in him.[16] The "authorities" most frequently cited in *Aradia*'s pages were thus poets — Byron, Keats, Wordsworth, Elizabeth Barrett Browning, Spenser, Chaucer. This lack of an orthodox scholarly apparatus, as well as the surprisingly intact survival of the rites, has made many readers suspicious of *Aradia*'s authenticity. Elliot Rose offered a damning critique of it in 1989 as not only a transparent polemic based on modern Christian sources but also "bad art."[17] Some suspicions do seem justified, and should be explored, if one is interested in the book as a fully factual record of ancient practices or in the influence it has had on modern Witches.

First, there are textual and archival issues. The manuscript of *Aradia* surviving in the Historical Society of Pennsylvania library is very definitely in Leland's own hand, not that of Maddalena, and there is no other manuscript of it that might be hers.[18] Leland hoarded items such as invitations, cards, and tiny diaries from the 1840s and scribbled notes on the back of slips from magazines — surely he would have kept something so important? But Robert Mathieson, who first analyzed the manuscript from the viewpoint of a medievalist scholar, suggests that Maddalena's material may have been returned to her.[19] Then, Leland's own text of *Aradia* in the Historical Society's collection is accompanied by further handwritten copies of some of the stories told in the published text and some remarks about the "general, genial spirit of creation of mythic tales, sorceries and quaint observances in ancient Italy."[20] Is this suspicious? It need not be — Mathieson has suggested that these fragments were also provided by Maddalena and simply translated by Leland, who revised his translations as he went along. Leland then commentated on his Italian material — as any reader of *Aradia* will see. He may have added to Maddalena's material and appreciated its rich poetic nature, said Mathieson, but he did not himself create it.

Yet the original dialect Italian that Leland reproduces is often incorrect and highly ambiguous — as Mario Pazzaglini, who retranslated the text with Dina Pazzaglini in 1998, shows. Would Maddalena and her sources have made such mistakes? These might be suggestive of sources from different regions, or of language difficulties on Leland's part, or of fabrication by Leland. Pazzaglini himself suggested that the texts were collected from scraps of paper bearing charms (which may have contained saints' names where once a pagan deity might have occurred), and from letters of description from Maddalena — not from a coherent, established witches' gospel. On top of this, Leland had considerable difficulties with translation. For Pazzaglini, the texts had a validity in reflecting a northern Italian "magical world" but were themselves significantly flawed and incomplete.[21] Mathieson, however, concluded that having begun his analysis in "two minds whether Leland might have invented *Aradia* by himself," he was "now . . . convinced that Leland had clearly written Italian texts, such as he said Maddalena had sent to him."[22] Meanwhile, it is clear that Leland dwelt very fondly on the idea of storytelling about witches, and they often played the role of muse for him. As he put it: "In my own voice, another voice seems known, the witch who is calling to me." This blending of voices is worrying, as is the way that signed creative work lies in Leland's papers alongside apparently collected material, without comment. His translation skills are equally an issue for readers who hope that the rites he offers to them are uncontaminated and original pagan formulae.

It has also been suggested that Leland's reputation creates a problem in taking what he said on trust. He was known as a raconteur and — as Ronald Hutton put it – "an unusually unreliable scholar." Chas. S. Clifton vigorously disputed Hutton's "libel," making a case that Leland was far more politically and socially conservative than Hutton thought, and so *Aradia* was not a "literary fraud" designed to mirror his beliefs.[23] But it is true that Leland's obituary in the highly influential journal *Folk-Lore* described Leland as a man who "liked to . . . allow his fancy to play about the stories and poems he was publishing."[24] And it is uncanny that *Aradia* comments on so many of Leland's own preoccupations, since it is supposedly a text based on oral peasant traditions, in a time and country very unlike his own. It privileges the role of women, in a way that Leland had been committed to throughout his life, both in his journalism and his creative work.[25] He had spent his whole life hankering after the mystic past:

Elizabeth Robins Pennell notes his early interest in tales of the witches of Pennsylvania such as Margaret Mattson, dime novels about the Salem case, and even Italian witches — to whom he referred in a number of letters written in his student days.[26] Leland ached to meet with Pictesses and to be "living in a bygone age" and *Aradia* fulfils many of these imaginative needs.[27] In addition to its political stance, it also deals with other favorite topics: tricksters, gypsies, fairies, tall tales. In particular, when *Aradia* is looked at alongside Leland's other, unpublished works, it seems exactly the same kind of book as "The Witchcraft of Dame Darrel," which makes no claim to authenticity and is clearly the private playfulness of a leisured, avid reader and writer. This does not mean it is purely a work of fiction, however. Leland wanted to meet real Italian witches, and apparently he did. However one looks at the textual evidence, it is hard to see *Aradia* as entirely Leland's own creation. The only way to do so would be to regard everything said about Maddalena (who is referred to elsewhere in Leland's letters and appears in a photograph in his biography) or written in Italian as an elaborate, conspiratorial forgery.[28]

There are, however, important historical problems with the material that he said he collected from Maddalena, Marietta, and others in Italy. First, Ronald Hutton pointed out that Herodias is a figure who originated in the Christian era, which creates difficulties in seeing her as an authentic pagan deity. Leland tried to explain that there were two different Herodias figures, but Hutton was not convinced.[29] The name might be explained away by etymological confusion (Aradia/Herodias is already a peculiar conjunction in its own right), or by changes during the transmission and translation of the myths. But there is also the matter of the Aradian rites' obvious debts to very recent writers, especially Jules Michelet, to be dealt with. Michelet had already, and with striking force, made witches into the forerunners of the eighteenth-century revolutionary, in a way that very few now accept as historically accurate. His medieval witches were sickened and turned to witchcraft by the cruel tyranny of feudal lords, with their droit du seigneur and arbitrary "justice." Michelet's peasant woman exclaims: "Why have I not a Spirit to protect me, strong and powerful. . . .

I see many a one carved in stone at the church door. What are they doing there? Why do they not fly to their proper home, the castle yonder, to carry off these miscreants and roast them in hell?"[30] And so she became a witch: the Sorceress, Medea, a Sibyl. Similarly, Leland's Aradia was seen as a rebel and defender of the common man and woman, promising her followers: "ye shall all be freed from slavery" and that eventually "the last of your oppressors shall be dead." This was a promise Leland saw both as stemming from ancient times and particularly relevant in the medieval period, from which he thought his texts might possibly date.[31] Like Michelet (and Joslyn Gage), Leland was convinced that the Middle Ages were a relentlessly terrible time, "in every palace tortures, in every castle prisoners," and that behind this was Catholic Christianity itself, behaving with "shameless, palpable iniquity and injustice."[32]

Yet Leland or his source had one vital difference from Michelet's account of the witch as rebel: the deity she worshipped was not Satan, as in Michelet's version, but a goddess. Michelet's witches were trapped in an intense sadomasochistic relationship with Satan, their "vile torturer" and "great sir." The witch permitted Satan to rape her, kissed his backside, and received in return "the power of working ill."[33] In complete contrast, Leland's witches were worshippers of "Queen of the Witches . . . the cat who ruled the star-mice, the heaven and the rain."[34] Each writer set his vision of rebellious witches in the same darkly gothic universe, but each demonstrably chose the form of resistance best suited to his character, time, and intent. Michelet, haunted by the Terror of the French Revolution, dwelt on torture, revenge, and madness – "fiery furnaces and boiling cauldrons," life as "one long-drawn moan of horror."[35] Leland, a jovial and positive man from an increasingly secure liberal democracy, wrote of freedom and pleasure — even of a Dianic charm that might allow a scholar to "find some rare old book or manuscript for sale very cheaply."[36]

It is not impossible, then, that Leland discovered some survivals from a pre- or anti-Christian past, but it is equally plausible that he found overall he wanted and imagined what he could not prove. This is not to suggest that he lied, or was tricked by his informants — although this is possible, too — but that both they and he had an investment in the "atmosphere of witchcraft" that he found in Florence.[37] For the people to whom he spoke, practicing folk magic and unwitching was both a traditional calling and a livelihood. They were not passive vessels of magical lore and may well have had their own understandings of its origin and meaning. Keith Thomas's and Owen Davies's work on English "cunning folk" of a similar kind suggests that while some folk magicians were self-confessed imposters, others believed sincerely in their own abilities. Some used an eclectic mix of religious and occult fragments, texts, and materials, and offered impressive-sounding accounts of their authenticity. None were quite like the pagan origins suggested for the Italian materials, but then England has a very different religious and social structure.[38] Whatever they believed, the Italian women's practices and stories were presumably important to them, and Leland offered them both a heroic, scholarly context for their profession and an opportunity to explore it further. He, meanwhile, was in his late sixties and recovering from a serious illness.[39] The attractions of making a great leap forward in folklore studies are obvious, and his excitement and pleasure seem quite genuine. He even began to practice Maddalena's rites himself, invoking helpful spirits to see what happened.[40]

Did he hope that publicizing a religion centered on women and freedom, with Aradia as the Goddess's messiah to witches, would help to change late-nineteenth-century society? Freethinking feminists like Joslyn Gage had headed in this direction, and Leland's fellow American radical Charlotte Perkins Gilman had imagined the power that witchcraft might grant such women in her story "When I Was a Witch." Here she used her witch powers to curb the cruelties, lies, and abuses of capitalist, masculinized life, and wished that "women, all women, might realize Womanhood at last; its power and pride and place in life."[41] But if he shared her aims, Leland can hardly have imagined the scale of his little book's impact on the world. In his unpublished "Prophecies for the Twentieth Century," written in the same year that *Aradia* was published, he entirely failed to note that by 2000 many hundreds of thousands of Americans would happily identify themselves as Witches.[42]

*Charles's Children: From Maddalena to Starhawk*

The resounding name of Charles Godfrey Leland is still frequently absent from the descriptions of how American Witches rediscovered goddess worship. But it is there now and again. The creator of Seax Wicca, Raymond Buckland, discusses *Aradia* in his *Witchcraft from the Inside*.[43] Goddess magic teacher Shekhinah Mountainwater calls on her in her ritual manual.[44] The High Priestess Phyllis Curott chose the name "Aradia" for herself at her initiation, as other Witches have done, but her account of Leland's influence on the feminist Craft is limited to his having provided some material for British Wiccan writers Gerald Gardner and Doreen Valiente, and a brief description of an unnamed book that helped Curott to choose her name.[45] One of relatively few modern American Witchcraft "traditions" to acknowledge Leland explicitly is — perhaps unsurprisingly — the Italian one. One of its chief proponents, Raven Grimassi, stated flatly in the mid-1990s that "it was Charles Leland who laid the framework for what became the modern religion of Wicca" — thus claiming not just Dianic Witchcraft but also the whole Wiccan movement for Leland and America. The Italian tradition is not explicitly feminist, and is thought of by adherents as "Stregheria" (the Italian word for witchcraft) rather than "Wicca," but nevertheless Grimassi saw the two as intimately connected, with Leland at their center. Grimassi believed that Leland "proved . . . that Italian Witches were alive and well in Italy and were worshipping the Goddess Diana."[46] As we have seen, this belief is complicated by an examination of his work and by surviving records. But Leland's name appears more frequently than it used to in books on the American Craft, and the new translation of *Aradia* in 1998 was accompanied by essays reflecting on his place in witchcraft history. In his popular history *American Witch*, Anthony Paige hedges his bets by describing *Aradia* both as "a preservation of what was once a dying tradition" and "not . . . anthroplogically sound." But he does credit Leland as the writer whose work would "spark a revival in Witchcraft."[47] And if Leland did, to any degree, create *Aradia* from his own fascination with Italian-American roots, then so much the better for American Witches. In *Aradia* they have a New World tradition of their own.

An interest in the originary cultures of Americans is a recurrent theme in American Witchcraft, whether those origins be in Italy, Africa, or England. But another distinctively American theme is a longing for the frontier, a Thoreau-like desire for the simpler, better life, often linked with Native American culture. Phyllis Curott's Wiccan circle discussed the philosophy of Suquamish Chief Seattle, and were told that "the Old Religion is a lot like Native American spirituality."[48] Witches worldwide bought Native American artifacts, like dream catchers, and built their own sweat lodges.[49] Some also took on new names that sounded Native American, like Silver Ravenwolf and Starhawk, and some practiced Native American magics, such as raising thunderstorms. The Wiccan and Isis worshipper Theodore Mills said of himself: "I'm what they call a medicine brother, to an Apache medicine man."[50] The pagan Don Two Eagles Waterhawk abandoned two careers, in law enforcement and the army, in his search for freedom as a "person of the land" after reading texts on Eastern philosophy. He returned to his Tsalagi/Cherokee roots, via an engagement with Seneca sweat-lodge traditions, as a "medicine" toolmaker.[51] But as Philip J. Deloria pointed out in his book *Playing Indian*, as well as actual Native Americans, many white Americans of the sixties and seventies found in the concept of "Indianness" a countercultural identity that they thought was inherently "communitarian, environmentally wise, spiritually insightful."[52] Along with New Agers, they participated in quasi-"Indian" ceremonies and chose totem animals. From 1968 onwards, many read the mystical, and supposedly Yaqui, revelations of Carlos Castaneda.[53] As so often, novelists and poets made the most striking contribution to public understanding of witchcraft, this time by making connections between Witch and Native American. In 2002, for example, the British writer Celia Rees achieved the perfect fusion of the two in her children's novel *Sorceress*, in which the Native American girl Agnes channels the spirit of Mary, a girl accused of witchcraft in seventeenth-century New England.[54] It seemed that, through a potent mix of fiction and fact, Witchcraft might be seen as a natural counterpart to Native American beliefs — literally, as a Native American religion.

This conviction is strengthened by the contribution to the reinvention of Witchcraft made by the Woodcraft movement. In the late 1890s, Ernest Seton Thompson, a Canadian-American living near Cos Cob, Connecticut, built an "Indian" settlement in the grounds of his home. Here he founded an organization that came to be known as Woodcraft. It was for boys and young men, who were encouraged to form self-governing tribes, and a girls' branch was founded during the First World War. There were also Red Lodges, which were for men and women, and had a ritual element partly based on European freemasonry. The Woodcraft movement spread to England, where Gerald Gardner encountered it.[55] In the middle years of the twentieth century, Gardner and, later, Doreen Valiente, then adapted and created many of the "pagan" rituals associated with modern Wicca: the chants to God and Goddess, the circle of worshippers, the formulaic actions with knife and chalice, the robes and initiation rites. As far as anyone can tell, these rituals developed alongside and possibly from Woodcraft rituals, while Gardner and his friends also drew on the writings of the British occultist Aleister Crowley, further elements from freemasonry, anthropology, and British and imperial folklores.[56] But Valiente in particular acknowledged Leland as a source, praising him as a "pioneer" collector, a "remarkable, many-sided," and talented artist.[57] *Aradia* does not seem to have been one of Gardner's original sources, and only later did Aradia's name appear in his texts. But appear it did. So, out of rituals already being practiced by their group and others in Britain, together with rewritings of diverse materials including Leland's and probably Seton Thompson's, was created a written Wiccan tradition now known as Gardnerian Wicca or Witchcraft.[58] A private ritual manual (Book of Shadows) called *Ye Bok of ye Art Magical* was produced by Gardner and updated over the years, and he wrote an insider's account, *Witchcraft Today*, to describe and publicize his beliefs and the ceremonial ways in which others might join him in expressing them.[59] Alternative American religion had crossed to Europe, from whence it had originally taken many of its ideas, and was now poised to recross the Atlantic.

*Witchcraft Today* was the first work of its kind, claiming that the practicing of Witchcraft, as the Old Religion, had survived to the present day, and that it could now be revealed to a more tolerant society by someone recently initiated into its traditions. Most scholars now dispute this view of history, and Ronald Hutton in particular has provided a very convincing account of how Gardner and others created and re-created their rites from a variety of practices and texts instead of inheriting a complete ancient tradition.[60] Whatever its precise origin, Gardnerian Wicca focused on a Horned God as well as the Goddess, unlike Leland's vision of Italian practices and more like Seton Thompson's Woodcraft. As it developed, however, Gardner and Doreen Valiente rewrote Leland's Charge of the Goddess for British Wiccans. Valiente's version became very popular, as some British Gardnerians, especially women, felt the first flickerings of a special commitment to the goddess. Gardner's initiate Patricia Crowther had a particularly vivid vision of a community of women offering her rebirth and succor in the "Moon Mysteries."[61] But the Gardnerian rites were very clear: as initiate Raymond Buckland was later to sum up, "both the God and the Goddess are important and should be equally revered."[62] Gardnerian Wicca, with its god and goddess in polar balance, spread throughout the sixties and seventies, and in this way an interest in Witchcraft returned to America. British teachers and publicizers such as Buckland and Sybil Leek found ready acceptance in the States, and "covens" practicing Gardner's and Valiente's rites were formed.[63]

The creative impulse had been augmented very substantially in this process of exchanges. Some Americans were content to take Gardnerian Wicca as it stood. Some followed British variants like Alexandrian Wicca.[64] Some added further traditions, rules, and hierarchies from their own experiences — Jessie Wicker Bell, for example, wrote a *Book of Shadows* and *The Magick Grimoire* to list her own rites and laws.[65] But, like Phyllis Curott's circle, some turned to Wicca for inspiration to produce a tailor-made goddess Witchcraft for themselves. They added elements from archaeology, anthropology, quantum physics, and anything else that seemed useful. They mirrored Gardner's own creative process, and that of Valiente, in borrowing from Leland and other writers. American goddess Witchcraft simply borrowed more, less, or differently, and they borrowed Leland right back. Many American Witches, like Zsuzsanna Budapest, also drew on family witchcraft traditions from Europe, a strand in Wicca that became known as Fam Trad, and blended it with Gardnerian, feminist, or other elements. Ironically, Budapest called her coven the "Susan B. Anthony Coven no. 1," rather than the Matilda Joslyn Gage coven, which might have been more appropriate.[66] In this climate of synthesis and experimentation, Leland was once again in the ascendant. He had provided raw poetic ritual largely unencumbered by prose history and theory, much of it filtered through the revered rewritings of Valiente. And in 1979 a Californian Witch, Miriam Simos, became his most obvious American heir. She published probably the most influential modern manual of the American Craft, *The Spiral Dance*.[67]

*The Spiral Dance* never once mentions Leland. But his ideas on the essential connection between womanhood and witchcraft, and his poetic desire to celebrate that connection, are at its heart. Effectively, Starhawk took Leland's broadest claims, that "in Witch Sorcery it is the female who is the primitive principle . . . the fully equal, which means the superior sex" and that "every woman is at heart a witch," and ran with them in exactly the same spirit as he had done.[68] It is not really surprising that she did not refer to Leland. His ideas had become, in her world of feminists and radicals, commonplaces. There was no pressing need for her to explore their local origin. So when Starhawk used Leland's Charge of the Goddess, she rewrote it to suit the needs of her community, and later said quite openly, "I did not know where the Charge originated." Ten years later, she had come to believe that Doreen Valiente was its original author, and still — in her twentieth-anniversary edition of *The Spiral Dance* — Leland's name is absent from her adaptation. Really, Starhawk was far more interested in the future than the past — she took the Charge without inquiry about provenance or ownership to make from it something that she thought she could use, and it is hard to imagine Leland disapproving.[69] Both he and Starhawk wrote in times of revolutionary change in the conception of women's role in society, and *The Spiral Dance* reads like a sequel to *Aradia* that would have warmed his heart. The Philadelphian scholar and the Californian activist have a surprising amount in common.

*The Spiral Dance* had grown out of a number of different factors in Starhawk's home state: feminism, hippy idealism, the existence of groups practicing versions of European Wicca, and an increased interest in Eastern and other spiritualities. Starhawk felt that the ideas she and others had been discussing, which revolved around women's empowerment and peace activism, should be made more public. These ideas sprang from Marxism, second-wave feminism, and humanism generally, but they also had roots as far back as the French and American revolutionary Romanticism that Leland so admired. As Starhawk said in her introduction to the twentieth-anniversary edition of her book, a number of works were published in the late seventies that encouraged her to believe that another revolutionary time lay ahead. "Women," she said, "were beginning to look at religion and spirituality as a feminist issue." Politics was an important factor, as it had been for Leland. The world was changing and there was a growing coalition of those opposed to such change, which they saw as a return to oppression and social divisiveness. Ronald Reagan, the governor of California, was about to be elected president and the nation was taking a turn to the right, toward what would become "trickle-down" economics. As Starhawk would later put it, "There're so many people who deserve to feel guilty. . . . There're people planning nuclear war. There're people using napalm in El Salvador. There's Ronald Reagan."[70] Starhawk and her friends began to define a cluster of ideas under the title "Reclaiming" — with an obvious imaginative connection to the feminist slogan "reclaim the night!" If women could reclaim the streets and even the dark, rapist-ridden alleys, why should they not also reclaim a connection with the spiritual, with justice and community, which they felt patriarchal religions had taken from them? And where Leland had looked to the

Classical and European world for inspiration, Starhawk examined the Christian and pre-Christian Middle East.

The idea that something was being taken back, rather than created from scratch, of course depended on a certain interpretation of history, one that built on the theory taken up by Joslyn Gage and others that society had originally been matriarchal. Starhawk, along with feminist Merlin Stone and some archaeologists — most prominently Marija Gimbutas — began to promote the argument that the original religion of humankind had been one of priestesses.[71] Humans had worshipped a maternal goddess or goddesses, embodying all the fertility and protectiveness that they needed to grow their crops and raise their livestock.[72] In her 1987 book *Truth or Dare*, Starhawk explored this notion in poetry, storytelling, and historical commentary. Following Gimbutas, she focused on ancient Middle Eastern myth, rewriting the story of the goddess Inanna and her priestesses, whose bodies channeled the goddess's sacred sexuality. Starhawk's re-creation, "A Temple Story," is more of a vision than an historical narrative. In it, the reader is imagined as Inanna's priestess: "you wake early and throw open the shutters of your east-facing window . . . you can smell the city below, the dampness of the canal, the freshness of the palm grove, the ripe odor of animal and human dung . . . you are Inanna's daughter, her vessel." The priestess goes to the temple to be bathed by attendants who praise the female body as they wash it: "Look at those lovely breasts — like ripe pomegranates! . . ."[73] Starhawk was careful to note that she described only "what might have been," but she also believed that priestesses and priests did enact the lovemaking of goddess and god as part of their rites, and this was how she ended her story. For her, as for Leland, the stories and their message were more important than scholarly provenance.

Starhawk was genuinely moved by what she and others saw as the loss of a feminized earthly paradise. She composed a number of poems memorializing its destruction. This one prefaces her chapter on "the dismemberment of the world":

And the circle was broken
And the people splintered
To rule or be ruled
To stand above or below
men over women, light skin over dark, rich over poor,
the few over the many
human gain over the living balance of the earth[74]

This was in terrible contrast to the poem that opened her book:

. . . remember the First Mother
. . . She is a being who is spinning, fire covered with a
sweet crust shell
Feel her pulse, remember in your nerves winks
the spark of the first fire
You are alive in her as she in you
You are her.[75]

Like Leland, Starhawk spoke most fervently through poetry, and this
idea — that a more-than-Edenic perfection had been snatched from
women by violent, polluting, capitalist patriarchs — underlay everything
that she wrote in *The Spiral Dance*. Here, as her subtitle promised, she set
out rituals for "a rebirth of the ancient religion of the great goddess."

The key ideas of Starhawk's old-new religion were sacredness and inter-
connectedness — of the earth, individual spirituality, female (and, later,
male) mysteries, and political action for justice of all kinds. Just as feminism believed that public space ought to be made safe and reclaimed by
women, so Starhawk thought it was time to give Witchcraft more of a
public presence. Her group created a Halloween ritual called "the spiral
dance" and her book took the same title.[76] The spiral dance begins with a
circle, which is broken in order to allow the line of people taking part to
snake back and forth into the center of a spiral pattern and out again, so
that each dancer passes (and in some versions kisses) all the others.[77] It
was intended to symbolize the sort of feeling the Jewish teenager Miriam
Simos had had when, in the summer of 1968, she was a hitchhiker camping on Californian beaches.

> I began to feel connected to the world in a new way, to see everything as
> alive, erotic, engaged in a continual dance of mutual pleasure, and myself
> a special part of it all.[78]

By 1979, her coven had its own Lelandian Charge of the Goddess and
manifesto. The creation of the spiral dance was a way of putting these
ideas into physical movement:

> I think of the Spiral Dance as a metaphor for community. We are all
> linked, and each person's motion affects everyone else down the line.[79]

It was characteristic of Starhawk to imagine an art form, dancing, as at
the heart of a new way of thinking and, in literary terms, to resort instinc-
tively to metaphor. She has described her writing, which would probably
be best categorized as a series of nonfiction manuals, as nevertheless a
"poetic thealogy."[80] Lelandian feminist Witchcraft — born in America,
exported and remade, rewritten, and "reclaimed" — had found its most
resonant expression.[81]

Starhawk has become increasingly comfortable with the idea that what
she and her many Witch followers are doing is taking part in a collab-
orative literary and artistic creation. Originally, as evidenced best in her
1982 book *Dreaming the Dark*, she had believed that the assumptions
underlying her rituals were not only pre-Christian, but had survived the
imposition of patriarchal religion — in western Europe, at least — and
that these survivals were what had prompted the witch persecutions
of the Middle Ages and Renaissance.[82] She had first discussed these in
*The Spiral Dance* and went on to devote further thought to the "burning times," as modern witches called the persecutions, as well as the pre-
Christian religions described in *Truth or Dare*. But by 1999 her thinking
had changed substantially. In her twentieth-anniversary introduction to
*The Spiral Dance*, she stated quite clearly that many of the beliefs and
rituals that "felt thousands of years old" were actually not so. Her naked
Winter Solstice night-bathing in the sea "was born out of a whim less
than twenty years ago, not Divine Decree lost in ages past."[83] She has

thus modified the assertions of some of those who originally inspired her: Zsuzsanna Budapest, practitioners of Faery or Feri magic and derivatives of English Wicca (to say nothing of Leland himself), who often claimed that their practices were ancient pagan rites preserved intact in oral tradition or newly rediscovered manuscripts.

In admitting this modernity unashamedly — and even with a kind of amused delight — Starhawk is pointing to something potentially much more interesting than the idea that what is being practiced by American Witches is unchanged and unchanging. A new and energetic tradition has certainly been created in America. Feminist and politically charged, it is very different from its Gardnerian past in Britain, but entirely true to the older ideas of Charles Godfrey Leland and Ernest Seton Thompson. Some of its Witches still see themselves as dogmatic missionaries, battling Christian and patriarchal hegemony. But because Witchcraft is now such an established presence in many American communities, Witches are more likely to be able to enjoy a role as poets, or actors who devise their own material, creating an ecstatic performance for themselves and each other. The eleventh principle of the short-lived American Council of Witches, agreed in 1974, is increasingly resonant:

> As American Witches, we are not threatened by debates on the history of the Craft, the origins of various terms, the legitimacy of various aspects of different traditions. We are concerned with our present and out future.[84]

This does not mean that American Witches' emotions and spiritual beliefs do not have roots, or are not deeply felt. But, like most religions, Witchcraft has an element of evolution, and a strong element of performance, poetry, and fiction in its sacred texts and signs. The Artemisian Witch Oriethyia told the editors of a collection of interviews with modern pagans that for her "poetry and ritual are synonymous . . . it's about speaking in metaphor."[85]

*Modernizing Magick: Hex and the City*[86]

In 1993 the American academic Cynthia Eller published a book exploring the many branches of the permanent revolution that constituted "the feminist spirituality movement" in the United States. Witchcraft was one of those branches, and it was noticeable that phrases like "center-stage" and "the divine play" came naturally to her in describing what witches do.[87] By the 1990s, the usual central rituals of goddess religion were well established — celebrants could modify them at will, but meetings would almost certainly include an element of ritual cleansing, the casting of a circle using invocations of the four compass points, the raising of energy in the group assembled, and the formal closing of the circle. Cleansing might be achieved with water or incense-burning, the circle cast with versions of Lelandian and/or Gardnerian recitations; energy might be raised by chanting or drumming, and the circle closed with ritual thanking and blessing, perhaps followed by a shared meal. There might be a meditation or sharing of individual visions and problems. A poem quoted by Eller in her discussion of yearning for the goddess shows how recent these seemingly fixed rituals actually are, however. In "Liturgy Circa 1976," Janet R. Price had written to her goddess as late as 1982:

> I want to love you perfectly . . .
> But I don't know how to dress or walk
> or where to put my hands
> or who to give my body to.[88]

Many Witches are still encountering the same problems, despite having a multitude of existing models to choose from. Ceremonies designed for one environment, gender, or income level do not meet everyone's needs, and Witches often define themselves through a strong commitment to individualizing their lives and beliefs. One of the most innovative responses to dissatisfaction with existing rituals is the invention of another modern Witchcraft tradition, often labeled "urban paganism," in American cities.

The idea that a Witch might be at home in an urban environment is inimical to some within the neopagan community. Many see cities as wasteful, polluting, and corrupting blots on the once-pristine American landscape, "boils upon the ass of Gaea," the earth goddess.[89] Thus they are no place for Witches, who should put Mother Earth at the heart of their practices. Paganism, after all, because of its Latin root implies country-dwelling, and so urban paganism is a contradiction in terms. In this respect, the vision of American Witchcraft that crystallized in the 1970s and 1980s owes, as has been suggested, a great deal to other defining American visions: the Frontier, Thoreau, the West. But what if a Witch happens to live and work in a city, has no desire or no money to flee to the country, and even likes city life? In the twenty-first century, Witchcraft's eminently adaptable view of tradition has found several ways forward for such people. Christopher Penczak's *City Magick*, published in 2001, offered the first approach. Penczak was working in Cambridge, Massachusetts, in the music business, when he began to explore ways of "reclaiming" (that key word again) the city environment. Drawing on Carl Jung's theory of the collective unconscious, he realized he believed strongly that cities are alive with archetypal spirits — just as they were with the gods of ancient Egypt or Mesopotamia. Nothing had changed in the human psyche, he reasoned, so why should modern cities be spiritually barren? "The city," Penczak asserted, "is the new primordial forest . . . both the concrete and the natural jungles are filled with their own beauty."[90] So he set out on a series of journeys of discovery, to find sites of power within cities, totem animals, and urban deities.

Informed by traditions ranging from Native American shamanism to Hindu metaphysics, he theorized freely, letting his mind open to the possibilities that pigeons, instead of being mere "rats with wings," might "have a special kinship to Mother Earth" because of their inexplicable homing instinct. Modern magic is often a blend of scientific (and pseudoscientific) ideas with the creative arts, so Penczak based his view of the pigeon totem-spirit on both scientists' suggestions that they homed using the earth's magnetic field, and the idea that pigeons "may work with trust issues," helping to bring home spiritually those who worked with them. Similarly, subways were not merely dark, dirty tunnels for trains, but "great electric serpents running through the city." Automobiles, too, had a sacredness: "if your car has trouble starting in the morning . . . help heal the car spirit." Best of all were airplanes, because they performed what, for Penczak, is a key service to Witches: the provision of readable signs for divination or "magickal" work. Airplane trails were "symbolic markers," and Penczak urged the would-be City Witch to "write down their shape and meditate on the new symbol to discover its magical purposes."[91] Detail was vital, in this world where everything might mean something. Penczak offers the startlingly powerful idea that "a whole new pantheon of gods may be lurking in the cities of North America," and follows it with the injunction that, in order to discover these gods' secrets, traffic noise should be recorded and played back to hear "the message."[92] Also, televisions can be used for visualization — an actual program should be watched, and the Witch should try to project him- or herself into the filming location, whether it be Egypt or South America. Penczak comments enthusiastically that, "news specials focusing on a troubled part of the world are good." If this is the type of program chosen, the Witch should try to project healing energies to help those on screen. Television screens, tuned so that the picture turns to "snow," can also be used as scrying (visual divination) devices like crystal balls. In a trance state, the Witch viewer simply asks the questions he or she wants answered, and waits for images to appear.[93]

It would be easy to caricature this spiritualizing of urban environments and modern technologies that most people see as wholly functional. Those who laughed at Leland would sneer at Penczak. It is easy to imagine many people's instinctive reaction to being told that there is a hidden message in traffic noise or in the white noise of the television. It may seem crazy, the construction of a mind obsessively searching for significance where none exists, a paranoid misreading of the world. It may even be seen as threatening or exploitative: do American Witches really want to use, say, the troubles of the Middle East or North Korea as an aesthetically satisfying backdrop for their own self-development? Penczak himself speculates occasionally on the borderline between the magic world of visions and spirit-conversations and the worlds of the mentally ill. He also returns to the images of playacting and poetry that sometimes make Witchcraft seem a mere metaphor, rather than a "real" belief, when he says, "entering a magical state is like playing pretend."[94] But for Penczak, the role-playing and healing through visualizing are deeply serious, carefully theorized, and benign exercises, for here the City Witch can contact the spirit world, and learn both to help themselves and other people. His world is certainly a rich and imaginatively compelling one. In it, Witches ascend to the plane of trance by imagining themselves in "a shamanistic elevator" in the Worldscraper, a skyscraper that, like the Norse concept of the World Tree, connects the real world with both an underworld and a higher realm. In this world, Spiderman is a shaman, moving between everyday life and the Marvel-lous beyond, by climbing buildings and flying miraculously through the city skyline. Not surprisingly, spiders are Penczak's favorite totem animals.[95] Even graffiti, the defining disfigurement of the urban environment, is of use, because it provides mystically charged sigils, magical words, to the observant Witch. A sigil found in graffiti, or based on a street map, can prove useful as a charm for finding a parking space or a new home.[96] Finally, the Internet can be used to create a cyber temple, with Witches from all over the world taking part in online, typed rituals in a chat room. "The wonderful thing about creating your own rituals," says Penczak happily, "is that there are no rules."[97]

The same empowering freedom can be found in Tannin Schwartzstein and Raven Kaldera's book *The Urban Primitive*. But it offers a different reading of city paganism, more playful than Penczak's and based more firmly on invention than reclaimed archetype. Penczak's book has roots in "olde worlde," old spelling Lelandian-Gardnerian magick, a tradition based on learning and ceremony. Penczak presents himself as a magus, beginning his book with acknowledgments to his "wisest teachers," and an explanation of terms from a distinct mystic tradition: *chakras* (energy centers in the body), *prana* (spirit energy).[98] That his teachers are not only writers but also musicians and comic book artists is simply an updating of the old high-magickal discourse. In contrast, the keynote of Schwartz-stein and Kaldera's book is make-do, "junkyard magic."[99] The book jumps straight into practicalities. A number of different traditions are immediately mentioned, including santeria and voudoun ("voodoo"), offering an inclusive, eclectic version of Witchcraft that can be based in any community. As Cynthia Eller documented, very few African-Americans, and very few people of Asian, Hispanic, or Native American backgrounds, identify themselves as Witches.[100] Witchcraft is a predominantly white, middle-class religion. Schwartzstein and Kaldera make an attempt to define it differently, but where they are really successful is in challenging its bourgeois associations. Charles Godfrey Leland and Gerald Gardner would hardly recognize as their disciple "a soccer mom with three kids who shields her tiny apartment with scattered Rice Krispies," or even the authors of *The Urban Primitive*, whose magical tools include toy soldiers and chewing gum.[101] They also favor cyber rituals, like Penczak, and include poetry on the subject from MagicRat:

> I am the Path
> And the Server
> And the Host . . .
> I am the Yule Login . . .
> First in the Printer Queue
> And the Passwyrd to Arcadia Online . . .
> I have crashed
> And gone down in Flames
> I have Doubleclicked the Bucket
> And been Recovered.[102]

If people decide to practice Witchcraft with old catfood cans, nail polish, and salt and pepper liberated from MacDonalds, so mote it be.[103]

And with these cheap, funky magickal tools, Schwartzstein and Kaldera offer an eclectic, postmodern mix of deities. The Greeks Athena, Zeus, and Apollo are there, as are the Norse Freya, Chinese Kwan Yin, Hindu Lakshmi, Egyptian Sekhmet, Yoruba Shango, and Celtic Brigid. The usual goddess of witches, Hecate, is there, but her role is minor and she does not even appear in the book's index — a further indication that this model of Witchcraft pays little heed to tradition.[104] The Classical gods and goddesses, however, have new homes in the modern city, and new links with like-minded deities from other cultures. Schwartzstein and Kaldera suggest that offerings for Apollo or Horus or Helios or Ra, all sun gods and all available to the modern pagan, may be left on the corners of solar panels. A good offering might be a sun made out of tinfoil and inscribed with the donor's wish.[105] This kind of eclecticism had been used by other groups, as far back as the earliest days of American Witchcraft.[106] But Schwartzstein and Kaldera have gone the final step and synthesized their own deities: "the Urban Goddess of America" and "the Triple Urban God." Each has three faces. The female deities are Squat, Skor, and Skram. Squat protects parking spaces if offered dirty jokes and doggerel, and can help find housing. Skor is the "Goddess of Yard Sales, Flea Markets, and especially Trashpicking," propitiated by gifts of recyclable trash or pennies on the sidewalk. Skram tells her adherents when to get out of wherever they happen to be, before something bad befalls them. Meanwhile, the three aspects of the God are Slick, Screw, and Sarge. Slick grants the mercurial art of fast thinking and persuasive rhetoric. Screw finds safe casual sex if he receives knotted condoms, hung up in public places or given out on the street. Finally, Sarge offers motivation — to face the landlord or the IRS. He also motivates other people. Sarge can be called simply by asking, and Schwartzstein and Kaldera tell the story of a Witch who ensured that her car parts were delivered when she "pictured someone looking vaguely like Sergeant Bilko leaning into the slack face of the truck driver, invisibly haranguing him."[107] These deities reek of the brashness of American city life, full of street-credibility and capturing perfectly the transatlantic essence of modern Witchcraft: experimental, sometimes self-parodic, always evolving.

This is Witchcraft for a young country, not in awe of Europe, or the prescriptive writings of dead white men. Leo Martello wrote of American Wicca more generally that while European traditions say that a Witch is born, not made, Anglo-American covens say, "A Witch is made, not born."[108] Although this distinction is not always true, it reflects perfectly the mythos of America and thus of her Witches, too: American Witches are generally self-made. Where Leland and Gardner concealed their weird, brilliant synthesis and innovation of traditions under a protective cloak of myth, many modern Witches are more likely to rejoice that their personal goddess was only conceived — or discovered — yesterday. Do we take these gods and goddesses seriously? It actually "doesn't matter," a phrase that recurs over and over again in more recent texts by Witches. Gardnerian Ed Fitch told researcher Margot Adler flatly that "It doesn't matter whether your tradition is forty thousand years old or whether it was created last week," a view espoused most vigorously by Aidan Kelly, founder of the New Reformed Orthodox Order of the Golden Dawn. The title of Kelly's organization was symptomatic of his evolving beliefs about the origins of modern Witchcraft: both new and re-formed, orthodox and ordered, with its roots in freemasonry and European occultism but its modern incarnation an "invention."[109] What does matter to American Witches, it seems, is the power and intensity of the experiences that such creations allow them. "Sometimes," as Schwartzstein and Kaldera put it, "a little skepticism lends a nice, tangy flavor to your sense of wonder."[110]

Because of this ability to stand back from dogma, to see merit in the beliefs of others and learn creatively from them, some Witches and other pagans have even begun a fascinating journey back to the churches where interest in witchcraft began to flourish so radically in the mid-nineteenth century. As Helen A. Berger has documented, an increasing number of Neo-Pagans are joining the Unitarian Universalist Association, which grew from the Unitarian and Universalist churches. Unitarian Universalism welcomes people of all creeds, rationalists, and social activists, and has both male and female ministers. The U.U.A. has even published works on goddess spirituality.[111] It has been a long journey from the pioneering history of the Unitarian minister Charles W. Upham, but in an ironic and unexpected way Salem Witchcraft has found its way home in the same way as Leland's *Aradia*.

*Historicizing Witchcraft*

In many ways, as I hope has been suggested, the embrace of inclusive creativity is simply a recognition of what was always true in modern Witchcraft. Each generation innovated, and added to the eclectic traditions handed down to it. Each Witch tried to find a way of making the Craft work for her or him — a dash of Buddhism here, or the feminist philosophy of Cixous or Irigaray there. Some Gardnerians objected, and some Witches even consider themselves "Gardnerian Heretics" because they have been so described by more orthodox practitioners. Judy Harrow founded her own sect, "Protean Witchcraft," in response to just this accusation. As its name suggests, it embraces change and metamorphosis: "We don't need our religion to ossify," she said.[112] But for those who like the world to be ordered and recordable, this endless variation made it important to construct a history (or histories) of Witchcraft, and to gather evidence about what Witches did and do. This project was particularly necessary since most Witches regarded themselves as being misrepresented in fictions dealing with both their past and their present. So while Starhawk was creating a poetics of Witchcraft, her fellow-Witch Margot Adler was trying to construct that definitive history. Her book, *Drawing Down the Moon*, was published on the same day in 1979 as *The Spiral Dance*. It was not that Adler was trying to pigeonhole Witchcraft: in fact, the opposite. In her second edition, in 1986, she summarized the book's message: "Strive to be comfortable in chaos and complexity.... Try to feel strong and whole and at home in a world of diversity."[113] But she did want to correct the misconceptions about Witches and their history that she saw around her, and this could only be done by adopting an approach recognizable to non-Witches. Adler distributed questionnaires, conducted interviews, and read a wide range of books. As someone from within the Neo-Pagan world, feeling her own religion to be inspired by classical deities, she was not writing from a position of scholarly objectivity. But it is inevitable that when writing about the postmodern fracturing of Western certainties that has helped to create modern paganism, no one can truly claim to be objective. Adler frankly included her own experiences as part of her data collection, and stressed repeatedly her own subjectivity.

Even so, Adler's book was quite an opinionated one. Her assertions were sometimes absolute, and some were based on a strict interpretation of a concept or phrase. A good example is her statement, "remember, no-one *converts* to Paganism or Wicca."[114] Actually, there were some testimonies in her text that would be considered fairly standard road-to-Damascus narratives in other contexts. In her interview with Sharon Devlin, Adler heard how Devlin had always been "deeply religious," had tried to enter a Catholic convent, had stumbled across books on alchemy and spellwork, tried some spells, and then "it flashed upon me that I was fulfilling something to do with my ancestry." After that, she regarded herself "a Witch because I knew that was what I was."[115] Adler took from this and similar stories, including her own, the truth that she saw: Sharon had always been a Witch, and had simply reconnected with her essential beliefs. But some readers may feel differently, if "conversion" is stripped of many of its negative associations. Cynthia Eller had no problem, fifteen years later, in using the word to describe the process of becoming a Witch.[116] Adler thus bravely tried to be both historically authoritative — retaining a concept of truth and "real life" that was not open to debate — and open-minded, genuinely committed to plural visions of truthfulness. *Drawing Down the Moon* must have been extremely difficult to write. Her approach was open to many questions, but it was vital if Witchcraft was to have a recorded presence outside its own circles.

One of the most interesting things that Adler did (and Cynthia Eller and Helen A. Berger have since done) was to interview large numbers of Witches and Neo-Pagans of various kinds, and print their responses. She did this both in the form of narratives, woven into an overall analytical account, and as statistics. It was a new approach to an often mystical and ungraspable faith. It suggested that American Witchcraft was not just about ecstatic creativity, but also was grounded in the everyday world. Witchcraft was shaped by, and had impacts on, the economy, education, technology, and social circumstances. Adler's 1985 questionnaire suggested, for example, that about 60 percent of Witches were formerly Catholic or Protestant, with a relatively small number from Jewish, atheist, or other backgrounds. Most had come to the Craft through feminism, an interest in occultism and magic, or the reading of significant books. Adler's own work and *The Spiral Dance* were the two most often mentioned. But most interestingly, a surprisingly high number of Witches were not counter-cultural dropouts, but computer programmers, students, clerical workers, counselors, and teachers.[117] Some were angry at being portrayed as eclectic and undisciplined, and worried about these tendencies toward "flakiness" in the movement, and one Witch said: "We are ordinary people. . . . We have families, jobs, hopes, and dreams. We are not a cult. We are not weird."[118] Adler's practical desire to historicize witchcraft, and connect it to worldly actualities, found an answering need among some Witches to move beyond the Romanticism and myth that had created their religion.

It is entirely possible to be both a Witch and a pragmatic operative in the everyday world. Laurie Cabot, the famous "official Witch of Salem" introduced in Chapter 2, is a fine example and she is not alone. Cabot is the author of a series of books, of which the best known is probably *Power of the Witch*, which she cowrote with freelance lecturer and shamanic counselor Tom Cowan, and she runs both a very successful business and a mail-order service. Her book, first published in 1989, accepted the traditional story of the Old Religion, the end of matriarchies, and the Burning Times. But she was very clear that Witches need not feel obliged to live in poverty because their forebears had suffered loss and persecution.

> Witches need to be prosperity conscious. . . . Read through the following statements. Many of them are part of our so-called folk wisdom . . . "Money seekers are hedonists." "Money corrupts." "Money is the root of all evil." "You don't need money to be happy." "The best things in life are free." "Rich people tend to be corrupt and selfish." "To walk a spiritual path you should give away your possessions."
>
> If you tend to agree with these comments, you may be creating psychic roadblocks to prosperity.[119]

Cabot's tradition is, on the one hand, conservative. It comes partly from the Gardnerian and Family Tradition teachings of Sybil Leek, the English witch who immigrated to America in the 1960s. It also incorporates elements of the theosophy of Helena Petrovna Blavatsky, whose writings fused Eastern mysticism with Christian and pagan beliefs, and Robert Graves's poetic musings in *The White Goddess*. Like many Gardnerians, Cabot wears a robe, which she believes is even more traditional than going "skyclad," because during the Burning Times it was "less conspicuous in the forest, where they went at night to do their rituals."[120] She also has a strong, literal understanding of the ways in which magic works: through traditional correspondences of elements, minerals, and star signs, for example, or the brain's alpha waves. Her American Witchcraft has strong affinities with the old European profession of the cunning man or woman, who used his or her magical skills (or his or her claim to possess them) to make money by offering divination, healing, and ritual acts and items for sale. But Cabot is also intensely modern, pointing out some decade before Penczak, Schwartzstein, and Kaldera that "we can use alpha to get a parking space."[121] What strikes anyone who looks carefully at the world of Witchcraft as it has been re-created in North America is that despite a number of common themes running through different traditions, Witchcraft is an amazingly diverse religion and its practitioners all have strikingly eclectic beliefs and practices. It is a religion that produces a Reformation every time a new book is published or a new coven formed.[122]

### Seeing Red: When Good Witches Go Bad

Yet despite this increasingly well-known history and broadly beneficent theology/thealogy, Witches were and are often portrayed in "the media" as dangerous radicals and satanist dropouts. One respondent to Adler's 1985 questionnaire wrote that the one thing s/he wanted to tell people was that "we do not worship the devil . . . we are not what you think we are from looking at T.V."[123] Some films and television series did and do continue to present a wholly negative image of Wicca and Witchcraft.

*Rosemary's Baby* (1968) is perhaps the best-known example, remembered and cited by angry Witches to this day.[124] In the film, the young, beautiful wife Rosemary (Mia Farrow) becomes pregnant, but gradually begins to believe that something is wrong with her baby. Is she suffering from delusions, wonders the viewer, or does some kind of sinister conspiracy really surround her pregnancy? In fact, it becomes clear that Rosemary's folksy elderly neighbors have been plotting with her husband to force her to bear the devil's child. The film juxtaposes the comfortable, domestic American setting of the adjoining apartments with the terrors of medieval Europe very successfully: just the other side of the wall was un-American horror. Rosemary's devil is the traditional witch-seducer of European folklore, a "black thing" in "the likenes of a Man."[125] Witches usually had sex with the devil as part of their bargain with him for power, but he also played another role, according to some demonologists, in that he impregnated other women with demonic seed. Skeptical English writer Reginald Scot summarized: "old witches are sworne to procure as manie yoong virgins for Incubus as they can, whereby in time they growe to be excellent bawds."[126] The notorious *Malleus Maleficarum* devoted a chapter to the subject:

> at first it may truly seem that it is not in accordance with the Catholic Faith to maintain that children can be begotten by devils, that is to say, by Incubi and Succubi.... But it may be argued that devils take their part in this generation not as the essential cause, but as a secondary and artificial cause, since they busy themselves by interfering with the process of normal copulation and conception, by obtaining human semen, and themselves transferring it.... For the devil is Succubus to a man, and becomes Incubus to a woman.[127]

The *Malleus*, however, was very definite: "of whom is a child so born the son? It is clear that he is not the son of the devil, but of the man whose semen was received."[128] The idea of the devil's child was a much simpler one, dismissed as peasant superstition by those who had given lengthy thought to the constitution of spiritual bodies, God's role in procreation, and how semen might be preserved for later use. However, by 1968 these distinctions had ceased to be important. What did matter was that the nice old lady next door was a witch, imperiling the innocence of the young wife in her care. The witch worshipped the devil, made magical potions, and organized satanic orgies. Nothing much had changed in five hundred years. Wiccans and Witches were keen to point out that "real witches aren't anticipating the birth of an Anti-Christ," but many believed that the film had done great damage to their public image.[129]

Witches like Starhawk and Cabot also saw the film version of John Updike's 1984 novel *The Witches of Eastwick* and the teen-movie *The Craft* in this light (and Updike's novel could be read in the same way despite its differences from its screenplay). In *The Witches of Eastwick*, filmed in 1989, three women are seduced by the devil, who — in the person of Jack Nicholson — comes to live in their small New England town. In an apparent reference to Shirley Barker's *Peace My Daughters*, his name is Van Horne. Each of his witches gets what she wants: sexual fulfillment, luxury, and power over her life and her community.[130] In the film's opening scene, the lecherous school principal is punished for his harassment of one of the women, and his patriarchal attitude toward the others, when his big speech is rained off by a sudden magically created storm. The viewer probably approves of this cheery feminist addition to the novel's plot. But later, the devil's interpretation of the witches' desires becomes increasingly malevolent. A woman is seriously injured, and then killed. The devil becomes a threat to the three witches themselves. This happens even more graphically in the book where the women kill their fellow witch by giving her multiple cancers, only to find that they are terrified of the consequences. Eventually, they must drive Satan out, but he is never entirely vanquished. In the film, he has also left the witches a legacy: each has a baby whose daddy is the devil. *The Craft* tells a similar story of temporary empowerment with serious consequences. Schoolgirl Sarah (Robin Tunney) comes to live in a new community following a history of depression and a suicide attempt. Here she joins forces with three girls who also have problems: bullying and racist classmates, a violent father. The girls, led by the goth Nancy (Fairuza Balk), experiment with witchcraft, taking their revenge on those who have hurt them. But Nancy goes too far. She invokes the god Manon (a name originally taken from the film *Manon des Sources* and suggesting a revengeful woman) who possesses her and quickly drives her mad. Soon Nancy is walking on water, flying, killing a former lover, and torturing Sarah with snakes and bugs. For her sins, she must be imprisoned in a psychiatric hospital. The coven falls apart in mutual recrimination, slapping down any ideas of women's empowerment through teamwork and friendship, and any idea that the practice of the Craft of Witchcraft might be about self-discipline or self-healing.[131]

In both films, witchcraft/Witchcraft is a seductive masculine power that lures women to it with a promise of legitimate gain, only to expose them to danger and self-doubt. Each film leaves the witches where they began — battling a demonic patriarchal force. At least the witches of Eastwick retained their friendship in the film, as they did not in Updike's novel, and the Wiccan community was perhaps less troubled by that film than *The Craft*. The major problem with *The Craft* was that, in the name of authenticity, its witches used charms and symbols based on actual Wiccan and Witchcraft rites. There were elements of the traditional initiation into a coven (as seen, for example, in *The Grimoire of Lady Sheba*) and the casting of a circle by calling on the Guardians of the Watchtowers (as seen, for example, in *The Spiral Dance*). Director Andrew Fleming had sought advice from Pat Devin, a respected authority within the Wiccan community, and he believed that this input meant that "this movie functions largely as a two hour commercial for the creed."[132] It is hard to see how this could be so, however. Dabbling in witchcraft led straight to insanity, murder, and despair for the film's four young protagonists. An attempt was, perhaps, made to suggest that Nancy in particular was being punished not for using magick but for her cavalier and selfish attitude toward the Craft. While Sarah had "natural" gifts as a witch, dressed in a mainstream, feminine fashion, and was basically a benevolent character, Nancy — with her black lipstick and trailer-park home — was an outsider, unfeminine and aggressive. Wiccan wisdom might be seen as embodied not in Nancy but in Sarah's sensibleness, or in the motherly keeper of a magic shop whom Nancy treats disrespectfully when she advises that evil spells done by Witches will return on them with triple strength. But this subtlety was not evident to the Witch community. It did not explain why all the Witches came out of the film so badly scarred by their experiences, and so isolated from one another. For Starhawk, *The Craft* was at best "trivializing," perpetuating an offensive connection made in the journalistic media between witchcraft and "horror and human sacrifice."[133] For Cabot, *The Witches of Eastwick* was precisely "*Rosemary's Baby* all over again." A desire to protest against the film led to her foundation of The Witches' League for Public Awareness. The League objected to "yet another film depicting the Witch as an evildoer . . . conjuring up the devil and having sex with him." They contacted the actresses playing the three witches, Susan Sarandon, Michelle Pfeiffer, and Cher, with "awareness packets," hoping to dissuade them from perpetuating the image of the witch as evil, and pressed for a disclaimer at the film's opening, stating that its content was not related to modern Witchcraft.[134] But none of these strategies bore fruit.

The most notorious recent example of the topos of the punished Witch is the fate of the characters Willow and Tara in *Buffy the Vampire Slayer*. *Buffy* was a film that died at the box office in 1992 and rose again as a television series in 1997. Buffy Summers (Sarah Michelle Gellar) had two sidekicks in the television series, Willow and Xander.[135] Willow (Alyson Hannigan), a childlike, awkward bluestocking, was scorned by most of her peers at Sunnydale High. But as the series progressed she became aware of her own intelligence and skill, particularly in researching and the use of computers. Yet it was hard to imagine in 1997 that in the not-too-distant future, she would become a powerful Witch. As Rhonda V. Wilcox points out, "Willow" sounded pliant but was often nicknamed "Will," and as her identity as a Witch developed, it was her will that became an issue for those around her.[136] Willow was developing the capacity to do exactly as she pleased. She learned some of her skills from the "techno-pagan" teacher Jenny Calendar, who was descended from Romanian gypsies. Jenny was not a witch, she said, but she knew a great deal about spells and magic.[137] After Jenny's death Willow took over her role as a spell caster and in the two-part episode "Becoming," she completed the magical task for which Jenny had been sent to Sunnydale, restoring the soul of the vampire angel.[138] For Angel, a punitive trip to Hell and back followed. For Willow, fast "becoming" an unusually powerful young woman, the consequence should have been rewarding. But instead it was to be a curious mirroring of Angel's, and indeed Jenny's, fate.

It seemed that Whedon and his cowriters were working toward empowering Willow in a variety of ways, and carefully managing her image so as not to offend Wiccans or, conversely, suggest that *Buffy* promoted paganism. Clearly Willow was not a standard Wiccan: few real Wiccans claim to be able to stick to the ceiling. Tanya Krzywinska argued that:

> Willow uses "magic," but she is not part of a cult or religious group. She may call herself a "Wicca," but she is never seriously linked to a Wiccan group . . .[139]

Willow certainly saw Sunnydale University's Wiccans as "wannablessed-be's," trendy and shallow. All they could talk about, she said, was "blah blah Gaia, blah blah moon, menstrual life force power thingy. . . ."[140] Her magic was different, and superior. This might have seemed insulting to Wiccans, but it could also have been an attempt to distance them from Willow in a protective gesture, for more controversial developments were to come. Willow's increasing proficiency in magic was being accompanied by greater confidence in her relationships. She moved into friendship with another Witch, Tara (Amber Benson), and at last they came out and began an open lesbian relationship.[141] The association of witches with lesbianism is a well-established one.[142] Ironically, lesbian sexuality was virtually invisible — maybe even "unimaginable" — at the time of the European witch hunts.[143] Early modern creative writers, however, had begun to open the door to a discussion of same-sex attraction between women. Shakespeare's plays from the turn of the sixteenth century contain a number of women who share intense friendships (*A Midsummer Night's Dream*'s Helena and Hermia, *As You Like It*'s Rosalind and Celia) or who fall in love with women disguised as men (*Twelfth Night*'s Olivia, *As You Like It*'s Phebe). These early modern hints of lesbian desire did not, however, appear in plays, poems, or

tracts about witches, and it was not until the "Enlightenment" that lesbianism began to be recognized as a definable and discussable phenomenon.
Whedon and his cowriters were thus attempting something fairly revolutionary, especially on American television, since it was only in the last
quarter of the twentieth century that it became possible to portray a lesbian
relationship positively and openly to a wide audience.

But the association of witches with lesbians came with other twentieth-
century baggage that was less suggestive of radical intent. The apparently
straight woman who becomes a witch as part of exploring lesbian and bisex-
uality was and is a recurrent character in gothic, and pornographic, horror
fictions.[144] This, of course, is why modern Witches have felt they needed to
"reclaim" a pure reading of female heterosexuality, lesbianism, nudity, and
community rituals. Witchcraft pornography often suggests that Witchcraft
is a religion based on unthinking promiscuity and sinister voyeurism. Second, it may be satanic. Certainly its adherents are usually drawn to dark
deeds and the satisfaction of their own lusts and ambitions. Third, closet
lesbians use it as a cover to allow them to prey on women under the guise
of offering mentoring and powerful role models. Vulnerable heterosexual
women are referred to as "normal" and "healthy," while the powerful lesbian
woman is stigmatized as unnatural and predatory. Her sexuality gives plenty
of opportunity for showing women naked together, however, in a depressing
double standard. Fourth, therefore, the portrayal of lesbian Witchcraft could
be seen as an excuse for the exploitation of actresses and models. Finally,
heterosexuality must triumph. The lesbian witch must die, nastily, stripped
of her power and dignity. Seen in this light, Joss Whedon's desire to develop
a lesbian storyline for Willow looks suicidally courageous.

In the service of that liberal aim, Willow and Tara developed a loving
and monogamous partnership, which was renewed despite a painful quar-
rel and lasted even when Tara became temporarily insane. The reasons for
their parting were troubling, however. They broke up because of Willow's
increasingly indiscriminate use of magic, which had come to be associated
with sex and particularly with her lesbian sexuality. Whedon explained

the relationship between witchcraft and sexuality on NPR when he talked about the creative process of writing Willow:

> we had thought about the idea of someone exploring their sexuality . . . Since we tend to work inside metaphor, for most of the show, we talked about Willow and her being a witch because it's a very strong female community and it gives her a very physical relationship with someone that isn't necessarily sexual. And then when we decided to go that way . . . someone had to be with Willow and it seemed like a good time for her to be exploring this and the question became, how much do we play in metaphor and how much do we play as her actually expanding her sexuality . . .[145]

Witchcraft rituals performed by Willow and Tara together helped build, and symbolize, the growing attraction between them, as "a substitute for romance and sexual tension."[146] In the tellingly titled "Who Are You?" viewers watched as Willow experienced a sort of magical orgasm at the climax of a ritual with Tara.[147] The witchcraft rituals were not, as in traditional portrayals, overtly sexual, but they did focus intensely on the relationship between the two Witches, and involved frequent hand-holding and ecstatic shared recitation. Magically speaking, then, by later using her sexy skill in secretive ways that Tara disapproved of, Willow was behaving promiscuously. She bewitched Tara to make her forget her concern about the overuse of magic, and then began to go out with another witch to seek thrills.[148] By 2000, magic seemed to be about sexual overconfidence, a symbol of too much experimentation, rather than a stable and loving bond between the two Witches.

But even more negatively, Willow's use of magic began to be imaged as an addiction, something from which she had to refrain in order to be healthy and engage in normal relationships. Sara Crosby commented angrily that "in the 2002 season [Witchcraft] suddenly stands in for heroin."[149] Willow became deceitful, selfish, sickly, and aggressive — stereotypical attributes of a drug addict whose only concern is for the next hit or, in this case, spell. Because the addictive substance — Witchcraft — had come to be equated with female empowerment and especially lesbian sexuality, its portrayal as damaging to its user was extremely confusing. Willow did not lose, or abjure, her magic powers in the series, and indeed they were instrumental in finally saving the world from destruction when the show ended in 2004. But it did seem that the message behind the storyline was that Willow had to curb her powers and only use Witchcraft wisely: not selfishly, not indiscriminately, not trivially. What did this metaphor really mean? Whedon had always liked his work to be open to many readings, on a "bring your own subtext" principle, and fans and critics are still arguing over the answer.[150]

The final, and for many viewers traumatic, events of the relationship between Willow and Tara (in Season Six episodes "Seeing Red," "Two to Go," "Villains," and "Grave") raised the strongest fears that Whedon had taken more from patriarchy and witch-porn than he had perhaps realized.[151] The two witches had been reunited after their rift, and were seen dressing after celebratory sex. Suddenly, Tara was shot and killed, by an assassin who had been trying to kill Buffy. There was no way back after this development: Tara had died naturally, and no magic could save her. Amber Benson, who played Tara, later said that in fact she had been asked to play an evil undead version of Tara, but had refused.[152] Willow, meanwhile, returned to her addictive use of magic and went on a witchcraft rampage that culminated in her torture and murder, by flaying, of Tara's killer. The title of the episode "Seeing Red," which marked her transformation, was revealing. "Red" was the vampire Spike's nickname for ginger-haired Willow, and the title suggested that viewers were — for the first time — seeing the Witch as she really was. Red was really Black — her hair and eyes changed color to match her evil essence. Willow then tried to use her powers to end the world. Her motivation may have been in itself humane — she wanted to put an end to all the world's suffering and pain by extinguishing it — but in becoming the agent of apocalypse, Willow was placed in the situation of every arch-villain since the series began. Amber Benson, written out of the series when Tara died, summed up the sadness and disillusion of many of her fans in an interview with *Diva*, a magazine for lesbian and bisexual readers. "I was really sad," she said simply, "it was so dumb . . . so traumatic for a lot of fans who had so much invested in her."[153] Tara's death and Willow's turn to villainy seemed to replay all the punishments meted out to both gay and Witch characters in fiction.[154] At least Willow was given a new girlfriend, Kennedy, in *Buffy*'s final season. But she was not another Witch. For many viewers, Whedon's brave experiment with Witchcraft failed because it fell into too many of the old traps, put there by patriarchal demonologists and modern pornographers to sustain its radical intent.

### The Blair Witch

Limits were also a key concern of the most famed witch-themed millennial event, *The Blair Witch Project*, also discussed in Chapter 2. As the story unfolded, several themes emerged: the relationship of outsiders with family and community, the role of history and myth in American life, the power of wilderness over the American mind, boundaries and frontiers. The directors and producers, and subsequent critics, have explored some of these: the character Heather as Captain Ahab, her quest as a frontier myth.[155] But the most interesting intersection was once again between the images of witch, Witch, and woman. The two *Blair Witch* films provided a complete tour of this cluster of ideas. The first film focused on the leadership of the filmmaking team by Heather Donahue, which was the name of both the actress and her character. It became more and more explicit in its attack on her. "Mike is the audience's character," commented the production team on the DVD commentary, and through the eyes of this team member Heather looked monstrous.[156] She became increasingly dictatorial, while her other collaborator Josh rebelled against her leadership. Mike offered an expressive face to both their cameras, and the producers saw him as echoing audience reaction to the two extremists. But it was his criticism of Heather, implicit and explicit, as well as Josh's open aggression toward her that they saw as particularly important. A dynamic was set up that pitted Josh against Heather, and then Mike against Heather, siding with Josh. The directors' and producers' commentary was later laced with remarks such as: "everybody in the audience wants to make fun of Heather," "very justified . . . the way she's been acting."

As the filmmakers, and the actors in reality, trudged through the woods, camping each night, they became increasingly lost. Finally, disgusted with Heather's insistence that they go on to complete the project and that she knew exactly where she was going, Mike threw her map into a creek and the trio were genuinely in trouble. Without a map, America yawned before them, as did the emotional landscape that their demonizing of Heather had created. It was a short step to the "mutiny" that the "boys" set up against Heather, during which they sang "The Star-Spangled Banner." Suddenly Josh's joke shot of Heather and a black cat was not so funny: like Elly Kedward, Heather was backed against a tree in the forest while all-American boys ranted at her. Heather wept — later she would weep again more famously. She filled up the time between by darning her male companion's clothes ("maternal control," the commentators muttered) and, when Josh disappeared, comforting Mike by putting her arm awkwardly round him. Then some bloody teeth of Josh's were found, wrapped in a scrap of his shirt and a bundle of sticks, like the stick-men hung in the trees and associated with the Blair Witch. Heather tried protectively to conceal this from Mike and again the producers commented on her "maternal" urges. But Heather was no good as a mother: seconds later she was washing the blood off her hands as the "fiendlike Queen" Lady Macbeth does,[157] and it was time for her "confession," as the producers called it. Really there is no other word. Metaphorically, Heather was the Blair Witch, and she knew it. This is what she said, crying and terrified:

> I just want to apologize to Mike's mom and Josh's mom, and I'm sorry to everyone . . . I am so so sorry for everything that has happened, because, in spite of what Mike says now, it is my fault, because it was my project, and I insisted. I insisted on everything . . . everything had to be my way, and this is where we've ended up, and it's all because of me that we're here now, hungry, and cold, and hunted. I love you Mom, Dad. I'm so sorry . . .

Heather Donahue wrote her own words for this speech. The equation between assertive women, lone women, and witches is inescapable. It was Heather who was the wicked woman alone in the woods here, apologizing to real mothers and good women. Heather should not have been practicing the magic of filmmaking, believing she was in control of words and

images. She was the child-killer, depriving Josh and Mike's mothers of
their sons. That she also fell victim to the witch at the film's end was little
comfort for female viewers hoping that, like witches tried by ordeal, if
Heather died she might be innocent. Viewers never saw the witch, but
they did not need to. It was obvious who she was: everyone died because of
Heather, including her guilty, executed self.[158]

The Blair Witch Project's revival of ideas of female evil personified
in the figure of a witch was controversial, although most discussion of
the film centered on its Internet-based marketing and its blurring of the
line between fiction and reality. Joe Berlinger, however, who was chosen
to direct the sequel, had noted that the Wiccan community was "quite
upset . . . by The Blair Witch Project because they felt it was one more
media example of how witches have been misportrayed and exploited
over the years."[159] So, in his sequel, an ironic reversal had taken place: the
human figure most likely to be associated with the Blair Witch, Erica,
was reworked as an innocent Wiccan. Was it coincidence that erica is the
Latin name for heather?[160] Erica (Erica Leerhsen) was threatening to men
in different ways than Heather had been — she was "a hottie," one said,
and sexually predatory — but the two women also had elements in common. Like Heather, Erica was accused of staging the frightening phenom-
ena that engulfed her group. She too believed that she was powerful, and
tried to take control of the situation in the woods, in this case by acting
independently to reverse the evil associated with the Black Hills. Some
of the threats associated with Heather were thus reworked in Erica, and
seen to be illusory. The second figure who might be mistaken for a witch
was the intellectual young woman Tristen (Tristen Skyler). Like Heather,
she had a "project," a book she was writing with her boyfriend Stephen
(Stephen Barker Turner) on witchcraft. She was also reluctantly pregnant,
establishing a problematic association with motherhood like Heather's. At
one point there was a visual joke associating her with Heather: Tristen
approached the camera in a moment that Berlinger described as an homage
to Heather's confession, but this time the actress smiled evilly. And these
two women, Erica and Tristen, became the film's chief victims, precisely

because their companions made the mistake of associating their assertive, independent qualities with witchcraft and murdered them accordingly.

Berlinger's idea was to undo some of the damage done to the image of Witches, and indirectly to women, by the first film, and, primarily, to show the dangers of teenage delusions. In this, he directly critiqued the first Blair Witch film, biting the hand that fed him.[161] Previously best known for *Paradise Lost*, a film about what he saw as the wrongful conviction of three Arkansas teenagers for murder inspired by satanism, Berlinger had strong views on the representation of the supernatural and its impact on children and young adults. Thus his own filmic riposte to *The Blair Witch Project* made a point on two levels, literal and symbolic.[162] The good Wiccan Erica was apparently the Blair Witch's first victim, just as Wiccans felt themselves victimized by *The Blair Witch Project*. Meanwhile, Tristen was executed by hanging simply because of her cleverness and because, following a miscarriage, her mind was disturbed. The film seemed to suggest that these factors had always been important in the selection of witches by hysterical groups of persecutors. The first film had encouraged this kind of antiwitch and anti-Witch hysteria, and this impression should be corrected. But Berlinger's film was — as he claimed in subsequent interviews — recut by the studio, which had envisioned a spooky reprise of the idea that the Blair Witch was both real and supernaturally evil. Berlinger's message was lost in shots of frenzied ritual killings, and narrative confusion blunted his defense of the American Witch.

Despite the growth of Witchcraft as a feminist religion, and despite the political correctness the movement had championed, at the turn of the twentieth century witches could still be represented as sexual predators, lesbian "deviants," and antimaternal villainesses. As actress Erica Leerhsen saw it, nothing had changed since 1640: "America loves to blame anything evil on witches, because it's so puritanical." But this could no longer happen without rebuttal. The "firestorm of protest" over the conclusion of Willow and Tara's story and the assault on *The Blair Witch Project* by its own sequel showed that for a significant number of Americans it had not been acceptable to suggest that assertive, clever, sexually assured women were witches, or that Witches were evil at all.[163]

# WITCHES IN THE FAMILY: COMEDY, DRAMA, AND THE ACCEPTANCE OF AMERICAN WITCHES

If we were to see one flying woman, we would instantly
know how to rise and join her.[1]

## *Witches and the Antifamily*

At the turn of the twentieth century, the United States was home to bubbling controversies over witchcraft and its modern manifestation as
Wicca. Was it right for soldiers to be granted the right to practice Wicca?
Would teachers who admitted they were Wiccans lose their jobs? Was
Wicca satanic, or criminal, or sexually deviant? A number of high-profile
court cases fed public interest in the subject. In 1994, for instance, the
three Arkansas teenagers championed by Joe Berlinger were convicted of
a series of child murders. The case was horrific in itself, but it became
nationally controversial when investigative journalists suggested that
the accused were being victimized because of their Neo-Pagan connec-

tions. Were Witches really still seen as child-killing devil-worshippers? Stories published in the *Arkansas Times* alleged that the convictions had been influenced by information given to the court that at least one of the teenagers had been interested in witchcraft. He had dressed in black and read the novels of J.R.R. Tolkien and Stephen King. It was alleged that this young man, Damien Echols, had changed his first name in tribute to the character in *The Omen* films who represents the devil. Echols, however, made the standard Wiccan defense of himself: "Paganism doesn't even acknowledge the existence of Satan." He argued that for his accusers "Everything that's not Baptist is satanic."[2] This had no impact on the court, and he was sentenced to death — a judgment that led to a vigorous and ongoing campaign pleading his innocence.[3] Elsewhere, Christian activists made a broad assault on Wiccan practices generally, often on Christian Web sites and in newsletters run by particular evangelical churches, but also in mainstream political campaigns. It was even suggested that Wiccans could be joining with abortionists to use "the blood of aborted children in their sacrifices" (although the author of this article was careful to point out that he had obtained no evidence of this activity) and that Wicca conspired with feminism and socialism in an "anti-family political movement that encourages women to leave their husbands, kill their children, practice witchcraft, destroy capitalism, and become lesbians."[4] This last assertion had been made in 1992 by the well-known Christian Coalition spokesman Pat Robertson.

It was the all-encompassing nature of this claim that would not fade from the public mind, because it summed up the fears of many Americans that their society was in total moral crisis by the millennial year 2000. Their concern was not just about local issues such as education, crime, and public safety, but focused on the White House itself, which from the right wing looked increasingly like the source of national corruption. Outgoing Democrat President Bill Clinton had survived impeachment proceedings, admitting marital infidelity but contesting accusations, made also against his wife Hillary, of improper business dealings. Mrs. Clinton was widely seen as a future presidential candidate herself, a Lady Macbeth more radical and far more driven than her fallible husband. And in the campaign for the 2000 elections, she, now a candidate for the U.S. Senate, was repeatedly portrayed as a witch. She was also compared by Republicans with Hitler, Stalin, Idi Amin, and Pol Pot, but the most striking image was the topical one of the Blair Witch. Mrs. Clinton appeared in cartoons as a child-stalking sorceress, ironically bearing her book *It Takes a Village* (to raise a child, as the saying goes). Her "Hillary 2000" bumper stickers were arranged in the shape of the Blair Witch's stickmen. A right-wing "wicked witch" Web site was set up to chronicle her alleged misdeeds.[5] Although pagans retorted with a bipartisan "Bless the Vote" campaign, targeted at Christian conservatives, the image stuck and was later used against the more appropriately named Cherie Blair, the wife of the British Prime Minister.[6] In 2006, the same antiliberal use of the word "witch" was deployed by the conservative columnist Ann Coulter against the "Jersey Girls," four campaigning widows of men killed in the terrorist attacks of September 11 2001: she labeled them "the Witches of East Brunswick" because they questioned the government's competence before 9/11 and policy thereafter.[7]

Today, then, a cluster of motifs has emerged in right-wing demonology: disaffected and rebellious teenagers, horror films and novels, rock music (especially by Marilyn Manson, whose high-profile goth flirtations with satanism make him a natural hate-figure), terrorism, antiwar and anti-Bush campaigners, Clintonite social and political liberalism (to say nothing of sexual scandal), and Wicca. A few more elements can be added or subtracted at will. In 2000 in Oklahoma, Brandi Blackbear, a schoolgirl whose classmates reported that she had gone "to seances and said she hexed people" was suspended from school after a teacher fell ill. Pupils were fearful, the school board declared, that she had put a spell on him. It did not help that Brandi, another Stephen King fan, was reported to have written horror stories that included a Columbine High–like school shooting. Brandi's father, meanwhile, believed that she had been discriminated against because of her Native American ethnicity and her class, as well as her interest in Witchcraft. The case quickly divided American sympathies. The American Civil Liberties Union sued the school on behalf of Brandi Blackbear, arguing that she had been exposed to ridicule by school authorities, that she was being denied freedom of speech because her writings had been confiscated, and finally that her religious freedom was imperiled because her inclination to explore paganism was being suppressed.[8] Witches have become a highly politicized symbol, a touchstone for both left and right.

### "Sorcery in a Stone":[9] Harry Potter in America

Surprisingly, however, the most explosive events in America's late-twentieth-century engagement with witchcraft surrounded a children's book imported from Britain. In June 1997 Joanne Rowling, a schoolteacher in Edinburgh, had her first novel published by the Bloomsbury publishing house in London. It was called *Harry Potter and the Philosopher's Stone* and was about a boy who attended a school for witches and wizards, Hogwarts. Although this premise was not entirely original, the book was witty, inventive, and packed with adventures set in a carefully imagined alternative world. It appealed to boys as well as girls. It also tapped into resurgent interest in magical fantasy among the young. So it was immediately noticed by the American publisher Scholastic. "I love this novel by this unknown woman in Scotland," said the editorial director Arthur A. Levine, and he was prepared to pay $105,000 for the rights.[10] Only one major change was made to the book in order to sell it to an American readership: for publication in the United States, the novel was retitled *Harry Potter and the Sorcerer's Stone*. This was done, with Rowling's permission, because it was thought that American children might not be familiar with the word "philosopher," or the concept of the mythical philosopher's stone. But ironically, the retitling of the first Harry Potter novel may have attracted, and sent precisely the wrong signals to, some of those who subsequently became vigorous critics of J. K. Rowling and her world of witches.

Although the change made the novel sound more accessible, it also made it sound more "magickal." As the Arkansas case had shown, sorcery was a concept with almost uniformly negative connotations: even Tolkien's Gandalf could be seen as anti-Christian in the right cultural context. Harry Potter might at best be seen as a sorcerer's apprentice (along with Mickey Mouse), but in many American Christian homes the word "sorcerer" simply conjured up images of their children falling victim to devil-worship. Ironically, the replaced phrase, "philosopher's stone," had plentiful Christian associations. The alchemical quest to discover it was widely regarded in the Middle Ages and the Renaissance as an allegory of the Christian search for purity and, through God's love, the elixir of eternal life — which, in Rowling's book, has been discovered by the real, historical alchemist Nicolas Flamel. Like the Holy Grail, only the pure might hope to find it, and its spiritual significance far outweighed any material or magical value.[11] So Rowling's novel echoed these Christian motifs: like any Gawain or Galahad, the hero Harry Potter battled the forces of evil personified in the dark Lord Voldemort and the vicious Malfoy family, whose names contain allusions to the power of death and bad faith. His own struggle was to keep his motivation pure, in a world where it would have been easy to succumb to hate (Voldemort had murdered Harry's parents), and arrogance about his own powers. The book's most striking symbol is perhaps the Mirror of Erised. Here, Harry faces a classic riddling temptation. As its name suggests, the mirror reflects his deepest desire, which is to see his parents alive and with him. Yet to pursue this dream, and sit looking into the mirror forever, would be to neglect the real meaning of their sacrifice: they died fighting evil and protecting Harry because they loved him, and it is this love that will help Harry defeat the forces of death and evil again. The next time Harry looks into the mirror, his desire is a pure and unselfish one: he must use the mirror to find the philosopher's stone before Voldemort can harness its power for evil. Rowling's original concept was thus a reworking of a traditional Christian image — something some American Christian writers perceived. For example, Connie Neal, a youth pastor who has become one of Rowling's chief Christian defenders, explicitly links the "philosopher's stone" theme of parental sacrifice and pure love with the crucifixion of Christ.[12] But by the time Neal published her analysis, the book's retitling had already rung alarm bells among sensitized American parents.

The claims of opponents of the book and its successors were consistent. They took two main forms: an uneasy fury that the books appeared to be promoting paganism, and expressions of dismay about the power that they granted children to challenge authority figures.

> The whole purpose of these books is to desensitize readers and intro-
> duce them to the occult. What better way to introduce tolerance and
> acceptance of what God calls an abomination, then [*sic*] in children's
> books? . . . Note how the adults are depicted as hateful and perhaps
> strict. Then note how these wizards and other creatures are the good
> guys. These types of writings are nothing more then Satan's way to
> undermine the family.[13]

This second accusation was motivated by Harry Potter's own family situation. With his parents dead, he had been left in Cinderella's predicament, in the custody of an uncaring aunt and uncle, who were "muggles" or nonwitches. Uncle Vernon and Aunt Petunia house Harry in a broom cupboard, and let their malicious son Dudley beat him up and blame him for everything that goes wrong. Naturally, Harry loathes them and the reader does, too, rejoicing when they are humiliated by their own crassness, or when Harry gets away with disobeying their unreasonable rules. Some American parents worried that their children might think that the author was generally sanctioning these attitudes toward parental control. By 1999, the Harry Potter books had become the volumes most often "challenged," which meant that a parent or other concerned party had objected to their presence on a school's curriculum or in its library.[14] Several books specifically devoted to an attack on Harry Potter appeared. The minister Richard Abanes summed up many Christian concerns in *Harry Potter and the Bible*, voicing suspicions that Rowling's world, by mixing historical figures and practices with imaginary ones, blurred the boundaries between fantasy and actual occultism. Abanes was concerned that the books, in a

sense, taught witchcraft, and that divination and other practices forbidden by the Bible were important aspects of life at Hogwarts School. He
objected to the use of swear words and blasphemies in the books, and that
Harry and his friends lied and broke rules frequently. The "good" adults in
the book were often poor role models, while the emerging and mysterious
connection between Harry and Voldemort, good and evil, was morally
confusing.[15] Abanes concluded his book with an account of Sean Sellers, a
teenager who had killed his mother, stepfather, and another victim while
under the influence of Satanism, and a discussion of the growth of occultism in "post-Christian America."[16] Fellow-minister Gary Greenwald went
even further with the unambiguously titled *Harry Potter: Satan's Trojan
Horse?*[17]

Much of the debate took place online, and the release of the Harry Potter
films intensified the proliferation of Web pages devoted to it. The Southern
Baptist churches were particularly active in their opposition to the Potter
phenomenon. Articles in the *Baptist Press* argued that children should not
be allowed to see the movie and criticized schools that organized trips for
their pupils.[18] In November 2001, the Arkansas Baptist State Convention
passed a resolution stating, "The Harry Potter book series and its subsequent materials are inconsistent with Biblical morality and ethics and
promotes pagan beliefs and practices." Delegates committed themselves
to speaking out against the books and notifying booksellers of their "anti-
Christian" content.[19] The Baptist assault on the Potter film was monotone
and ubiquitous enough for the satirical, liberal "Betty Bowers" Web site to
parody it, especially its "anti-family" jibes:

> Hollywood is coming after the hearts of our children with tales of mysti-
> cal powers even more appealing than those in the Bible. . . . In the world
> of Harry Potter, children wave 11-inch rods to cast spells and routinely
> backtalk adults. In the Old Testament, adults use 11-inch rods to beat the
> stuffing out of children (Proverbs 13:24) — and stone them to death if
> they backtalk (Deuteronomy 21:18–21). Clearly J. K. Rowling has a defter
> touch than our Lord when it comes to writing a book that children will
> kneel before their beds at night and pray is true.

For good measure, "Betty" pointed out that witches were "virtually indistinguishable from the Mary-genuflecting Catholics" and Harry was a "homosexual recruitment poster boy."[20] Material from another satirical Web site found its way back into the attack on Harry Potter when its fictitious contents were taken as accurate representations of the views of J. K. Rowling ("these books guide children to an understanding that the weak, idiotic Son of God is a living hoax . . .") and her readers ("I want to learn the Cruciatus Curse, to make my muggle science teacher suffer for giving me a D").[21]

For a number of Christian right-wingers, Harry Potter fitted the devil-shaped hole in American life. Like Clinton, Brandi Blackbear, or Damien Echols, he symbolized all that was wrong with American society and the American family. One of the remarks that Rowling had made about her books was that:

> the idea that we could have a child who escapes from the confines of the adult world and goes somewhere where he has power, both literally and metaphorically, really appealed to me.[22]

This was quoted over and over again in support of the belief that she was telling children to rebel against their parents, and become witches. J. K Rowling and her fans were bemused, and they often responded with flat denial that further outraged her critics. Asserting baldly that the books are "not about witchcraft," "not trying to influence anyone into black magic," or that "the truth is very different," and moving quickly to discuss the books' concerns with racism, education, or sexuality, was ineffective.[23] Rowling has become increasingly resigned to criticism. Interviewed by the BBC's Jeremy Paxman in 2003, she was surprised to hear that *Harry Potter and the Goblet of Fire* was longer than the New Testament. But immediately she responded: "the Christian fundamentalists will find a way to turn that into a reason to hate me as well. She's more verbose than God."[24] It is clear that neither camp can imagine the moral universe of the other. To fans, accusations that Rowling promotes Satan or encourages children to rebellion seem like lunacy. But seen in the context of the Columbine-related panic about influences on America's children, it is easy to imagine why Harry Potter caused such a furor in America. As the Reverend Lori Jo Schepers remarked on CNN, of Harry Potter readers:

> as we expose our kids to the occult, we expose our kids to blood, to violence and desensitise them to that . . . What I can expect is those kids, as they mature, have a very good chance of becoming another Dylan Klebold and those guys in Columbine.[25]

Perhaps the fuss surrounding Harry Potter and his allegedly anti-Christian, antifamily values was not so surprising after all.

The books' Britishness was also part of the problem for critical American readers. With her English and Scottish inspirations, Rowling had wondered why they had become so popular with American children: "They are such *British* books," she said. In fact, she had defended her books' un-Americanness vigorously, refusing to translate English into American unless absolutely necessary.[26] Like many liberal Britons, she seemed suspicious of American cultural imperialism and was antagonistic to any suggestion that she might modify her story to maximize sales in the United States. "You are not going to get an American exchange student brought in at Hogwarts," she announced.[27] So, like many ideas that cross the Atlantic, something was lost on the journey. Those Americans who expected Harry's world to be the god-fearing, conservative, and patriotic one in which they were trying to raise their children found Harry and his friends Ron and Hermione foreign in almost every way. These were independent-minded, disrespectful heathens, who swore, disobeyed parents and teachers, held dangerously liberal views, and never went to church or spoke of God. Most British readers recognized instantly in the mildly eccentric, anarchic world of Hogwarts school their culture's stereotypical virtues and vices: embarrassment at "speechifying" or public displays of spirituality, suspicion of authority and uniformity, interest in the oddities of history and folklore. Harry Potter fitted for them into the British genre of the "boarding school story," like the *Malory Towers* series or *Tom Brown's School Days*, rather than the "children's conduct book."[28] Britain was also the land that, as historian Ronald Hutton points out, gave the world the modern religion of Gardnerian Witchcraft, and most Britons regard it with tolerance — whether they perceive it as New Age nonsense or ancient wisdom.[29] Most Christian Britons were accustomed to their children reading about witches and meeting people who regarded themselves as pagans, and they were used to the idea of religion as a private matter. So were their non-Christian neighbors. These readers would all have squirmed at overt godliness or attempts to preach the ideology of good versus evil, however pleased they might be by the books' implicit morality: many Americans squirmed at the absence of everyday pieties. In part, the Harry Potter controversy developed because Britain and America were divided by a common culture and language, differently interpreted: just as in the seventeenth century, they had different beliefs about the proper response to witches.

Not all American Christians found the books and films threatening, however. One of the most notable pro-Potter voices was that of Charles Colson, a former adviser to President Nixon jailed for his involvement in the Watergate scandal. Now a Christian campaigner, Colson argued that "some Christians may try to keep their kids from reading these books, but with 8 million copies . . . floating around American homes, it's almost inevitable that your own children or grandchildren will be exposed to them." Instead of resisting, he urged American parents to "help them to see the deeper messages . . . contrast the mechanical magic in the Potter books to the kind of real-life witchcraft the Bible condemns."[30] Colson and others believed that because the books were based on a literary, nondemonic version of magic, that did not involve actual conjuration, they were safe to read and might offer positive models of bravery, goodness, and loyalty to child readers. His view was attacked by Abanes and others.[31] Berit Kjos went so far as to accuse Colson and his camp of helping "lure kids to witchcraft."[32] It seemed that Harry Potter was indeed doing the devil's work, as the controversy over his status divided Christians. So vicious was some of the debate that pastor Connie Neal wrote *What's a Christian to Do with Harry Potter?* to advise Christians to stop fighting each other and "work through these perplexing issues within the body of Christ." She believed that the Potter books and films emphasized ethical behavior, did not promote Wicca or Satanism, and even that they could be used to preach the gospel. Children liked the books, she said, because they wanted hope, empowerment, self-esteem, affirmation of their emotions and tools to help deal with them, knowledge that they could face and conquer fear, a sense of belonging, love, and good friends. The books answered all of these needs, providing examples of children taking responsibility for decisions and their consequences, dealing with depression and grief, and so on. The fact that children yearned for such comforts, and for a supernatural context for these

> reflects the longing in our kids' souls for God . . . Harry Potter is not the real thing. Which is why many Christian parents are concerned about it. Nor is it the best way to satisfy our kids' desire. But you can use the Potter craze to get kids and grandkids into something that leads them on to the real thing.[33]

As Neal's argumentative strategy shows, for many Americans the crucial question is whether the classic images of American witch and all-American family can be reconciled. Will American children still love and defer to their parents and grandparents if they read about Harry Potter? Or will Wicca cause them to murder their families? Are family values actually compatible with witches, creatures once thought to be archetypally antisocial? But, as Neal's words demonstrate, where the two images of family and witch can be harmonized, the result is positive. Where the witch is alone, without a proper family context, he or she is usually seen as predatory and a conduit for evil forces. Where witchcraft can be seen as family-friendly, or a witch is domesticated and anchored within a family community, he or she is often seen as safer. This is true of child-witches Harry Potter and his friends, but is also true of the female witches, wife and mother figures, who so richly populate other American fictions. Women and children out of patriarchal control are dangerous, as can be seen from the unpleasant and undomesticated women-witches discussed in the last chapter. But what about witches who do have a home to which to go? To understand America's obsession with keeping witches in the family and explain the trend toward positive portrayals of witches and Witches in recent American popular culture, we must go back to the 1930s, to a resurgence of interest in witchcraft and a rewriting of the image of the witch.

### Marrying a Witch

In the early 1930s, the American novelist Thorne Smith had an idea for a new story. He had been writing fantasy fictions, often with a clever, funny twist, for years, and his most popular book was the comic ghost story *Topper*. Smith's new story was simple enough: man marries witch, wishes he hadn't. It was not entirely original, for there are a number of English fictions, dating as far back as 1634, in which unfortunate men find themselves amusingly married to witches.[34] Smith made evident the point of the old, misogynist story, saying of his hero:

> He was, in fact, acting like many husbands, most husbands. They marry some camouflaged monster, and there they are — married to it — so they do their best not to know too much about her, while she generally does her best to make the worst visible as neon signs on a country road.[35]

But *The Passionate Witch*, unpromising as it looks to modern eyes, became the grandmother of all modern American witch-comedies. It can claim as its direct descendants plays (*Bell, Book and Candle*), TV series and films (*Bewitched*), comic strips (*Sabrina the Teenage Witch*) and novels (*Practical Magic*), among many others. If we want to understand how America feels about witches in the twenty-first century, we must look back at the origins of a new twentieth-century story about them. And we must start with the place where the old story, of the witch as satanic temptress, meets the new, the witch as a cheerfully empowered wife, mother, or sister — Everywoman.

As I suggested in Chapter 3, the first stirrings of this redefinition came with L. Frank Baum's *The Wonderful Wizard of Oz* in 1900. The 1938 film

of the book kept Baum's Good and Wicked Witches, with Glinda's character amalgamated with Baum's Good Witch of the South as a lovely fairy
godmother. But more important for the future evolution of good witches
in American popular culture was the relationship between Thorne Smith's
book and the film made from his story, *I Married a Witch. The Passionate
Witch* was a comic novel of a saucy kind. It built, perhaps, on vaguely satirical witch-fictions like the English novelist Sylvia Townsend Warner's *Lolly
Willowes* (1926) and Esther Forbes's *A Mirror for Witches* (1928).[36] In *The
Passionate Witch*, a witch arrived in a New England town, and seduced its
meek, abstemious insurance broker, T. Wallace Wooly. Wallace had only
just plucked up the courage to ask his secretary Betty out to dinner and
seemed set for a happy marriage with her. But instead the witch, Jennifer,
bedded him, married him, and proceeded to make his life hell. When he
found that his new wife went out at night to ride a goat and sacrifice cock-
erels, Wallace made her read the Lord's Prayer. Jennifer could only do this
backward (a new variant on an old superstition) and so her witchcraft was
discovered. She agreed to leave her husband in peace, but instead cast a
spell that made him able to hear other people's thoughts — most of which
were extremely uncomplimentary. She also set fire to the town church
and, happily for Wallace, was killed by a falling masonry cross. As she was
not buried at a crossroads with a stake through her heart, however, she
rose again and her spirit occupied — of all things — Wallace's horse. Wallace, meanwhile, was trying to placate Betty, who had become his mistress
during his short but terrifying marriage, and in this quest he ended up
dressed as a woman, being driven from a Turkish bath, and put on trial
for transvestism, drunkenness, resisting arrest, lewd conduct, assault, and
battery. Betty perjured herself to save him, proving her true love. And,
at last, Jennifer-the-horse was killed in a bizarre accident at a crossroads
where she fell fortuitously into a deep hole, while being speared through
the heart with a crowbar. The reader emerges from the story surprised at
the sexual license allowed to pulp fiction of the thirties, and dimly aware
that behind the oddly structured plot is simply the old story of the witch
as — as the inquisitor's manual *Malleus Maleficarum* put it through the

golden mouth of St. John Chrysostom — "a natural temptation, a desirable calamity, a domestic danger, a delectable detriment, an evil of nature, painted with fair colours."[37] As Wallace puts it, his wife is "an evil thing . . . a draggletailed harpy, a trull, a conspirator against the public and the natural order."[38]

Beyond the shrew-taming comedy is a tragedy, and a reason for the book's disjointedness. Thorne Smith did not live to see *The Passionate Witch* complete, as he died of a heart attack in 1934, aged only forty. But the book was taken on by Norman Matson, who completed it. In 1942 he helped to make it into a film, starring Fredric March and Veronica Lake, and in doing so he and his fellow-writers changed almost everything about it. In the process, almost by accident, they made possible a happy ending for a witch tamed by marriage. To begin with, the project was retitled *I Married a Witch*, and its "passionate" elements were toned down.[39] The film, as before, told the story of Jennifer (Veronica Lake), but this time it gave her a motive for hating men, and Wallace Wooley[40] in particular. Jennifer had been (with little regard for history) burned at the stake in New England "long, long ago when people still believed in witches." Her accusers were Puritan ancestors of Wallace Wooley, who took pains not only to kill Jennifer but also her father, and to have both their spirits trapped in subterranean torment by planting a tree on their grave. Like her counterpart in *The Passionate Witch*, however, Jennifer did not die passively: she cursed all the line of the Wooleys, so that each would make an unhappy marriage. In modern times the tree was damaged in a storm, and the present Wallace Wooley (Fredric March), a political candidate on the eve of wedding his principal backer's daughter, became the target of a more personalized revenge. As in the book, the reincarnated Jennifer ensured that Wallace rescued her from a fire and was found in compromising situations with her. But now her evil plan was far more sympathetically portrayed, and the woman she replaced in Wallace's narrow, unfulfilled life was not loving Betty but his intolerable fiancée. The entire ending was changed — as in the book, Jennifer set out to make Wallace fall in love with her (the idea being that, married to the wrong woman, he would also be tormented by forbidden passion) but now she mistakenly drank her own love philter and fell in love with Wallace herself. The witch was tamed in part, but further taming followed. The plot became twisted as Jennifer's father opposed her plan to break Wallace's engagement and marry him herself. His machinations against the lovers were defeated, but the price was important: Jennifer was stripped of her powers and became a mere "mortal." Thus, she could marry Wallace and they might even live happily ever after.[41]

*The Passionate Witch* and its reincarnation, *I Married a Witch*, help explain why American culture so strongly affirms to this day that domesticated witches, whether women or children or both, are the only good kind. The problem with undomesticated ones is the threat they pose to the omnipotence of the American male, and women are particularly dangerous because they are so "fascinating," "bewitching," and "enchanting." The relative dating of novel and film is important: in the 1930s America was battered by the Depression, broken and looking for scapegoats. Women were being pushed out of the workforce to make way for men with families to feed, and patriarchy was in desperate crisis. Smith's book includes not only satire on grasping wives ("I do *so* much shopping. It's exhausting!") but attacks on intellectual women, too ("a female pighead, an opinionated ass in petticoats"). Betty Jackson, Wallace's secretary, is turned quickly into a sex object when she loses her job and becomes her employer's mistress, while the book's only other professional woman is a French maid whose major contribution to the plot is to get drunk, "bounce and jounce and jiggle."[42] But by 1942 America had regained her confidence. American men were advancing the world over to avenge Pearl Harbor, and women were working alongside them. The economy was on a war footing, and in the year after *I Married a Witch* Norman Rockwell would celebrate publicly the virtue and utility of American women in *The Four Freedoms* and *Rosie the Riveter*. Economically speaking, times were good for women at home and even at work, and so they were better for witches, too. But it was still clear that the best place for a woman was at home, even if that meant the home front. After the war, the expectation was that women would be glad to get back to the kitchen and the nursery. That was where Jennifer, the married witch, had ended her story.

Some women, of course, did not want to do this. And the witchcraft-comedy reflected this reluctance, its dangers and pleasures, in its next incarnation. In 1958 *Bell, Book and Candle* began where *I Married a Witch* began: with the dangers of a "bewitching" woman. Its theatrical trailer went straight to the point by making witchcraft and women's other powers interchangeable: "a very bewitching comedy, on a very enchanting subject — sex," it promised.[43] Sixteen years after the novel's publication, it borrowed a wordplay from *The Passionate Witch*, describing itself as a sex comedy, or "sex hex."[44] It was a more sophisticated, flirtatious film than *I Married a Witch*, implying that the mysteries of instant attraction are just as magical as any spell, and just as dangerous to men. Although it reduced the ribaldry of its source, *I Married a Witch* was not without titillation: the witch spent the night before her victim's wedding in his bed (although he was fully clothed and confined himself chastely to holding her hands), and she was naked for much of the early part of the film (although the viewer saw nothing except smoke and castoff clothing). But the impression that women's witchcraft was a straightforward metaphor for sex was strengthened immeasurably by *Bell, Book and Candle*, especially because the film starred James Stewart and Kim Novak, who had both appeared in the same year in *Vertigo*, Hitchcock's tragedy of sexual obsession. *Bell, Book and Candle* contained sly references to this: a hat falling from the roof of the Flatiron Building, Stewart rushing downstairs. But revealing plot similarities also reinforced the equation of witchcraft with women's sexual power.[45] A fine upstanding American citizen could be ruined by a woman or a witch — the difference was apparently minimal.

Like *Vertigo*, *Bell, Book and Candle* began with Stewart's character (Shep Henderson) violently attracted to Novak's beautiful, morally questionable, woman (Gillian Holroyd). Gillian was a successful businesswoman, running an art shop, and she had literally bewitched him. Moreover, she had stolen him from his bride-to-be (Miss Kittredge, surely named after the author of *Witchcraft in Old and New England*?) on their wedding day.

Shades of *I Married a Witch* were evident, but this time the love spell had taken its sinister effect on the male victim: Shep, a publisher, was distracted from his work and every other aspect of his neat, once-controllable life. The audience learned that witches could not themselves fall in love, and that Shep was in deep trouble. After several weeks of clearly sexual unmarried bliss, however, he discovered Gillian's spell, and employed another witch to break it. But as the film progressed, a comedic ending did become possible, just as with *I Married a Witch*. If witches fall in love, the second film's dialogue explained, they can no longer be witches. Gillian did fall in love with Shep and, instead of being destroyed by his attraction to a mysterious, deceitful woman, Stewart's character was rewarded for his unwilling constancy. The catch for Gillian was that, like Jennifer, she was by then no longer a witch. Both films thus ended with the sexy witch safely domesticated. "I'm only human," said Gillian, contentedly diminished. "Love is stronger than witchcraft," said Jennifer, only slightly more upbeat.

This was in stark contrast to the point reached when Shep, still under Gillian's spell, had first proposed marriage — only to discover that traditional sexual roles had been unsettlingly reversed.

> GILLIAN: I hadn't thought of marriage.
> SHEP (lightly): Darling, that's the *man's* remark — usually . . . I'm going crazy . . .
> GILLIAN (keeping up banter): And how do you think marriage would cure that?
> SHEP: I don't know. I don't care. But we can't go on like this.
> GILLIAN (leaning away): Darling — that's the girl's remark — usually![46]

Gillian was happy with her bachelorette lifestyle, her shop, her flat, and her pet cat's company. With power relations topsy-turvy, and no prospect of containment within a family to hand, witchcraft must be crushed at once. The title of *Bell, Book and Candle* was a reference to the rite of exorcism designed to defeat it. Witches' loss of power was signaled in each film by a loss of control of themselves and their environment. Jennifer could no longer make fire and seemed doomed to die at midnight because she had told her lover about her powers; Gillian had acquired the dubiously desirable abilities to blush and cry. Jennifer survived her father's attempts to punish her but traded his deadly patriarchy for the more comfortable prison of the governor's mansion. She put up her long blonde hair, started knitting, and had children with Wallace. Gillian abandoned the tight black and scarlet dresses and the glamorous accessories that marked her out as a femme fatale. By the film's end she was in full Doris Day mode: New Look white and yellow. Most interestingly, she restocked her African and Oceanic art shop with pretty shells and renamed it "Flowers of the Sea" — surely a less profitable venture! Her cat familiar, Pyewacket (who was named after one of the familiars "discovered" by England's Witch-finder General Matthew Hopkins), left her, and her feline self-possession did, too.[47] But at least she was allowed to keep her business, and her public role. This was a slightly more encouraging ending for female viewers than the play on which the film was based, John van Druten's *Bell, Book and Candle*. In this, Gillian ended the play where she had begun it, in her apartment. It was now stripped of "all the objects savoring of witchcraft" that had made it "interesting" in Scene One. A brass bird, African god and goddess, a witch ball, masks, a mortar and pestle, and statuettes had been replaced by plants, vases of flowers, an herb jar, and a china mug. All of these items spoke of nurture, cooking, and housekeeping, a complete retreat into private life.

The play *Bell, Book and Candle* was first performed in New York in 1950. As well as leaving Gillian a little more domesticated than the film, the play had a few "magickal" differences. The film placed less emphasis on "magick" as such: witches had no "manual" on which they swore oaths as most Americans do on the bible, and spells were done by humming, not by the more obviously un-Christian chanting of names. Hollywood was probably not ready for America's beloved Jimmy Stewart to star in a film about anti-Christian activities. The film also showed more concentration on witchcraft's connection with what were unself-consciously called "primitive" societies (Africa, the Caribbean, South America). This was mostly because Gillian's mask- and carving-filled shop was put onscreen, indeed was the background for the opening credits. Each actor or crew member was represented by a mask or statuette — a little image magic. But this jokey beginning in an art gallery had two serious functions: as we've noted, it gave Gillian a setting outside the home, where she served customers and made business decisions just like Shep, but it also gave witchcraft a safe, distant context, at least at first. It was a matter for travelers, anthropologists, and scientific men, rather than being domestic satanism. In both book and film, Sidney Redlitch (Ernie Kovacs), a character writing books on magic in "the jungle and the tropics," went on a journey similar to that of the audience in that he began by studying magic in Mexico and ended with the startling discovery that magic was equally at home in Manhattan. It was especially at home in the Zodiac club, the witches' headquarters. The club in the film had a potent mix of tom-tom beats, smoke, and raffish finery: a fakir acted as doorman, and a male singer writhed sinuously to his own French song. The dialogue between exotic and domestic continued here: witchcraft was more distanced from ordinary New Yorkers in one way, but in another it was closer to home. One feels more than a suspicion that the witch club in the 1950 play and 1958 film is based on New York's gay scene.

Van Druten was himself gay, and his play *I Am a Camera* was the basis for *Cabaret*, which explored issues of personal freedom in a nightclub setting in Nazi Germany.[48] In *Bell, Book and Candle*, the Zodiac and the witchcraft emanating from it similarly suggested gay sexuality as a counterpart of the "dangers" of female sexuality to patriarchal repression. The play and film's male witch, Gillian's androgynously named and unmarried brother Nicky (Jack Lemmon), worked at the Zodiac. The play, if anything, took the possibility of male witches a little further than the film: everyone, male and female, had the potential to be a witch — "queer," subversive. While in both play and film, witchcraft was clearly learned rather than innate, in the play it was suggested that even Shep could become a witch if he learned the right way. There seems an obvious parallel with van Druten's other work, although the possibilities of gay sexuality are carefully closed down and married off by the film. So, the witch club was underground in more ways than one. Play and film were haunted also by the separation between America's liberal intellectuals and her governing culture. This focused the play on communism, as with the contemporary *The Crucible*. When Gillian decided to confess all to Shep, he asked: "Have you been engaging in un-American activities?" She replied: "No. I'd say very American. Early American!"[49] This line cut several ways in 1950: a joke about colonial witch-hunting, a swipe at McCarthyism, an assertion that witchcraft, communism, and maybe even women's empowerment are all legitimate American traditions. But overall, the play and film conservatively reaffirmed women's place in society, as in *I Married a Witch*. Having been given the space for alluring independence at first, they must be "shepherded" into marriage. Gillian had initially proposed that her cat familiar give her Shep as a Christmas present: but it was she who would be given away in the end. It was, however, better than ending up dead with a stake through your heart, and the next evolution of the witchcraft-comedy made the pleasures of marriage for a witch, as well as its constraints, very clear.

*Bewitched and the Domesticated Goddess*

*Bewitched*, the American television comedy that ran from 1964 to 1972, is the best-known example of the taming of the witch. It had obvious roots in *I Married a Witch* and *Bell, Book and Candle*. But, most notably, it took further the idea that a married witch might be a good woman, boldly breaking new ground. In *Bewitched*, Darrin Stephens, a successful advertising executive played by Dick York (and later by Dick Sargent), was married to Samantha, a witch played by Elizabeth Montgomery. Like Jennifer and Gillian, Samantha kept her witchcraft a secret during her courtship. However, this was no *Passionate Witch* horror story: after a revelation in the first episode, "I, Darrin, Take This Witch, Samantha," Darrin came amicably to terms with his wife's abilities and she was able to retain them.[50] Samantha was not like Jennifer and Gillian as we first meet them: she was a model of traditional femininity. She was pleasant and morally sound, she stayed at home or shopped sensibly while Darrin worked in his office, she cooked and cleaned, and she supported her husband's career. It was very clear that she had forsworn magical practices such as flying and the ability to walk through walls. After their wedding, Darrin had made her promise not to use them. Sol Saks, who created *Bewitched* with Harry Ackerman, said he had initially had in mind a sitcom that was very spooky and witchy, like *The Addams Family*. It was William Asher, soon to be the show's director, who saw the possibilities of the witch being, as he put it, the girl next door.[51] In his version of the show's genesis, then, the witch dwindled into a wife just like Jennifer and Gillian. But in many ways *Bewitched* pushed harder at the constraints it put on its witch. After all, this was Kennedy and Johnson's America, not Roosevelt's or Eisenhower's.

Clearly, against the background of an increasingly vicious battle between conservatives and radicals over women's place in society, a potentially more liberating analogy was being drawn between the witch's magic and the woman's independence of mind and body despite her family role. Elyce Rae Helford describes *Bewitched* as "an innovation in the representation of women in entertainment television," in her book *Fantasy Girls*. In the early 1960s, she notes, programs incorporating an element of fantasy helped television producers address

> the changing role of women in America . . . without risking a reduced viewership among conservative, white, middle-class viewers, or making plain that the culture was losing faith in the post–World War II American Dream.[52]

In fact, *Bewitched* producer Danny Arnold had said the same thing in 1965:

> Fantasy can always be a jumping-off place for more sophisticated work. . . . What we do in this series doesn't happen to witches; it happens to people. But the messages are funnier when they happen to a witch — and therefore less offensive.[53]

What couldn't be discussed openly without causing offense could be discussed covertly, using witchcraft or other magical powers (as also in the contemporary genie sitcom *I Dream of Jeannie*) as a metaphor for women's aspirations. Samantha could be both married and powerful — her witch-craft was not ended by love.

Cultural norms could not be expected to change overnight, however. Samantha's renunciation of power had obvious conservative elements. She had surrendered her autonomy of mind and body to Darrin through marriage, and she did not intend to take them back. Sometimes she and Darrin would fall out, but reconciliation would always be the way forward and the happy end of the episode.[54] She even spent several episodes reconciling other married couples, who had been divided by some misunderstanding.[55] Refusing to be a witch had a gendered economic symbolism as well as a moral one. Samantha did not usually use magic to clean her house or whip up meals. Instead, she exemplified the housewife's version of the American frontier virtues of making do and working hard, without magical advantages *or* expensive gadgets. There is a long history of equating witchcraft with labor-saving technology, and making the two interchangeable. One of the world's first steam engines was called the *Lancashire Witch*, several pioneering steamships were dubbed the *Water Witch*, and even an early computer was named W.I.T.C.H.[56] Samantha chose to do without such technological help and without its traditional magical equivalents as well. Instead, she washed, scrubbed, chopped vegetables, and roasted meat like generations of homemaking women before her. This promoted the idea that the tensions surrounding women's place in the workforce that had been so evident in the thirties, forties, and fifties were a thing of the past. If women would accept their role in the home, their work there would be respected and they could join with men in sharing the benefits of the affluent society. So Samantha's hard work was rewarded with modern furniture, fashionable clothes, and a smart car. Apparently even witches stayed home to bake cookies and raise children, and ordinary women might well do the same.

But the show would have been very dull if the witch had never used her magic, and Montgomery's character far less appealing if she had not exercised her own judgment and skill. As Harry Ackerman said, the show had liberal aspirations, although it compromised them heavily to sweeten the pill. Many episodes therefore flirted with the pleasing danger that Samantha's witchcraft, like her subversive independence, might pose to Darrin's position as the "man of the house." The challenges of female witchcraft to male omnipotence were very traditional and often came, interestingly, from the oldest European demonology rather than colonial American beliefs. Spells might, for example, freeze or silence Darrin, while his wife went about her own business.[57] This was the traditional way that witches managed to absent themselves in order to go to a Sabbath, leaving their husbands insensible.[58] The plot of "Mixed Doubles," in which Samantha inadvertently caused Darrin's boss to mistake her for his wife, while Darrin mistook Mrs. Tate for Samantha, could be taken verbatim from the *Malleus Maleficarum*: "Devils can by witchcraft cause a man to be unable to see his wife rightly, and the converse."[59] But there was always the reassurance that Samantha had Darrin's best interests at heart. If she turned him into, say, an old woman, it was intended to protect him from being beaten up.[60] Her relatives were less choosy about their motives: Circe-like, they cheerfully changed Darrin into a pig, a gorilla, a werewolf, and the Fisherman's Memorial statue at Gloucester, Massachusetts. They also gave him donkey ears.[61] This last trick had been a witch's party piece since at least the time of St. Augustine. In the 1580s, Reginald Scot derided French demonologist Jean Bodin's claim that a Cypriot witch had once turned a young Englishman into an ass, describing it as a "foolish fable" and "the starkest lie that ever was invented."[62] Most "Early American" colonists agreed with him: such tales were for "Papists" who believed in miracles, not sensible Protestants. In this way, *Bewitched* writers' glee in playing with ludicrous transformations, rather than taking them as genuine threats, is typically American as well as an example of a liberal containment strategy for witch-women. More especially, it is typical of the modern portrayal of witchcraft as something to be doubted in sensible Connecticut, where Samantha and Darrin lived at Mercy Disborough's old hometown, Westport.[63]

But other ways in which Samantha or her family might threaten Darrin would have seemed more likely to colonists: frequently one of the witches would create just the type of "specter" that had caused so much anxiety at Salem and elsewhere. This specter was the illusion of her own or another's presence, a projection by a witch or, originally, a devil. There were many analogous moments in *Bewitched*, often revolving around a threat of incest: the time Samantha's mother (whose birthplace was Salem) impersonated Samantha in "Which Witch Is Which?"; when Samantha's daughter Tabitha made a fake Samantha to get herself more attention; or when Samantha's cousin Serena replaced her, completely fooling Darrin.[64] Specters would usually visit their bewitched victims at night, hanging over their bed to make threats, or offer temptations. In 1692, for instance, Susannah Sheldon described how the specters of accused witches Bridget Bishop, Mary English, and Giles Corey came to her to proffer wicked books, pray to the devil, and assault her.[65] Just as with earlier stories of spectral visits, Endora's, Tabitha's, and Serena's transformations and fake Samanthas created a variety of obvious threats to Darrin. His home had been invaded by strange females, posing as his dear wife. He might even have ended up in bed with his mother-in-law, his wife's cousin, or a fake wife, a kind of pseudosuccubus. Witches were certainly thought to be able to work with devils to create succubi, demonic doubles of beautiful women who tempted men to have sex with them. In the event, everything was set to rights when the transformations were discovered — but not before Endora (Agnes Moorehead) had embarked on an affair with Darrin's friend Bob. Naturally, the Stephens's neighbors believed that Samantha was being unfaithful, another kind of threat to family unity.[66]

Another classic theme was the threat that witches might pose to children. Whilst this was a well-developed European obsession long before America was colonized, the early settlers made it their own, and *Bewitched* echoed this concern. In "There's No Witch Like an Old Witch," Samantha's Aunt Clara (Marion Lorne) got a job as a babysitter. Soon she was entertaining her charges with stories of flying from the roof, and bringing their toys to life. Their parents became worried that witchcraft was at work, and, astonishingly for the 1960s, Aunt Clara was taken before a magistrate. It was only because he was prepared to believe that she was just a children's entertainer that she avoided serious consequences.[67] It is impossible not to think during these episodes of the many cases collected by the Mathers of children accusing old women of harming them or tempting them into danger: Elizabeth Knapp, Katherine Branch, and perhaps most evidently the Goodwin children, who accused their laundress of bewitching them in 1688.[68] Anxiety about witches and newborns was also reflected in scenes on the maternity ward when Samantha gave birth to her children. Here, the matron was pitted against invasive female witches, who brought unsuitable flowers and flouted visiting rules. Endora even abducted her granddaughter from the hospital.[69] With witches interfering at every turn and breaking every medical rule, there were echoes of their supposed role in childbirths, such as the Stamford woman Abigail Debell's near-fatal 1667 labor, for which she blamed the witchcraft of William Graves, or Blanche Bedortha's 1647 agonies at Springfield, blamed on Hugh Parsons. Like these women, Samantha looked besieged and enfeebled. The sight, too, of Endora hovering over rows of cots might well have stirred queasy memories of Miller's Ann Putnam lamenting her dead infants only a decade before:

> I have laid seven babies unbaptized in the earth. Believe me, sir, you never saw more hearty babies born. And yet, each would wither in my arms the very night of their birth. . . . They were murdered, Mr. Parris![70]

However, the show's basic assumptions meant that the threat of witchcraft was present only to be closed down, its potency contained by mutual respect and amity. Samantha was an exemplary mother and wife. Not only were witches seen to be quite safe with children, but Endora and Darrin even made a brief, tearful peace as they shared their joy at Tabitha's birth. Far from creating division, children connected witches and mortals, women and men. Women's domestic magic was saturnalian — an explosion of excitement and disruption into everyday life, that could easily be quelled and that served, in fact, to reaffirm the usual family values pleasantly. In the 1960s and '70s, women's social, cultural, and economic power was seen to be in need of careful control. But resistance to that control was more sustained and attractive than ever before, and the power itself was less of a threat.

## A Radical Witch?

*Bewitched* created a template for later depictions of witches, modifying the one inherited from *I Married A Witch* and *Bell, Book and Candle*. The tension between radically empowering women and conservatively affirming the need to control them was played out each week, and was left unresolved. The plot of each episode was more or less the same: wife's witchy heritage creates havoc, husband suffers, but wife puts things right. A typical storyline would revolve around Darrin's clients, who experienced some magical mishap that left them unwilling to sign a vital contract. One was turned into a dog, another unexpectedly met Queen Victoria, a third found that Darrin could suddenly speak nothing but Italian.[71] Once again, economics were to the fore: not only the bright young man and his bright young career were in peril but so was the glamorous, masculine world of advertising, which in the Cold War period so often symbolized America's modernity and capitalist success. Darrin's boss, Larry Tate (David White), would usually threaten to fire him, and Samantha would save the situation by contriving an explanation that satisfied Larry and reconciled Darrin with his client. Her methods varied: with or without Darrin's knowledge, she might make the unfortunate victim believe he or she had ESP or was having visions and simply needed a rest, she might travel back in time to rearrange the past, or she might transvect (magically transport) herself or someone else.[72] Thus her magical, independent abilities were carefully presented: to be used only in extreme need and, best of all, when yoked firmly to her fulfillment of her husband's needs and wishes. Darrin often repeated his prohibition on the use of magic, and Samantha reiterated her acquiescence, just to drive the point home.

But *Bewitched* did also offer more subversive pleasures to those who equated witchcraft with women's lib. Samantha might overtly have renounced the use of witchcraft at will, but she was always "needing" to use her powers in petty ways when Darrin wasn't looking. Her life was simpler and more fun accordingly. She might mend his broken clock, or run out of time with the washing up and cast a soapy spell. More aggressively, she could cause a rainstorm that ended whatever sport he was watching on TV so that he would get up and teach her to drive — giving her an alternative freedom in place of the forbidden flying.[73] And where Samantha would not resort to magic, her strident, hedonistic mother Endora undoubtedly would. She was named after the biblical witch of Endor, a prophetess who raised spirits and foresaw the death of the king who consulted her. Like her namesake, Endora stood in challenging relation to male authority. She was also the classic joke mother-in-law figure. She was unable to remember Darrin's name (her name for him, Durward, is probably a reference to Durward Grinstead, the author of the witchcraft novel *Elva* and one of the writers for the 1937 film *Maid of Salem*).[74] She despised his personality, lifestyle, and mortality. But she was also a deliciously uncompromising rebel against the strictures of patriarchal human society. Most surprisingly, she had separated from Samantha's father and enjoyed a single life that included flings with much younger men.[75] While Samantha's method of spell-casting was a coy and easily disguised twitching of her nose, Endora cast her spells with theatrical arm-waving and, often, clouds of colored smoke. She was a foil for her conservative daughter, but also an inspiration. She served to remind viewers that Samantha still had her powers and could use them without hindrance any time she chose. Scriptwriter Lila Garrett saw Endora as offering an alternative to liberal women viewers who "were a little annoyed at times to see a woman like Samantha, who was that capable, insisting on staying at home all the time."[76]

Endora and Samantha's potential as icons of empowered womanhood was also important for Elizabeth Montgomery's own satisfaction. Her own life and her liberal views sometimes sat uneasily with her screen persona. She had already divorced twice when she began *Bewitched*. During its run she worked closely with her new husband, the show's director William Asher, on developing and producing it. She was a working wife from the start, and had two children during her career as Samantha. Asher supported her throughout, and says he even encouraged her to continue work after their marriage against her own initial inclinations.[77] Once she had begun *Bewitched*, however, there was no stopping her. She was a very public figure, living a life that some still regarded as controversial and even improper. In an interview for *TV Photo Story* in 1965, she described her anger at being unable to make choices that suited her life, and having to "fit into a mold" created by "Madison Avenue types" (ironically, advertising executives like Darrin). They had told her, for example, that being filmed while pregnant would "detract from my sex appeal, whatever that is."[78] Seeking a more realistic female role model, she chose Lucille Ball, with whom Asher had formerly worked, and argued that Ball's pregnancy during *I Love Lucy* had actually boosted ratings. This strategy gestured pointedly toward the genealogy of *Bewitched*: Ball and Montgomery were both pioneering comediennes working in husband-and-wife partnerships on and off screen. Both demanded and gained greater respect for female performers. Like Lucille Ball, Montgomery won her arguments and Samantha accordingly gave birth to onscreen children Tabitha and Adam.[79] Tough-minded working wife Elizabeth thus formed an interesting counterpoint to domesticated Samantha. Their relationship summed up the differing roles available to women in the 1960s.

It was after the dispute over her pregnancy that Montgomery and Asher's unease with women's traditional roles was manifested on screen by the creation of the new witch Serena. Serena appeared first in the episode in which Tabitha was born, and was Samantha's cousin.[80] Actually, she was played by Montgomery herself. Split-screen technology allowed a split personality. Serena was single, "wild," a relentlessly fashionable and funky socialite — Samantha's "alter-ego," as Montgomery called her, who had certainly not given up witchcraft or any other power.[81] She was much more like Endora, her aunt, and as if to signpost her significance Montgomery adopted the soundalike pseudonym Pandora Spocks to play her. Pandora appeared on the cast-list week after week, a standing joke. It was a typically double-edged gesture — distancing Montgomery from Serena, but also loudly announcing her subversiveness. Pandora has always been a figure associated with rebellious women, like Eve, because in the myth she disobeyed her orders and opened the box out of which all the world's troubles came. But she also let out the last creature in the box, Hope, and similarly Serena gave Montgomery an outlet for her more radical side. Serena, for instance, had a changeable beauty mark on her face, which one week might take the form of a Campaign for Nuclear Disarmament peace symbol, the next a question mark. Montgomery's opposition to the Vietnam War thus surfaced in Serena.[82] She also wore a number of variations on the symbol for femaleness, including a combination of female with male symbols. Serena was part of the wider witch family, and so made safer than the traditional solitary witch-figure, and her character may also have been made acceptable because viewers could tell that really she was the same actress as sweet Samantha. But she was undoubtedly a smuggling into the show of non-family-values and possibilities for women (and witches) beyond the family — hippie, radical, single lifestyles. These had been seen as too daring in 1963 when the show was conceived. When Montgomery's screen-daughter Tabitha was the focus of a 1977 spin-off series developed by William Asher, it was notable that she was more Serena than Samantha. Like Montgomery, she was a woman working outside her home as a television producer.[83] The show's publicity marketed her with explicit reference to *Bewitched* as "single, liberated and more sophisticated than a television witch would have been 14 years ago."[84] *Bewitched* thus redefined the parameters of witchcraft-comedy, and set up new ones that could be explored further by later shows. Its ambiguity was probably its most useful legacy: witchcraft could be read in different ways by conservatives and liberals. It was open to many interpretations.

*Bewitched* was an American icon by the time it ended in 1972, so much so that in 1994 Quentin Tarantino could define his character Vincent Vega in *Pulp Fiction* by the question: "Are you a *Bewitched* man or a *Jeannie* man?"[85] The symbolism of its suppressed witchcraft has been interpreted in many different ways. For Vincent, who replied, "*Bewitched* all the way, though I always dug how Jeannie always called Larry Hagman 'master,'" choosing *Bewitched* might have had something to do with his preference for cool, self-possessed women, like Mia Wallace, who asked him the question. Vincent's world revolved around TV, cocaine, and killing people who had displeased his boss. In which case, according to Herbie J. Pilato, who wrote the definitive fan's guide, he had missed the point of *Bewitched*, which was very simple:

- No matter how much one tries to suppress one's natural idiosyncrasies in order to fit into modern society, it will not work.
- Spirituality must always prevail over matters of commerce.
- Love conquers all.[86]

Therefore, like *Bell, Book and Candle*, "*Bewitched* is a sort of gay allegory," announced *The Advocate* in 1992, "the ultimate closet story." Elizabeth Montgomery agreed: "Don't think that didn't enter our minds at the time . . . this was about people not being allowed to be what they really are."[87] Montgomery was involved in campaigning for gay rights after her costar Dick Sargent, the second Darrin, revealed in 1991 that he was homosexual. Her comments also raised other possibilities for reading the show's witchcraft. In 1995 Camille Paglia saw Samantha as emblematic of every outsider in Johnson and Nixon's America. She likened *Bewitched* to *The Crucible* in suggesting that both debated

> the tension between individualism and middle-class normality. Aspiring toward good model citizenship, Samantha forever remains the alien trying to "pass." Her spirited relatives are like flamboyant ethnic immigrants refusing to conform to the requisite WASP persona.[88]

In this double reading, witches appear again as Milleresque Communists associated with foreign exotica, another echo of *Bell, Book and Candle*. Samantha's distancing of her extended family after her "marriage out" is seen as an attempt to become more American by becoming less witchy both "politically" and "ethnically." This begs the questions of what witch politics might be, and how racially different *Bewitched*'s witches were from mortals.

The series does not answer these questions straightforwardly. In one episode, Samantha got involved in local American politics (as Jennifer had before her), supporting a clearly mainstream candidate against a corrupt incumbent. But his party and policies were coyly left unidentified.[89] Perhaps Samantha and Darrin's "mixed" marriage might have been evidence in itself of their political liberalism, if each was taken as emblematic of an ethnic community. In "Just One Happy Family" Darrin certainly told Larry Tate that he was English and Samantha Norwegian — thus they had a mixed marriage.[90] This was certainly how their relationship was read by high school students from Los Angeles who submitted a script for an episode about racial prejudice in 1970. The episode, "Sisters at Heart," showed Tabitha becoming friends with a black girl, Lisa. When told that people of different skin colors couldn't be friends, Tabitha made "black" spots appear on her own skin, and "white" spots on Lisa's. This child-magic (which, interestingly, went unremarked) allowed Samantha to explain that "you can be sisters without looking alike . . . all men are brothers, even if they're girls." The episode won the Governor's Award at the 1971 Emmy ceremony.[91] But the possible issues of intermarriage were more usually skated over. One Stephens child was discovered to be a witch, the other mortal — a neat symmetry involving no dangerous discussion of hybridity. Samantha's integration, and avoidance of un-American activities, was thus spectacularly successful. But it was achieved only at the expense of her individual freedom, and by minimizing her difference from mortals and her witch heritage. Endora's disapproval of the way her daughter lived with Darrin can be seen as the playing out of a classic American story through the metaphor of witchcraft — the disappointment felt by immigrants when their children repudiate traditional customs and beliefs, and "marry out."

Contrastingly, at a *Bewitched* online discussion forum, Adam Blair saw Endora's conflict with Darrin as one of class, not ethnicity, nationality, or politics. Witches were "old-money" while mortals were "blue-collar," he suggested. Endora spoke of "rubbing elbows with European nobility" and literati, while "for the rootless, classless American, these still hold nearly as much magic as the incantations uttered by the various witches and warlocks."[92] In fact, one concept that William Asher had suggested for the show, before hitting on the idea of witchcraft, was that Darrin should be a poorly paid gas station attendant while Samantha would be a rich girl.[93] *Bewitched*'s Darrin, however, was hardly a manual worker: his status was bourgeois and Endora's objection to him was more likely to be his showy, nouveau-riche materialism. She disapproved of his work ethic and apparently of his capitalism — maybe witches *are* Communists. *Bewitched* certainly upset its sponsor, Chevrolet, with an episode in which Endora criticized Darrin for making people "buy things they don't really want or need," such as new cars. The story was, unsurprisingly, never filmed.[94] It is, however, clear from surviving episodes that Endora was disgusted that Darrin and Samantha lived in suburbia, owned a huge, sky-blue convertible, and spent their leisure time in dining out, playing golf, and taking handicraft classes. They lived the American Dream, and Blair is right to note that the show both endorsed and, through Endora, criticized their preoccupation with it. In this reading, the recent revival of witchcraft as a spiritual alternative to the materialism that Samantha had accepted echoes Endora's disdainful rejection of the physical world. Paglia is right to call Samantha's relatives "spirited" and Herbie J. Pilato to emphasize the show's priority as the spiritual rather than the material. Nevertheless, Asher saw a message of self-help behind the scripts, which did suggest the importance of worldly rewards of hard work. "Samantha could have had anything or anyone she wanted. Yet, she chose not to take the easy way out," sums up Pilato. Asher imagined viewers saying:

> Hey, they're not going for the easy way out. They want to earn their way. If Samantha doesn't think life as a mortal is so horrendous, I guess I don't have it so bad after all.[95]

Here, *Bewitched* functions as a kind of anti-*Crucible,* the opiate of the masses, but also as an endorsement of the idea that men and women could work in partnership for economic and social success.

Although the series attracted increasing interest as a commentary on the lifestyle of the modern American woman, relatively little fuss was made about its supernatural content — which might surprise readers and viewers habituated to the recent struggle over Harry Potter. In the mid-twentieth century, after *The Crucible* and *Bell, Book and Candle*, witches were still seen as reasonably reputable creatures, to be viewed through the lens of Enlightenment skepticism about their reality. They were metaphors for modern concerns (sex, social issues, politics), amusing stereotypes. Nevertheless, the president of ABC initially rejected *Bewitched*, because he believed it would offend Bible Belt viewers. He had reckoned without the alliance between witchcraft and commercial good sense that the show represented. It seemed likely to be a success, and ABC was persuaded to take it — rather than have it go to CBS — by the bald argument, "It's only a TV show." Later, cast and crew would occasionally encounter a concern about satanism, which they saw as unexpected, puzzling and "a bit off the mark."[96] For them, Samantha and her family were good, unthreatening all-Americans. They didn't even have *The Crucible*'s and *Bell, Book and Candle*'s potentially problematic equation of witchcraft with black, Native American, and Asian cultures, a link made both through the historical Tituba and through modern readings of witchcraft as "primitivism." A publicity shot for the show featured the all-right, all-white family standing in front of the Capitol, beside an American flag. Witchcraft and the American family were entirely compatible, without a hint of Gillian's "early American" irony: indeed Samantha met the Washingtons, Benjamin Franklin, Paul Revere, and other patriotic worthies on a regular basis.[97] Her family took part in Halloween celebrations because, despite their concerns that these might involve disrespect to witches, they wanted to belong.[98] They even visited seventeenth-century Salem to reconcile witches with other early Americans. With deliberate irony, it was Darrin who was accused of witchcraft during their visit (because he struck a match) and Samantha who knocked the nation's Puritan forefathers into shape with a plea for liberty and justice for all. She blamed witchcraft accusations on the inability to tolerate difference — in speech, manner, appearance, and name — concluding:

> Is this what we seek in this new world? Methinks not. The hope of this world lieth in our acceptance of all differences and a recognition of our common humanity.[99]

This summed up *Bewitched*'s "platform," interpreted by Pilato as: "the show is about . . . prejudice. Looking past differences, and concentrating on what makes people the same."[100] Witches (liberated women; politically, racially, and sexually diverse Americans) could be part of the big, happy American melting pot, if they would just consent to be part of the family.

### After Bewitched

Like all fantasies, then, *Bewitched* raised deep issues of class, race, economics, and politics. But its writers and actors seemed most interested in the ways that it could be read as a metaphor for concerns about women's role inside and outside the modern American family. In this respect, it was a model for later films and television series that wanted to present witches as acceptable women living unthreatening lives — or perhaps women as acceptable witches. Further positive portrayals were built on the foundation of *Bewitched*, where witches were allowed a number of modern freedoms but again made safe by being contained within a family. The 1990s TV series *Sabrina the Teenage Witch* and *Charmed*, and the 1998 film *Practical Magic*, based on Alice Hoffman's novel, used this trick to domesticate their witches. In all three cases, witchcraft ran in the family of the main characters, as it did in Samantha's. Thus becoming a witch was not seen as an individual's acquisition of power as with *The Craft*, *Eastwick*, and *Buffy*, but as a respectable inheritance — indeed, a family affair from the outset. The leading witches of *Sabrina* and *Practical Magic*, Sabrina and Sally, both lived with their witch aunts. Both were pretty, heterosexual, and keen to please those around them by working hard and doing domestic chores, even the ones their families despised or preferred to do by magic. Sally, says the novel, "was the one who cooked healthy dinners of meat loaf and fresh green beans and barley soup, using the recipes from a copy of *Joy of Cooking*."[101] She was "Glinda good witch," perceptively says Sandra Bullock, the actress who played her in the film.[102] Like Samantha Stephens, Sally married and had children of her own. Sabrina had a boyfriend, Harvey, whom she eventually married.

The three witches of *Charmed*, now past its sixth season on American TV, are likewise beautiful, heterosexual, and live in an immaculate family home in sisterly harmony. They are watched over by a grandmother in the next world, a more-or-less absent but still living father, and the memory of their mother.[103] The show is explicitly about the sisters' relationship, WB's official show Web site explains, a "bond that reached far beyond petty sisterly grudges."[104] Since the series was developed in the 1990s and is still running, the sisters have careers but, crucially, these do not interfere with screen time at home with each other (although they do sometimes clash with the women's magical commitments). They make time for partners, and even children, when necessary. When one sister, Prue (Shannen Doherty) died in battle, she was replaced by another "long-lost" half-sister, Paige (Rose McGowan). Family, the dialogue repeatedly insists, is vital for the women's power as "the power of three": witchcraft runs in their veins, literally. In "Astral Monkey," a doctor accidentally acquires it while testing their blood.[105] The ultimate weapon used by their adversaries is to turn the sisters against each other, so that the power of three will be lost.[106] Sisterliness thus also limits their freedom. They must act together or be powerless, often as spiritual chaperones to each other, with decisions and action taken communally seen to be far wiser and more effective than whatever each woman once thought or did as an individual. When Phoebe betrayed her sisters in favor of her romance with the demon Cole, the consequences were serious and the relationship disastrous. Phoebe ended up as Queen of the Underworld, bearing an evil baby that must be removed — a sharply gendered warning against breaking sisterly solidarity to trust a mere male.[107] The sisters keep each other in check because the commitment to sisterhood is always seen to be stronger than that to any man, enterprise, or idea. As Michael Abernethy says, "The show's focus is sisterhood," even at the expense of a sensitive portrayal of "Wicca."[108] This is because to be acceptable, a witch still needs a family — not an ideology.[109]

The same was true of the 1995 novel and 1998 film *Practical Magic*. Both explored family relationships between witches. The film was more explicit about the specific need for sisterhood than was the novel, and in the film this private commitment was what forced the witches to seek help — and find public acceptance — from the nonwitch community. Sisters Sally and Gillian (the latter's name a reference to *Bell, Book and Candle*?) were played by Sandra Bullock and Nicole Kidman, respectively, and these women were clearly the film's "stars." One lover and two grown daughters were deleted to allow uninterrupted focus on their sisterliness for most of the film's one-and-a-half hours. Two further important changes to the novel's story made their relationship more central. As a girl, the film's Sally was traumatized by seeing what unhappy love can do to women, and cast a spell that effectively prohibited her from falling in love. She specified that she could only truly love a man with what she conceived to be impossible attributes, including one green and one blue eye. Thus she trapped herself in permanent immaturity, in the safe world of the family. Gillian, meanwhile, a sexual time bomb just like Kim Novak's Gillian, eloped early in the film, but before she did so she cut her hand and her sister's and they affirmed a "blood-sisterhood." This added tie to her family was what saved Gillian at the film's end. Sally and Gillian were seen to share a telepathic connection, a strongly stressed bond that ultimately enabled Sally to save Gillian's life. And to effect this, she called in the women of her community, who all performed witchcraft with her to heal Gillian. Loyalty to family directly created public acceptability.

The book was strikingly different: both women found happiness with good men, and Sally's two daughters were major characters in their own right who grew into young adults and found partners of their own. Outsiders were a welcome part of the witches' world, and happy sexuality drove the story. The story of witchcraft was clearly a story about sex again, and no bell, book, and candle exorcism was needed to drive it away it this time. But the film contained only two good men, and there was an exorcism. This addition to the film literally showed a witch repossessing her sister from a man outside the family, Jimmy (Goran Visnjic), at an all-female "Tupperware exorcism party": an exorcism of male possessiveness needed because of the sister's overconfident sexuality.[110] Families, the film suggested, are good and safe for witches. Independence, and especially sexual freedom, are still bad. Producer Denise di Novi and Sandra Bullock recorded a commentary for the DVD, and they acknowledged this male marginality. "Poor Goran," said Bullock. Both repeatedly emphasized the film's focus on women (actresses, designers, and production staff) working together and on the "sister bond." Thus the film ended with an all-female act of solidarity by the witch-family as they stepped off the roof of their house and flew, applauded by their newly sympathetic female neighbors. This was a positive, feminist film, but its affirmation of sisterhood had all the limitations of family as well as its strengths. At the film's close, when Sally did meet her man, Gary, Gillian was a lonely, immature figure. Moreover, it was revealed that Sally's spell, coupled with Gary's wish for a girl like her, brought him to her. Thus even he was a safe, fitting part of the witch world — not really an outsider at all. The witches had become acceptable, but only through the discovery that the world outside the family was dangerous. It might embrace, but it could also reject and threaten, and this threat came especially from contact with men and the release of sexual energy. Only Sally might marry, and while this seemed (delightfully, but for no apparent reason) to break the family curse that doomed all the witches to lose their lovers, it seemed also like a concession to the viewer's expectation of romance rather than a logical plot development.

The novel's focus was also on family, but lone, available men were included as an essential, wonderful part of life. Sisterhood was a key theme, but so were relationships with lovers. The book offered at least four good men to be cherished: the lovers of Sally, Gillian, and Sally's daughters, Kylie and Antonia. Its last line was: "Fall in love whenever you can."[111] The book contained less violence against men and less suspicion of them. It was revealed that Gillian did not actually kill Jimmy with her spiked magical drink, as the reader had thought: he died of unknown causes. Jimmy's surname was not the ominous Angelove, which suggested that romantic love is a honey trap, but prosaic Hawkins. Gillian's lover, Ben Frye, who was not in the movie, was a conjuror — albeit of the rabbit-out-of-a-hat kind — and thus, like the other men, had a magic all of his own. It was he and not Sally who redeemed Gillian by showing her that she could fall in love safely and that not all men are abusers. Finally, the film invented its witches' curse on men. Sally and Gillian's ancestor Maria Owens was hanged as a witch, it explained, but her power inexplicably broke the rope and she was banished to an island (a modern witch appears as Circe again). She waited for her lover to come to her as he had promised. He did not, and so a curse fell on all the men the Owens women would ever love: they would die young. The curse reminds the viewer of *I Married a Witch*. In *Practical Magic*, Sally's husband Michael fell victim to this curse and so, presumably, did Jimmy. It was broken (it appeared) by the sisters' blood bond and its expulsion of Jimmy, allowing a happy end for Sally. The other women remained curiously infantilized, like the *Charmed* sisters and Sabrina. Witchcraft was something that set them apart, forcing them to remain in their family home like a fairy-tale castle. Any would-be Rapunzel, seeking nonwitch love, got the witchy punishment due to her. And even in the book, with its positive males and the possibility of growing up, there was a circular return to the family home that could be affirmation, or could be a curse in itself. The lone witch is still too dangerous to be comfortably accommodated in American culture

Sarah Projansky and Leah R. Vande Berg explore why this might be. In "Sabrina the Teenage . . .? Girls, Witches, Mortals and the Limitations of Prime-time Feminism," they argue that Sabrina (whose show was and is usually aired at times when it will be accessible to girls and housewives) is a role model of limited use to female viewers. This is because, despite a feminist gloss, the series' affirmation of traditional patriarchal feminine concerns with physical beauty, acquisition of heterosexual male attention, and responsibility to others undermines Sabrina's access to independence.[112]

In conservative American society, they argue, women (and thus witches) are still expected to be self-denying, sexually secondary homemakers, even where they are allowed access to traditional male perks. Sabrina, say Projansky and Vande Berg, spent far too much time worrying about her appearance, competing for male attention, and either holding back her powers or using them selflessly to benefit others rather than advancing or pleasing herself. Like *Charmed*'s witches, she experienced severe difficulties if she used her magic for personal gain. Even though she was only a teenager, she was repeatedly saddled with moral responsibilities, and — because her own parents were absent for magical reasons — sometimes acted in a quasi-parental role to her accident-prone aunts. It might certainly have been expected that late-twentieth- and early-twenty-first-century texts would offer more of a challenge to this state of affairs. The powerful, popular figure of the witch offers a perfect opportunity. *Sabrina the Teenage Witch* might have been particularly likely to take up the gauntlet and transcend the limitations of its original source, 1960s comic books, because its star, Melissa Joan Hart, and her producer and mother, Paula Hart, had such a grip on the show through their production company, Hartbreak Films. Both were thus by definition committed to smashing glass ceilings, and asserting "girl power." Paula Hart certainly intended Sabrina to be an improvement on earlier TV witches: "Samantha had to use her magic on the sly, while Sabrina is encouraged by her aunts to use hers to the fullest," she said.[113] But it is precisely "girl power," a media-friendly pseudofeminism, that is the problem. Today's witches in popular culture are being denied the right to grow up.

*I Married a Witch, Bell, Book and Candle,* and *Bewitched* were — surprisingly — in some ways more radical departures from the conservative taboos about representing witch-hood than are later dramas. These women had no truck with the idea that witchcraft was not to be used for personal gain. They were old enough to resist the tutelage of aunts, and were not encumbered with "weird sisters." Jennifer had a father, but she defied him and imprisoned his spirit in a bottle. Gillian had a brother, aunt, and coven, but lived alone and was strikingly autonomous, a shop-keeper and woman-about-town who had fallen out with the chief witch. She made her own decisions in chilly independence. Despite Darrin, her children, and her relatives, Samantha, too, is the ancestress of the danger-ously free and single witches of Eastwick, *The Craft,* and Willow as well as of the comfortably domesticated Prue, Phoebe, Piper, Paige, Sabrina, Sally, and (second) Gillian, as the recent *Bewitched* feature film (2005) showed. Samantha had no coven to depend upon and frequently defied her mother, father, and other witches, as well as disobeying Darrin. She made up her own mind, challenging the Witches' Council. And then there were Ser-ena and the grown-up Tabitha, independent witches born of *Bewitched.* Jennifer, Gillian, Samantha/Serena, and Tabitha were fully adult women, not limited by a need to return to familial protection, strong in their own right. They were in some ways more dangerous creatures than the 1990s teen and twentysomething witches policed by their families. Has Ameri-can society become less tolerant of possibilities, and more concerned about policing the aspirations of the young, and of women? Or is it that paganism, and indeed satanism, are now seen as real threats to society, not just metaphors? Viewers and readers, especially young people and women who feel disempowered, are desperately keen to read and watch stories of witches, while parents and pastors are desperately worried that they will become witches themselves. What better solution than to leach the economic, sexual, and social power from the image of the witch, even as it becomes a vehicle for the promotion of self-empowerment?

Twentieth-century fictions began by freeing witchcraft from its associa-tion with evil, but then by depriving adult female witches of power, espe-cially once they were married. Thorne Smith and Norman Matson's story and the film that came out of it set up an exchange of witch-women's power for marital bliss that proved irresistible for another twenty years. Then *Bewitched* allowed women to keep their powers after marriage, provided they exercised strict self-control over them. On the one hand this trend of greater empowerment has continued: witches can keep their powers indefinitely, and need not marry at all, although they must not use magic for personal gain. But a parallel impulse has been to whittle away their autonomy in less obvious ways. Then in 1997 came a threat from an unexpected quarter — British child-witches who actually did have "power, literally and metaphorically." The significance of suppressing witchcraft in America is just too symbolic for witches to be allowed complete liberation in this way. Many Americans are well aware of the biblical analogy: "Rebellion is as the sin of witchcraft."[114] Few fictions dare to let witches of all ages and sexes live like real, free people, and the Harry Potter furor demonstrates perfectly what happens when an author tries to do so. Immediately, accusations of satanism are made, and a revolt of witches, "an Horrible Plot against the Country by Witchcraft" as Cotton Mather put it, is predicted.[115]

In American culture, the novel *Practical Magic* and the 2005 film *Bewitched* perhaps come closest to the liberal ideal of a witch — adult or child — exploring her powers and growing in independence, judgment, and strength. Patriarchal structures, whose purposes are to protect women and children from dangerous and corrupting empowerment and keep them under the watchful male gaze, are less evident and potent in *Practical Magic* than anywhere else. *Bewitched* allows its heroine, Isabel Bigelow, a real witch who is playing Samantha Stevens in a remake of the sitcom, to have a career, female friends, marriage, and witchcraft powers, bringing Hollywood's stuffed men to their knees with confidence and charm. Its writers, Nora and Delia Ephron, deliberately set out to remove from the original *Bewitched* premise the limitations on the witch's power, and they largely succeeded.[116] So, with a remake of *I Married a Witch* also planned, audiences may be treated to a breakthrough in modern American culture — the portrayal of a disempowered witch-figure empowered without condition, without strings. Or they may not. As the modern witch Starhawk said, "I'm waiting for the TV witch who happens to be an auto mechanic, an engineer, or a molecular biologist."[117] When Rosie the Riveter herself becomes a witch, then the evolution of Thorne Smith's Jennifer and her seventeenth-century coconspirators will be complete.

# NOTES

## Introduction

1. John Demos, "Underlying Themes in the Witchcraft of Seventeenth-Century New England," *The American Historical Review* 75:5 (June 1970): 1311.
2. A note on terminology: I have throughout the book used "colonial" as an adjective for all early modern American polities, since other adjectives ("provincial," "proprietorial") proved confusing to the reader.
3. Robert Frost, "The Road Not Taken," *Selected Poems* (New York and Avenel, NJ: Gramercy, 1992), 163.

## Chapter 1

1. John W. De Forest, *Witching Times*, ed. Alfred Appel (serialized 1856–57; New Haven: College and University Press, 1967), 211; Lawrence Buell, *New England Literary Culture: From Revolution through Renaissance* (Cambridge: Cambridge University Press, 1986), 245.
2. These figures include: slander suits; accusations that were pursued no further than an initial naming or "complaint" against a suspect; each separate trial of a suspect tried several times, but not each separate indictment; witchcraft cases referred to in diaries, letters, and other sources up to 1730, where the writer may be credited with knowledge of the events described; cases where the suspect's name and/or the outcome is not known; cases of persons tried for executing a "witch" on shipboard; and cases of magic, medical practice, or conjuration that a contemporary record represents as amounting to a charge of demonic contact. Nevertheless, as this book argues, the process necessarily relies on interpretive choices: statistics are, in my view, poor guides to "truth," but necessary bases for a discussion of interpretation and myth.

3. The overall totals are the best available at present: I have drawn on John Demos's *Entertaining Satan: Witchcraft and the Culture of Early New England* (Oxford: Oxford University Press, 1982); Richard Weisman's *Witchcraft, Magic and Religion in Seventeenth-Century Massachusetts* (Amherst: University of Massachusetts Press, 1984); Carol F. Karlsen, *The Devil in the Shape of a Woman: Witchcraft in Colonial New England*, 2nd. ed. (1987; New York and London: W.W. Norton, 1998); Amelia Mott Gummere's *Witchcraft and Quakerism: A Study in Social History* (Philadelphia, 1908) at http://www.strecorsoc.org/gummere/contents.html; Frederick C. Drake's "Witchcraft in the American Colonies 1647–1662," *American Quarterly* 20:4 (Winter 1968): 694–708; George Lincoln Burr's *Narratives of the New England Witchcraft Cases* (1914; Mineola, NY: Dover, 2002); Samuel G. Drake, *Annals of Witchcraft in New England and Elsewhere in the United States* (1869; n.p.: Kessinger, 2006), I. Marc Carlson's online list of "Witches in History" at http://www.personal.utulsa.edu/~marc-carlson/witchtrial/na.html; Richard Beale Davis's "The Devil in Virginia in the Seventeenth Century," *Virginia Magazine of History and Biography* 65 (1957): 131–49; Carson O. Hudson's *These Detestable Slaves of the Devil: A Concise Guide to Witchcraft in Colonial Virginia* (Haverford, PA: Infinity Publishing, 2001); and Diana Lyn Laulainen Schein's unpublished Ph.D. thesis "Comparative Counterpoints: Witchcraft Accusations in Early Modern Lancashire and the Chesapeake," University of Minnesota, 2004, as well as on my own research and other accounts that confirm the findings above. See also Mary Beth Norton, *In the Devil's Snare: The Salem Witchcraft Crisis of 1692* (New York: Alfred A. Knopf, 2002) and Tom Peete Cross, "Witchcraft in North Carolina," *Studies in Philology* 16:3 (July 1919): 217–87. Robert Calef, in his *More Wonders of the Invisible World* (London, 1700) says that by October 1692 one hundred and fifty people were in prison at Salem and elsewhere, with another two hundred accused on top of that (references are to George Lincoln Burr's edition of Calef in *Narratives*, 373). I have counted George Burroughs as a Maine case, because he was arrested while still living there. Although Beale Davis and Laulainen Schein identify Paul Carter as a witch, this was a regular murder case with a magical attempt to reveal the killer and must be discounted. I have omitted cases from New France, the Caribbean, and South American countries: a list of publications on these can be found in Brian F. Le Beau, *The Story of the Salem Witch Trials* (Upper Saddle River, NJ: Prentice Hall, 1998), 255–56.

4. Hudson, 54–55, Richmond County Court, October 1730; *Pennsylvania Gazette* (October 22, 1730): 3–4. It was reprinted as a true story in London ("Melancholy Effects of Credulity in Witchcraft," *The Gentleman's Magazine* 1 [January 1731]: 29–30). Franklin was not alone in his skepticism, of course, but debate was ongoing. In 1733, for example, Josiah Cotton wrote a manuscript demonology, "Some Observations Concerning Witchcraft," condemning evidence against witches such as that summarized in Joseph

Glanvill's *Saducismus Triumphatus* (London, 1681) as "ABSURD." But he also pondered why "the horrible Tragedy at Salem" had not eradicated belief in such evidence (MS Am 1165, Houghton Library, Harvard University).

5. Each set of figures should be seen as being prefaced by the words "at least": in particular, Richard Weisman's meticulous search of Massachusetts records and Diana Lyn Laulainen Schein's parallel work in the Tidewater states need to be replicated across all of New England, New York, and the Carolinas. I have no doubt that there are undiscovered texts to be found.

6. The best general account is Sally Smith Booth, *The Witches of Early America* (New York: Hastings House, 1975).

7. David Hackett Fischer, *Albion's Seed: Four British Folkways in America* (Oxford: Oxford University Press, 1989), 527; Burr, *Narratives*, 81–84.

8. For the Witchcraft Act of 1604, see Marion Gibson, ed., *Witchcraft and Society in England and America 1550–1750* (Ithaca and London: Cornell University Press and Continuum, 2003), 5–7.

9. Burr, 47–8; *The Public Records of the Colony of Connecticut from April 1636 to October 1776*, 15 vols. (Hartford, 1850–90); General Assembly minute 12 May 1664, http://www.colonialct.unconn.edu (consulted 20 June 2006).

10. Burr, 85–88, 42–43, 48–52; Gummere.

11. Joseph Smith, *Colonial Justice in Western Massachusetts 1639–1702* (Cambridge, MA: Harvard University Press, 1961), 13. The nearest English parallel would be the trials conducted by justices of the peace and ministers in the 1640s when the Assize system was interrupted by the Civil War, but the legal analogy is inexact. For a detailed discussion of English judicial processes, see Marion Gibson, *Reading Witchcraft: Stories of Early English Witches* (London and New York: Routledge, 1999), especially Chapter Two.

12. See Timothy B. Riordan, *The Plundering Time: Maryland and the English Civil War 1645, 1646* (Baltimore: Maryland Historical Society, 2004).

13. Massachusetts Archives Middlesex County Court records folder 15 (1:670).

14. N. B. Shurtleff, ed., *Records of the Governor and Company of the Massachusetts Bay*, 5 vols. (Boston, 1853–54), vol. 3, 273.

15. See Massachusetts Archives folder 1352–16 and Suffolk County Court files 13:1228 (and Demos 315–39); Edgar J. McManus, *Law and Liberty in Early New England: Criminal Justice and Due Process 1620–1692* (Amherst, MA: University of Massachusetts Press, 1993), 74.

16. There were important exceptions, and one is discussed below: county courts were not created in Connecticut until 1662, and in Plymouth not until 1685; New Haven had plantation or town courts; Rhode Island devolved its powers to town meetings, which were replaced by a circuit (traveling) court with no county courts, and then a fixed court; New Hampshire and Maine had county courts, with New Hampshire developing an internal circuit court after its separation from Massachusetts in 1679 (McManus, 79–89). The county courts played the biggest role in witchcraft prosecutions in Virginia and Massachusetts, because they were set up there as early as 1624 and

1643, respectively (Philip A. Bruce, *Institutional History of Virginia in the Seventeenth Century* [1910; Gloucester, MA: Peter Smith, 1964], vol. 1, 484; McManus, 74).

17. Bruce, vol. 1, 484, 540.

18. Essex Institute, files of Essex County Court 2:46:1.

19. McManus, 74.

20. Bruce, vol. 1 647–53, 657, 665–66, 690–1, 279, 281. There are no records of witches being tried and condemned by lower courts, or availing themselves of the right of appeal to the king himself, which was briefly introduced in the 1680s. H. R. McIlwaine, *Minutes of the Council and General Court of Colonial Virginia 1622–32 and 1670–6*, ed. Jon Kukla, 2nd. ed. (1924; Richmond, VA: Virginia State Library, 1979), vii, ix–x.

21. The Provincial Court records can now be read online, and the court systems are outlined here, too: http://guide.mdarchives.state.md.us.

22. McManus 79–81. See also James Deetz and Patricia Scott Deetz, *The Times of their Lives: Life, Love and Death in the Plymouth Colony* (New York: W.H. Freeman, 2000), 92–97.

23. McManus 83–84, 87–89 — no Rhode Island cases reached the upper levels of her judiciary, so the Particular and then General Court are not discussed here; New York and Pennsylvanian cases are discussed above.

24. "Second Book of Records of the Acts of the County Courts and Courts of Probates, in the County of Hartford," Connecticut State Library, Hartford, title page. See also Anon, *Connecticut's Courts* revised ed. (Hartford, CT: State of Connecticut Judicial Branch, 1999), 31–32; and *Connecticut Historical Society Collections Volume 2: Particular Court 1639–1663* (Hartford, CT: CHS and the Society of Colonial Wars in the State of Connecticut, 1928), vii–viii.

25. *Public Records of the Colony of Connecticut* vol. 1, 391, 397, 399, 407–8, 415, 426–27; the records do demonstrate the General Assembly's awareness of the witchcraft cases, minuting such items as the payment of a fee to the surgeon who examined the body of one of the "bewitched," and the administration of the estate of one of those who had fled (vol. 1 396, 401); McManus, 82; William K. Holdsworth, "Law and Society in Colonial Connecticut 1636–1672," Ph.D. thesis, Claremont Graduate School, 1974, 401–2.

26. On the legality of the proceedings see Calef and George Bancroft, *History of the Colonization of the United States*, 9th ed. (1840; Boston, 1841), vol. 3, 88.

27. William Elliot Woodward, *Records of Salem Witchcraft* (Roxbury, MA, 1864); http://extext.virginia.edu/salem/witchcraft/. The records were also the subject of a Works Progress Administration transcription project (1938), published in parts by Nova Anglia, a Salem-based company, in the 1990s; and see also http://www.nationalgeographic.org/salem.

28. For short histories see Charles J. Hoadly, "A Case of Witchcraft in Hartford," *Connecticut Magazine* 5:11 (November 1899), 557–61, and R. G. Tomlinson, *Witchcraft Trials of Connecticut* (Hartford, CT: Bond Press, 1978), 27–37.

29. Proceedings and Acts of the General Assembly 2 September–26 October 1723 (vol. 34, page 678), Maryland State Archives.

30. See note 69; Gummere; Drake, 173.

31. Washington Irving, *The Complete Tales of Washington Irving*, especially "Rip van Winkle" and "The Legend of Sleepy Hollow," ed. Charles Neider (New York: Doubleday, 1975); Karl Herr, *Hex and Spellwork: The Magical Practices of the Pennsylvania Dutch* (Boston and York Beach, ME: Weiser Books, 2002), Don Yoder, *Discovering American Folklife: Essays on Folk Culture and the Pennsylvania Dutch* (Mechanicsburg, PA: Stackpole Books, 1990) and from a modern Wiccan perspective, Silver Ravenwolf, *American Folk Magick: Charms, Spells and Herbals* (St. Paul, MN: Llewellyn, 1999). In the twentieth century, the rhetoric changed with changing perceptions of immigrants and Germans. In particular, the 1929 murder of a suspected wizard provided an opportunity to deplore the "rot" believed by Pennsylvania Germans, reinforcing existing prejudice (see M.V.B. Perley, *A Short History of the Salem Village Witchcraft Trials* [1911; n.p.: Kessinger, 2005], 11, and Jesse N. Bowen, "Lecture to the Lawyers' Round Table of Maryland," 7 December 1929, p. 18, Maryland Historical Society). As we shall see in Chapter 4, it was in Pennsylvania that American Witchcraft was reinvented.

32. Charles Wentworth Upham, *Salem Witchcraft*, ed. with an introduction by Bryan F. Le Beau (1867; Mineola, New York: Dover, 2000), 3; Charles H. Levermore, "Witchcraft in Connecticut," *New England Magazine* 12:5 (July 1892): 636.

33. Massachusetts Archives, records of Middlesex County Court folder 25, County Court at Cambridge 3 April 1660. Not all the documents here are numbered. Winifred was the widow of William Holman (see Lucius R. Paige, *History of Cambridge, Massachusetts, 1630–1877* (Boston, 1877), 587–88. For similar carefulness, see Susan Topan's evidence against Elizabeth Morse, in which she corrects the supportive testimony of Elizabeth Titcomb which she says "is true [inserted over line "for the substance"], onely there is a mistake . . . [in] w[hi]ch she might easily mistake [inserted over line "her"]. (Trials for Witchcraft in New England collection, Houghton Library, Harvard University.)

34. Essex Institute Phillips Library, records of Essex County Court 15-61-1.

35. Essex Institute Phillips Library , records of Essex County Court 32-130-3, 32-133-3.

36. Massachusetts Archives, Middlesex County Court folder 15, group 1. See also Smith, *Colonial Justice*, 94–96.

37. This was not unheard of in English courts, but was comparatively much rarer. See J. S. Cockburn, *Introduction to Calendar of Assize Records. Home Circuit Indictments. Elizabeth I and James I* (London: HMSO, 1985) and J. M. Beattie, *Crime and the Courts in England 1660–1800* (Oxford: Clarendon, 1986).

38. Records of the Court of Assistants, CSL, 11 May, 12 October 1669, 30 May 1670; "Petition for the Investigation of Katherine Harrison," Connecticut Historical Society MSS, Hartford; Wyllys Papers, John Hay Library, Brown University, "The Answers of Some Ministers . . .," 20 October 1669.

39. "Second Book . . . of the County Court . . . of Hartford," CSL, 6 and 13 June 1662; 9 Oct 1661.

40. Records of the Court of Assistants, CSL, 8 July 1665 and 18 May 1666. A document in the Wyllys Papers, John Hay Library, Brown University, records a split verdict also in 1662, including the reasoning of the jurors such as "about the buisnes of fliing the most part thought it was not legally proved" (Box 1).

41. "Second Book . . . of the County Court . . . of Hartford," CSL, 6 January 1662, 2 July 1663; Records of the Court of Assistants, CSL, 26 June 1665, 18 May 1666.

42. Massachusetts Archives 135: 22, 23, 24; writing in 1702, John Hale explained that "the Governour Simon Bradstreet Esq. and some of the Magistrates repreived her, being unsatisfyed in the Verdict." They thought that spectral evidence — in which it was alleged that visions of a "spectre" of Morse had appeared to her victim — was not good enough to condemn her. Also there were no two witnesses to any one of the crimes she was charged with committing. There were more than two witnesses in total, but this did not seem to them to meet the accepted standard of evidence required (John Hale, *A Modest Inquiry into the Nature of Witchcraft* (Boston, 1702) in *Witchcraft in Europe and America*, Reel 48 [Woodbridge, CT: Research Publications], 15).

43. George Francis Dow, ed., *Records and Files of the Quarterly Courts of Essex County, Massachusetts*, vol. 1 (Salem: Essex Institute, 1911), vi.

44. On English generic constraints, see Gibson, *Reading Witchcraft*, 78–109, Marion Gibson, "Understanding Witchcraft? Accusers' Stories in Print in Early Modern England," and Peter Rushton, "Texts of Authority: Witchcraft Accusations and the Demonstration of Truth in Early Modern England," in Stuart Clark, ed., *Languages of Witchcraft: Narrative, Ideology and Meaning in Early Modern Culture* (Basingstoke, England: Macmillan, 2001), 41–54 and 21–39.

45. Informal records were, moreover, often kept in court files when they would undoubtedly have been thrown away in older jurisdictions, where storage space was limited by existing piles of medieval documents – see Cockburn, *Introduction*.

46. Princess Anne County Order Book 1 1691–1709 part 1, 6 June, 5 July, 10 July; Minutes of Council folder 17, item 6 (28 March 1706), Library of Virginia.

47. Library of Congress Thomas Jefferson Papers, series 8, Virginia Records Manuscripts 1606–37, available online at http://memory.loc.gov/service/mss/mtj/mtj8/064/0200/0290.gif (also image 291). Accessed 24.06.2006.

48. Increase Mather, *Cases of Conscience Concerning Evil Spirits Personating Men* and Cotton Mather, *The Wonders of the Invisible World* (Boston and London, 1693). *Witchcraft in Europe and America*, Reel 66 (Woodbridge, CT: Research Publications); Cotton Mather, *Memorable Providences, Relating to Witchcrafts and Possessions* (Boston, 1689).

49. Deodat Lawson, *A Brief and True Narrative of Some Remarkable Passages Relating to Sundry Persons Afflicted by Witchcraft* (Boston, 1692); Samuel Sewall, *The Diary of Samuel Sewall*, ed. M. Halsey Thomas, 2 vols. (New York: Farrar, Straus and Giroux, 1973); see also Richard Francis, *Samuel Sewall's Apology* (London, England: Fourth Estate, 2005); Samuel Parris's records of the Salem examinations at http://extext.virginia.edu/salem/witchcraft; Joshua Moody to Increase Mather, Boston Public Library, Mather Papers, Prince Collection Ms.Am. 1502 v. 5 no. 36, John Whiting to Increase Mather Ms.Am. 1502 v. 1 no. 28, Nathaniel to Increase Mather, Ms.Am. 1502 v. 5, no. 84, and Samuel Willard, "A Brief Account of a Strange and Unusual Providence," Ms.Am. 1502 v. 2, no. 3.

50. Christina Larner, *Witchcraft and Religion: The Politics of Popular Belief*, ed. Alan Macfarlane (Oxford: Blackwell, 1984), 4, 14, 124. Robert Muchembled and Joseph Klaits also focused on the role of the state in facilitating witch-hunting. Robert Muchembled, "Satanic Myths and Cultural Reality," in Bengt Ankarloo and Gustav Henningsen, eds., *Early Modern European Witchcraft: Centres and Peripheries* (1990; Oxford: Clarendon, 1993), 139–60, and Joseph Klaits, *Servants of Satan: The Age of the Witch Hunts* (Bloomington: Indiana UP, 1985). These ideas on state-building seem to have been in part a response to the concern in the 1980s with the relationship between government and society, loosened most notably by Ronald Reagan and Margaret Thatcher.

51. Although in rather more stereotypical terms. Kai T. Erikson, *Wayward Puritans: A Study in the Sociology of Deviance* (New York: John Wiley, 1966).

52. In response to Larner, who put problematic emphasis on the persecutory role of the "ruling classes," Brian Levack has argued that many national elites attempted to suppress local attempts to prosecute witches. But, modifying Larner's theory, it can be argued that these Hathornes and Danforths were engaged in their own state-building exercise. It was below the level of the nation state, but it was certainly an act of self-definition in the terms that Larner described. Both Levack and Larner might, then, be right about the role that American witches played in building states: they were persecuted by the community around them rather than a big government far away, but their communities had significant aspirations to self-government. Local leaders were acting very like national leaders elsewhere (Brian P. Levack, "State-Building and Witch-Hunting in Early Modern Europe," in

Jonathan Barry, Marianne Hester, and Gareth Roberts, eds., *Witchcraft in Early Modern Europe: Studies in Culture and Belief* (Cambridge: Cambridge University Press, 1996), 96–115 — Levack considers the North American colonies on pp. 109–10).

53. Demos, "Underlying Themes," 1311.

54. Two good accounts of the general historiography of "Salem" are Frances Hill, ed., *The Salem Witch Trials Reader* (New York: Da Capo, 2000), 215–305, and Marc Mappen, *Witches and Historians: Interpretations of Salem*, 2nd. ed. (Malabar, FL: Krieger, 1996). For Tituba see Chapter Three.

55. Documented most recently from a literary-cultural perspective by Buell and John McWilliams, *New England's Crises and Cultural Memory: Literature, Politics, History, Religion 1620–1860* (Cambridge: Cambridge University Press, 2004), and in witchcraft studies by Marilynne K. Roach, *The Salem Witch Trials: A Day by Day Chronicle of a Community Under Siege* (Lanham, MD, New York, Dallas, Boulder, Colorado, Toronto, Oxford: Taylor Trade Publishing, 2002).

56. Calef, 368, 372, 369, 360–61.

57. See Bernard Rosenthal, *Salem Story: Reading the Witch-Trials of 1692* (Cambridge: Cambridge University Press, 1993), 129–50; Upham, *Salem Witchcraft*, 518–19, 564–66; Kenneth Silverman, *The Life and Times of Cotton Mather* (New York: Welcome Rain, 1984), 87, 100–1, 110, 114–18, 130–35; Robert Middlekauff, *The Mathers: Three Generations of Puritan Intellectuals 1596–1728*, 2nd. ed. (1971; Berkeley: University of California Press, 1999), 159–60. Increase Mather, Cotton's father, had also written his book on the trials, *Cases of Conscience*, which gave more weight to doubts about the evidence. But as Perry Miller points out, Increase also endorsed the verdicts and executions, yet his name is sometimes coupled with Cotton's in execration, sometimes not. See Perry Miller, *The New England Mind: From Colony to Province*, 2nd. ed. (1953; Boston: Beacon, 1961), 192–204. Surprisingly, the most insightful and balanced portrayal of Mather and his Bostonian context that I have found, despite some poetic license, is in Amelia E. Barr's almost unknown novel *The Black Shilling* (New York: Dodd, Mead and Co., 1903).

58. Bancroft, 75–88.

59. Hannah Adams, *A Summary History of New England* (Dedham, MA, 1799), 163, Jedidiah Morse and Elijah Parish, *A Compendious History of New England* (London, 1808), 165; Abiel Abbot, *History of Andover* (Andover, MA, 1829), 172–73; Charles A. Goodrich, *A History of the United States of America* (New York, 1829), 6.

60. Anon, *Salem Witchcraft* was published serially in *The New York Literary Journal and Belles-Lettres Repository* (September–November 1820), issues 3–4, pages 329–35, 417–20, and 17–27; Anon, *The Witch of New England: A Romance* (Philadelphia, 1824); John Neal, *Rachel Dyer* (1828; Amherst, New York: Prometheus Books, 1996); James Nelson Barker, "The Tragedy of Superstition" in Arthur Hobson Quinn, ed., *Representative American Plays*

*from 1767 to the Present* (New York: Appleton Century Crofts, 1953). See also John W. Crowley, "James Nelson Barker in Perspective," *Educational Theatre Journal* 24:4 (December 1972), 363–69.

61. Philip Gould, *Covenant and Republic: Historical Romance and the Politics of Puritanism* (Cambridge: Cambridge University Press, 1996), 173–74, 175, 176; Bancroft, 98. On Bancroft's "seductive populism," see McWilliams, 161, 169–70, 175–76. See also Philip Gould, "New England Witch-Hunting and the Politics of Reason in the Early Republic," *New England Quarterly* 68:1 (March 1995): 58–82.

62. John McWilliams has suggested that "from the Enlightenment until at least the Civil War, dwelling on the Salem witch trials . . . offered the ready assurance that an outbreak of so deadly a spiritual mania could never recur." But this makes histories of witchcraft in the mid-nineteenth century seem quite safe, whereas in fact it was the urgent (and futile) attempt to still such fears that animated the debate about early American witchcraft and made it so pointed (173).

63. Upham, *Salem Witchcraft*, 519, 564–70, xxviii. See also James Russell Lowell, "Witchcraft" in *Among My Books* (1870; London and Toronto: Dent, 1925), 115.

64. William F. Poole, "Cotton Mather and Salem Witchcraft," *North American Review* 108 (April 1869) 337–97, *Cotton Mather and Salem Witchcraft: Two Notices of Mr. Upham his Reply* (1870; n.p.: Kessinger, 2006) 5–6, 12, 21–23; *Dictionary of American Biography*, ed. Dumas Malone (New York: Charles Scribner's Sons, 1936); Charles W. Upham, *Salem Witchcraft and Cotton Mather: A Reply* (Morrisana, New York, 1869). The controversy is discussed in Frederick C. Drake, 694–95. It continued as Poole accused Abner C. Goodell of partiality on Upham's behalf (*Two Notices*, 29–30, and see also Abner C. Goodell, *Further Notes on the History of Witchcraft in Massachusetts* [Cambridge, MA, 1884] and G. H. Moore, *Final Notes on Witchcraft in Massachusetts* [New York, 1885]). Poole's was not the first attack on Upham by conservative churchgoers, although it was the most vehement and sustained (Le Beau in Upham, *Salem Witchcraft*, xvi).

65. Forrest Morgan, "Witchcraft in Connecticut," *American Historical Magazine* 1 (1906): 237; Charles H. Levermore, "Witchcraft in Connecticut," *New England Magazine* 12:5 (July 1892): 636.

66. J. Hammond Trumbull, ed., *The Public Records of the Colony of Connecticut* (Hartford: Brown and Parsons, 1850), vol. 1, 573. Trumbull found Connecticut's first witchcraft case (Alse Young, 1647), although the record that he saw first gave her no name, as related in Annie E. Trumbull, "One Blank of Windsor," *Hartford Courant Literary Supplement* (December 3 1904): 11.

67. Demos, *Entertaining*, 340; Wethersfield Historical Society Teachers' Pack; Sherman W. Adams and Henry R. Stiles, *The History of Ancient Wethersfield* (1904; Wethersfield, CT: New Hampshire Publishing and Wethersfield Historical Society, 1974), vol. 1, 680 (original emphasis); *DAB*.

68. Gummere; John M. Taylor, *The Witchcraft Delusion in Colonial Connecticut 1647–1697* (New York: Grafton, 1908), 36, 25.
69. Adams and Stiles, 680, 684.
70. Samuel G. Drake, preface to *The Witchcraft Delusion in New England*, 3 vols. (Roxbury, 1866), vol. 1, lxiii.
71. Charles H. Levermore, "Witchcraft in Connecticut," *The New Englander and Yale Review* 44:189 (1885): 788–89.
72. As Drake points out, 76, 86. New England did first disregard witchcraft accusations: Maryland and England both held their last witch trials in 1712 (Virtue Violl and Jane Wenham), and Virginia in 1730 (above), while in New England they ceased after the trial of Winifred Benham in Connecticut in 1697. The records of Knapp's case are now lost. New Haven did not convict its witches, but did banish two of them (Nicholas Bayley and his unnamed wife) and imprisoned a third upon suspicion before a final release (Elizabeth Godman, above); Plymouth tried and acquitted Mary Ingham of Scituate in 1676, and Rhode Island's accused witches did not proceed to trial (see Demos, *Entertaining*, 402–9, and Laulainen-Schein, 410–12 for summary tables, and Phyllis J. Guskin, "The Context of Witchcraft: The Case of Jane Wenham 1712," *Eighteenth-Century Studies* 15:1 (Autumn, 1981): 48–71).
73. 7 August 1655, "New Haven Town Records 1649–56," 175, New Haven Colony Historical Society, Whitney Library.
74. Levermore, "Witchcraft in Connecticut," *New England Magazine*: 637.
75. Levermore, *New Englander* 789, *New England Magazine*: 637–38, 641.
76. Drake, *Annals*, xxxiv–xxxv.
77. W. C. Elam, "Old Times in Virginia and a Few Parallels," *Putnam's Magazine* 14:20 (1869): 207. Elam described himself as a Virginian, and his article reflected the division in Virginia itself between Confederacy and Union.
78. Edward Ingle, "A Virginia Witch," *Magazine of American History* 10:5 (November 1883): 425–27; John Esten Cooke, "Grace Sherwood, the One Virginia Witch," *Harper's Magazine* (June 1884): 99–102; Edward W. James, "Grace Sherwood the Virginia Witch," *William and Mary Quarterly Historical Magazine* 3:2 (1894): 96–101; 3:3 (1895): 190–2; 3:4 (1895): 242–45; and 4:1 (1895): 18–22. The editorship of the modernizing college president Lyon G. Tyler must have encouraged James's writing. He also mentioned the cases of Barbara Wingborough (1657), Katherine Grady (hanged at sea, 1658), Alice Stephens (1668), and an anonymous woman and her children who brought a slander suit (4:1, 18); 3:2, 96, n.1 and published "Witchcraft in Virginia," WMQ 2:1 (July 1893): 58–60 and "Witchcraft in Virginia," WMQ 1:3 (January 1893):127–29.
79. Elam, 208–15; the rhetoric of race in witchcraft history will be discussed in Chapter Three.
80. John Gorham Palfrey, *History of New England* (Boston, 1877), vol. 3, 131.

81. George Lyman Kittredge, *Witchcraft in Old and New England* (Cambridge, MA: Harvard University Press, 1929), prefatory note, 329–39, 357, 359–61, 364–65, 367–70. Chapter 18 of the book is an almost unchanged version of Kittredge's "Notes on Witchcraft" in the *Proceedings of the American Antiquarian Society*, new series 18 (1907), 148–212.

82. See Ian Bostridge, *Witchcraft and Its Transformations c. 1650–c. 1750* (Oxford: Clarendon, 1997); Stuart Clark, *Thinking with Demons: The Idea of Witchcraft in Early Modern Europe* (Oxford, England: Clarendon, 1997), made the latter point to deserved acclaim.

83. George Lincoln Burr, "New England's Place in the History of Witchcraft," in Ronald H. Bainton, *George Lincoln Burr, His Life* with Lois Oliphant Gibbons, ed., *Selections from his Writings* (Ithaca and New York: Cornell University Press, 1943), 354.

84. Bainton and Gibbons, eds., 353–56.

85. Bainton and Gibbons, eds., 4–5, 312–13, 375–77. Burr explored these notions also in "The Literature of Witchcraft" *Papers of the American Historical Association* 4:4 (1889–90): 37–66. The Kittredge-Burr debate is also discussed in Frederick C. Drake, 695–96.

86. Alice Robertson, "A Biographical Study of George Lyman Kittredge," M.A. thesis, University of Maine, 1947, 41; Clyde Kenneth Hyder, *George Lyman Kittredge, Teacher and Scholar* (Lawrence, Kansas: University of Kansas Press, 1962); the Bok prize was regarded as so un-American by some that it was investigated by the Senate Special Committee on Propaganda — see Elaine M. Anderson, "Eleanor Roosevelt and the Bok Peace Prize," *Historical Perspectives* (March 2004): 1–14.

87. Shirley Jackson, *The Witchcraft of Salem Village* (1956; New York: Random House, 2001), 1.

## Chapter 2

1. Richard Malcolm Johnston, "Our Witch," *Century Magazine* 53 (n.s. 31) (March 1897): 760; William Carlos Williams, *Tituba's Children* (1948) in *Many Loves and Other Plays* (New York: New Directions, 1961), 288.

2. Charles L. Crow, ed., *American Gothic: An Anthology 1787–1916* (Oxford: Blackwell, 1999), 113.

3. Henry Wadsworth Longfellow, *Giles Corey of the Salem Farms* in *The New England Tragedies* (London, 1868), Act 5, Scene 4, lines 13–14. A similar line is taken by Mary E. Wilkins (Freeman)'s play *Giles Corey, Yeoman* (New York, 1893).

4. William P. Upham, *Account of the Rebecca Nurse Monument* (Salem, Massachusetts, 1886), 3–5. For the Upham family's witchcraft industry see also Caroline E. Upham, *Salem Witchcraft in Outline* (Salem, 1891). Caroline was Charles's daughter-in-law.

5. William P. Upham, 12 (from Milton's Sonnet XV, "On the Late Massacre in Piedmont").

6. As Longfellow's play suggests, the three other best-known candidates for memorialization would have been Giles Corey (litigious and suspected of beating a servant to death), Bridget Bishop (thought to be a tavern-keeper who wore a racy red bodice — but see Rosenthal 67–85), and Tituba (enslaved, Indian although often thought to be black, suspected of having really practiced some kind of magic, and thus politically problematic in a range of conflicting ways — see Chapter 3).

7. William P. Upham, 3, 29, 24, 5.

8. For Poole, see Chapter One.

9. William P. Upham, 15–17, 22.

10. William P. Upham, 29–30, 25–26.

11. See also John Greenleaf Whittier, *Legends of New England* (1831; Gainesville, FL: Scholar's Facsimiles and Reprints, 1965) for other writings on witchcraft. There are many rather undistinguished fictions of this period which like "O Christian martyr" romanticize innocent witches, such as Pauline Bradford Mackie's *Ye Lyttle Salem Maide: A Story of Witchcraft* (1898; Boston: L.C. Page, 1903).

12. Williams's play has the Puritans and witches of 1692 transform onstage into senators and accused Communists, while Miller's remains in the seventeenth century throughout. See also Kim Newman, "The McCarthy Witch Hunt," a short story in which Goodwife Samantha Stevens is interrogated by the Committee on Un-Christian Activities, at http://www.infinityplus.co.uk/stories/mccarthy.htm (accessed 18 October 2006).

13. Marvin Dana, *The Puritan Witch: A Romance* (New York and London: Smart Set Publishing, 1903).

14. James J. Martine, *The Crucible: Politics, Property and Pretense* (New York: Twayne, 1993), 61–3; Arthur Miller, "Why I Wrote *The Crucible*," *The New Yorker* (October 21 and 28, 1996), reprinted in Hill, *Salem Witch Trials Reader*, 386 and Miller, *The Crucible: A Screenplay* (London: Methuen, 1996). See also Martin Gottfried, *Arthur Miller: A Life* (New York: Da Capo, 2003), 203–26, 266, 286–92, and Sarah Churchwell, *The Many Lives of Marilyn Monroe* (London, England: Granta, 2004) 253–66.

15. Miller may also have drawn inspiration from Marion Starkey's portrayal of John and Elizabeth Proctor and their servant Mary Warren, who dislikes Elizabeth, feels that she makes her husband miserable, and is pleased when she is "put away," but feels "respect if not . . . love" for John (Marion L. Starkey, *The Devil in Massachusetts: A Modern Inquiry into the Salem Witch Trials* [1949; New York: Time Inc., 1963], 87). On the play's misogyny, see Joseph Valente, "Rehearsing the Witch Trials: Gender Injustice in *The Crucible*," *New Formations* 32 (1997): 120–34; and Wendy Schissel, "Re(dis)covering the Witches in Arthur Miller's *The Crucible*: A Feminist Reading," *Modern Drama* 37 (1994): 461–73.

16. Personal conversations in Salem, summer 2003.

17. Richard B. Trask, *"The Devil Hath Been Raised": A Documentary History of the Salem Village Witchcraft Outbreak of March 1692*, rev. ed. (Danvers, MA: Yeoman Press, 1997), 6.

18. Pamela E. Apkarian-Russell, *A Collector's Guide to Salem Witchcraft and Souvenirs* (Atglen, PA: Schiffer, 1998) — the book is dedicated the memory of the "witches" and to Holocaust survivors; Roach, 586.

19. For example, David C. Brown, *A Guide to the Salem Witchcraft Hysteria of 1692* (n.p.: n.p., 1984) and Frances Hill, *Hunting for Witches: A Visitor's Guide to the Salem Witch Trials* (Beverly, MA: Commonwealth Editions, 2002); *Three Sovereigns for Sarah*, dir. Philip Leacock, Night Owl Productions/American Playhouse/National Endowment for the Humanities, 1985.

20. John Hardy Wright's *Sorcery at Salem* contains photographs of many of Salem's witches, their rituals and businesses, as well as of the witchcraft memorials (Charleston, SC: Arcadia, 1999).

21. The show has been variously reviewed as "though simplified . . . the best available introduction to the witch trials, bringing the events and people to life" (Hill, *Hunting*, 88) and "one of the worst things I've ever seen. A complete joy" (Sandi Toksvig, *The Gladys Society: A Personal American Journey* [London, England: Little, Brown, 2002], 247).

22. Trask, x.

23. Roach, 587–88.

24. The name is spelt variously (see below) but I have standardized it in my own text as Disborough, the most common spelling.

25. 29 May 1654, Court of Magistrates records, 51–58, New Haven Colony Historical Society, Whitney Library.

26. The surviving documentation is split between the Wyllys Papers at Brown University (John Hay Library) and Samuel Wyllys Papers at the Connecticut State Library, Hartford. The quotations above are from the Brown collection (Wyllys Papers Box 1).

27. Wyllys and Samuel Wyllys Papers; Ronald Marcus, *Elizabeth Clawson: Thou Deservest to Die* (Stamford, CT: Stamford Historical Society, 1976).

28. Wyllys Papers Box 1. See also, *Richard Godbeer, Escaping Salem: The Other Witch Hunt of 1692* (Oxford: Oxford University Press, 2005) and Tomlinson.

29. Anon., *The Witches: A Tale of New England* (Bath, 1837); Frank Samuel Child, *A Colonial Witch: Being a Study of the Black Art in the Colony of Connecticut* (New York, 1897), 9–10, 235–37, 276. Child was well informed about Connecticut's witchcraft history — more so than most of the historians of his day. His sources included the records of the General Court and some knowledge of the Essex county trials, as well as reading on some English cases.

30. Child, 35, 15–18, 94–95, 42, 56, 61, 74, 86, 96–98, 115, 200, 245–247, 265.

31. Mary Wilson, "Witchcraft and Witches" in *A Story of Fairfield: Essays Delivered by the Honor Students of the Class of 1932* (Fairfield, CT: Roger Ludlowe High School, n.d.), 7–8.
32. Stephen Taylor Squires, "Search for Westport Relative Uncovers Truth about Witches" and "Man Finds Odd Coincidences in Family History," *Fairfield Minuteman* 9 March (pp. 3, 30) and 26 October (pages B3, B6), 1995.
33. Michael S. Disbrow, *Descendants of Thomas and Mercy (Holbridge) Disbrow* (Manton, MI: Disbrow Family Association, 1992), 45.
34. Lawrence Cortesi, "Was Mercy Desborough In League With the Devil?," *Connecticut* (October 1972): 27, 46; and "The Beautiful Witch of Fairfield," *Cobblestone* (January 1981): 16–19.
35. Disbrow, 33–4, 45.
36. Susann Disboro-Davis, "God Hath Mercy: The Journal of Mercy Holbrook Nichols Desborough" (unpublished typescript, gift of the author to Fairfield Historical Society, now Fairfield Museum & History Center).
37. For witch ancestry see also Associated Daughters of Early American Witches at http://www.adeaw.us/.
38. Mike Patrick, "Within the Circle of the Craft," *Connecticut Post* 11 August 1996 A1, A12–13. Mercy Disborough was also the subject of *The Accused*, a *Hallmark Hall of Fame* dramatization, in 1953. *The Accused*, written by William L. Stuart and directed by Albert McCleery, starred Sarah Churchill and was broadcast on 1 March. The broadcasts were usually transmitted live and the performance is probably lost: Hallmark has no knowledge of the whereabouts of the screenplay.
39. For Karlsen see Chapter 3.
40. Mary Jeanne Anderson Jones, *Congregational Commonwealth: Connecticut* (Middletown, CT: Wesleyan University Press, 1968); interpretive panel, "Hearts Against Hearts" exhibition. Courtesy of Wethersfield Historical Society.
41. Essays by E. K. Beyer, D. Andrews, L. Dzionkonski and M. Myers, D. Ruffino and R. Skolnick, S. Hale, E. W. Charlson, and J. Stratton, Wethersfield Historical Society.
42. For comparison, see http://www.pem.org/visit/ed_curriculum.php (Peabody Essex Museum, Salem, teachers' pack).
43. Elizabeth George Speare, *The Witch of Blackbird Pond* (1958; New York: Bantam Doubleday, 1987), 24–25, 83, 128–29. See Karlsen, 84–89, for an approach to Harrison that represents her as a threat to her neighbors in economic, social, and gendered terms.
44. Speare, 221.
45. John Carrington was said to have sold a gun to Native Americans, while Harrison was disliked for her litigious and quarrelsome behavior. Mary Johnson was also confused with Elizabeth Johnson, who had been convicted of adultery. That Mary should be sexually transgressive was a gift for those who believed Puritan intolerance caused witchcraft accusations.

See William K. Holdsworth, "Adultery or Witchcraft? A New Note on an Old Case in Connecticut," *New England Quarterly* 48:3 (September 1975): 394–409.

46. Speare, 250.

47. Catharine Maria Sedgwick, *Hope Leslie: Or, Early Times in the Massachusetts* (1827; New York: Penguin, 1998), 107–17; Native American spirits were frequently mentioned as associating with Christian witches, but Native Americans were not drawn into subsequent investigations despite the later creation of laws to facilitate this (e.g., Drake, 136–37).

48. Shurtleff, ed., vol. 4, part 1, 96, and Records of the Court of Assistants 13 May 1651, 24 October 1651; Hale, *A Modest Enquiry*, 19.

49. See Stanley Waters, "Witchcraft in Springfield, Massachusetts," *New England Historical and Genealogical Register* 35 (1881): 152–53 for some of the "missing" depositions.

50. There are a few other related works, none of them historically grounded. For example, in the Springfield-born writer Herbert Gorman's *The Place Called Dagon* (1927; New York: Hippocampus, 2003) the nearby towns of Leominster and Marlborough are home to a sect of devil-worshippers descended from those who fled Salem in 1692.

51. Josiah Gilbert Holland, *The Bay Path: A Tale of New England Colonial Life* (New York, 1891).

52. Buell, 251.

53. Holland, vii–x, 5.

54. Buell, 252.

55. J. G. Holland, "God, Give us Men!" from *Wanted* (New York, 1872), 122.

56. Similarly in De Forest's *Witching Times*, Samuel Parris is made an ignorant Cockney and the Salem witches' other accusers are equally oafish (39, 48, 103).

57. Holland, 218, 254, 261, 265, 280. As he says of Mary Pynchon, "moral and intellectual growth" cease in a woman while she is "waiting for a mate" (73).

58. Holland, 291–94.

59. Records of Hampshire County Court (HCC), Connecticut Valley Historical Museum, Springfield 27 September 1664, 26 September 1665, 27 March 1666, 29 September 1672; S. G. Drake, 225; Stephen Innes, *Labor in a New Land: Economy and Society in Seventeenth-Century Springfield* (Princeton: Princeton University Press, 1983), 70–71.

60. Demos, *Entertaining*, 263–65. Lyman was later a selectman and committeeman, who died in 1662 leaving an estate valued at over £500.

61. Massachusetts Archives Middlesex County Court records fol. 15, group 1; HCC 30 January 1669; S. G. Drake, 228; Innes, 101–03. Innes sees Matthews as irascible and slothful, but the evidence of neglect of his business, his child, and of drinking is primarily from the period after Pentecost was murdered by Native Americans in 1675.

62. Holland, 25, 30–31, 62, 91–92, 19–20, 218, 280, 353.

63. Demos, *Entertaining*, 246, 257, 260–69.
64. Demos, 258–59.
65. Demos, 258, 262, 267.
66. http://ccbit.cs.umass.edu/parsons/hnmockup/ and http://ccbit.cs.umass.edu/parsons/goodyparsons. Thanks to Kerry W. Buckley and Bridget Marshall at Historic Northampton for explaining their project.
67. Massachusetts Archive Middlesex County Court records fol. 15 group 1. See also Chapter 4.
68. See *The Great Pink Scare*, dir. Tug Tourgrau and Dan Miller (PBS/Independent Lens, premiered 6 June 2006) and http://www.pbs.org/independentlens/greatpinkscare; Christopher Heredia, "Joel Dorius — Gay Professor in '60s Porn Scandal," *Chronicle,* 19 February 2006 (obituary), n.p.
69. Beale Davis; Laulainen-Schein; Isobel Gough, "Witchcraft — Northumberland County Style," *Northumberland County Historical Society Bulletin* 5 (1968), 52–57; Ivor Noel Hume, "Witchcraft and Evil Spirits: Weird Sisters, Hand in Hand," *Colonial Williamsburg* 21:1 (Autumn 1998):14–19; Florence Kimberley Turner, *Gateway to the New World: A History of Princess Anne County, Virginia 1607–1824* (Easley, SC: Southern Historical Press, 1984), 78–82; Ed Chews, "A Shadowy Side of Early American History: Witch Bottles, Hidden Shoes, Amulets and Charms," *Colonial Williamsburg* 23:2 (Summer 2001): 32–37; Elizabeth Dabney Coleman, "The Witchcraft Delusion Rejected," *Virginia Cavalcade* 6:1 (Summer 1956): 28–34; Virginia Lunsford, "The Witch in Colonial Virginia: A Question of Gender and Family Relations," *Northern Neck Historical Magazine* 43:1 (1993): 5007–16; W. Preston Haynie, "Witchcraft — An Outcry of Public Hysteria, Paranoia or a Belief of the Time?," *Bulletin of the Northumberland County History Society* 28 (1991): 33–39.
70. Personal conversations in Virginia 2004, 2006; S. E. Schlosser, *Spooky South: Tales of Hauntings, Strange Happenings, and Other Local Lore* (Guilford, CT: Globe Pequot Press, 2004).
71. Louisa Venable Kyle, *The Witch of Pungo* (Virginia Beach, VA: Four O'Clock Farms Publishing, 1973) 43–52; Beverly Campbell, "When Virginia Ducked Milady Witch," *Richmond Times-Dispatch* 30 December 1934 archived at http://richmondthenandnow.com/Newspaper-Articles/Witch-Grace-Sherwood.html (accessed 28 March 2005); George Holbert Tucker, *Virginia Supernatural Tales: Ghosts, Witches and Eerie Doings* (Norfolk, VA: Donning, 1977), 97–104. A badly written and racist novel, James T. Bowyer's *The Witch of Jamestown*, invented a witch called Mrs. Grindon to be a scapegoat for political tensions during Bacon's Rebellion (Richmond, VA, 1890).
72. Carson Hudson, *Cry Witch!*, performance at Colonial Williamsburg 5 July 2006. Voting not guilty: 30 including myself; voting guilty: 47. See also John Witt, "Story of Accused Sorceress' Trial by Water in State is Bewitching Tale," *Richmond Times-Dispatch* 31 October 1989.

73. Ian Shapira, "After Toil and Trouble, Witch is Cleared," *The Washington Post*, Metro section, 12 July 2006, B1–2.

74. Tamara El-Khoury, "Witchduck Witch Ducked for Re-Enactment," *The Virginian-Pilot*, 11 July 2003, archived at http://home.hamptonroads.com/stories/story.cfm?story=56802&ran=28970 (accessed 5 September 2003).

75. *The Blair Witch Project*, dir. Daniel Myrick and Eduardo Sanchez, Artisan, 1999; *Blair Witch Two: Book of Shadows*, dir. Joe Berlinger, Artisan, 2000. The fake documentaries made by Ben Rock and other production team members to publicize the films perpetuate their fiction in a number of ways, alongside Web sites. One way is by making multiple, naturalistically differing, versions of the central myth. Some characters in the "mockumentaries" regard Heather, Josh, and Mike's disappearance as a student prank. One film, *The Burkittsville 7*, suggests that Rustin Parr's hostage, Kyle Brody, who escaped to reveal Parr's crimes, is actually the perpetrator or inspiration for them himself. The documentaries (*The Curse of the Blair Witch*, *Shadow of the Blair Witch*, and *The Burkittsville 7*) are available on the DVD versions of both movies.

76. See Philip Love, "Witch of St. Mary's Moll Dyer Lives on in Legend — and a Rock," *Baltimore Sun* supplement (20 October 1974): 24–26.

77. Alyce T. Weinberg, *Spirits of Frederick* (Frederick, Maryland: Studio 20, 1979), 69, 59, 54, 67; George C. Carey, *Maryland Folklore and Folklife* (Cambridge, MD: Tidewater, 1970), 38; Madeleine Vinton Dahlgren, *South Mountain Magic* (Boston, 1882) 162–75. See also Annie Weston Whitney and Caroline Canfield Bullock, *Folk-Lore from Maryland* (New York: American Folklore Society, 1925).

78. "Still Valley," *The Twilight Zone*, dir. James Sheldon, 24 November 1961. The episode was written by Rod Serling, based on a 1939 story, "The Valley was Still" by Manly Wade Wellman (Jean-Marc and Randy Lofficer, *Into the Twilight Zone: The Rod Serling Programme Guide* [London: Virgin, 1995], 39).

79. The nearest thing to a full history is Francis Neal Parke's pamphlet *Witchcraft in Maryland*. It has no publication details and is undated, but was based on "Witchcraft in Maryland," *Maryland Historical Magazine* 31 (December 1936) and is at the Maryland Historical Society.

80. Carey, ix, 93.

81. For Maryland's strengthened interest in folklore, see, for example, http://www.wam.umd.edu/~dschloss/Legends/index.htm (University of Maryland Legends Collection). See also David Dishneau, "Witchcraft as a Part of Maryland's Past," *Washington Times*, 11 October 2004, at http://washingtontimes.com/metro/20041010-102416-3747r.htm (accessed 12 October 2006).

*Chapter 3*

1. L. Frank Baum, *The Marvelous Land of Oz* (1904) in *Fifteen Books in One: The Original Oz Series* (n.p.: Shoes and Ships and Sealing Wax, 2005), 52.
2. See Barbara Weisberg, *Talking to the Dead: Kate and Maggie Fox and the Rise of Spiritualism* (New York: HarperSanFrancisco, 2004).
3. See David D. Hall, *Witch-hunting in Seventeenth-Century New England: A Documentary History 1638–93*, 2nd. ed. (Boston: Northeastern University Press, 1999), 22.
4. George M. Beard, *The Psychology of the Salem Witchcraft Excitement of 1692 and its Practical Application to our own Time* (1882; Stratford, CT: John E. Edwards, 1971), vi; on Nicholson see Rhodri Hayward, "Demonology, Neurology and Medicine in Edwardian Britain," *Bulletin of the History of Medicine* 78:1 (March 2004): 37–58. Beard's electrization treatment — the passing of a mild current through the patient's body — was part of S. Weir Mitchell's famous "rest cure," which inspired Charlotte Perkins Gilman's *The Yellow Wallpaper*. See also Dona L. Davis, "George Beard and Lydia Pinkham: Gender, Class and Nerves in Late Nineteenth-Century America," *Health Care for Women International* 10:2/3 (1989): 93–114.
5. There are similar tendencies in more recent medical theories about witchcraft: Ernest Caulfield, "Pediatric Aspects of the Salem Witchcraft Tragedy," *American Journal of Diseases of Children* 65 (May 1943): 788–802 (hysteria) and Linnda R. Caporael's "Ergotism: The Satan Loosed in Salem?," *Science* 192 (2 April 1976): 21–26, echoed in Mary Kilbourne Matossian, *Poisons of the Past: Molds, Epidemics, and History* (New Haven and London: Yale University Press, 1989), 113–22. The ergot theory has been rebutted by Nicholas P. Spanos and Jack Gottlieb, "Ergotism and the Salem Village Witchcraft Trials," *Science* 94 (24 December 1976): 1390–94.
6. Beard's use of the "Salem" trials as a background to his theory is a tradition that has continued: most recently with Richard A. Gardner, *Sex Abuse Hysteria: Salem Witchcraft Trials Revisited* (Cresskill, NJ: Creative Therapeutics, 1991) and Stuart Bell, *When Salem Came to the Boro: The True Story of the Cleveland Child Abuse Cases* (London, England: Pan, 1988). See also Lynley Hood, *A City Possessed: The Christchurch Civic Creche Case* (Dunedin, New Zealand: Longacre, 2001), on witch hunting and allegations of child sexual abuse.
7. D. R. Castleton, *Salem: A Tale of the Seventeenth Century* (New York: 1874), 58–59.
8. Anon., *Salem: An Eastern Tale*; for Dana see Chapter Two; Henry Peterson, *Dulcibel: A Tale of Old Salem* (Philadelphia: John C. Winston, 1907); Henry William Herbert, *The Fair Puritan: An Historical Romance of the Days of Witchcraft*. The novel was published as a fragment in 1845, in parts in 1853, and prepared for publication in book form in 1856, but printing was stopped when the publishers went bankrupt. It was rediscovered and published by J. B. Lippincott in 1875. See G. Harrison Orians, "New England Witchcraft in

Fiction," *American Literature* 2:1 (March 1930): 62, an indispensable list of such fiction including some works not discussed here (although also omitting some).

9. Nathaniel Hawthorne, *The Scarlet Letter*, ed. Seymour Gross, Sculley Bradley, Richmond Croom Beatty, and E. Hudson Long (1850; New York and London: W.W. Norton, 1988). See also, Karl P. Wentersdorf, "The Element of Witchcraft in The Scarlet Letter," *Folklore* 83 (Summer 1972): 132–53). "Young Goodman Brown" in Crow, ed., 113–20. For a story that, like *The House of the Seven Gables*, links past and present in a meditation on fiction and memory, see "Alice Doane's Appeal" also in Crow, ed. 106–13.
10. Nathaniel Hawthorne, *The House of the Seven Gables* (1851; London: Dent, 1970), 40–41, 77, 34, 52.
11. Hawthorne, *House*, 90, 45, 154.
12. Hawthorne, *House*, 197–203.
13. Matilda Joslyn Gage, *Woman, Church and State* (1893; Amherst, NY: Prometheus Books, 2002), 278. For a history of occultism in America, see Howard Kerr and Charles L. Crow, eds., *The Occult in America: New Historical Perspectives* (Urbana and Chicago: University of Illinois Press, 1986).
14. David D. Hall, "Witchcraft and the Limits of Interpretation," *New England Quarterly* 58:2 (June 1985): 274.
15. Leila R. Brammer, *Excluded from Suffrage History: Matilda Joslyn Gage, Nineteenth-Century American Feminist* (Westport, CT: Greenwood Press, 2000), 1–19.
16. Jacob Kramer and Heinrich Sprenger, *Malleus Maleficarum* (1486), ed. and trans. Montague Summers (New York: Dover, 1971).
17. Jules Michelet, *La Sorcière*, retitled *Satanism and Witchcraft*, trans. A. R. Allinson (1862; London: Tandem, 1965); Joslyn Gage, 231, 236–37, 238–39, 249, 272, 510.
18. Sally Roesch Wagner confirms that many of the books used by Joslyn Gage are in Syracuse University library and that she probably also used the Onondaga County Public Library. E-mail correspondence 10 August 2006.
19. Starkey, *Devil*, ix–xii.
20. The Emory psychiatrist Erikson's *Wayward Puritans* is the classic mythic statement of this "school."
21. Starkey, *Devil*, 10–11.
22. Starkey, *Devil*, 8–9. Her portrayal had not changed by 1973 when Starkey wrote *The Visionary Girls: Witchcraft in Salem Village* (Boston and Toronto: Little, Brown), although Starkey was now happy to admit that "I have invented the scenes with Tituba . . . but they are what I believe really happened" (ix), and Tituba had become softer and more honest (13, 17–18).
23. Starkey, *Devil*, xxiv.
24. W.W. *A true and just Recorde* (London, 1582) 2A7–v.
25. For example, Keith Thomas, *Religion and the Decline of Magic* (1971; London: Peregrine, 1978), and Barbara Rosen, *Witchcraft in England 1558–1618* (1969; Amherst: University of Massachusetts Press, 1991).

26. Barbara Ehrenreich and Deirdre English, *Witches, Midwives and Nurses: A History of Women Healers* (New York: The Feminist Press at the City University of New York, 1973), 3, 6–8, 14, 17–18, 41–3. On Ehrenreich and English, and feminist histories of witchcraft generally, see Diane Purkiss, *The Witch in History: Early Modern and Twentieth Century Representations* (London and New York: Routledge, 1996), 19–20 and 7–29.

27. See David Harley, "Historians as Demonologists: The Myth of the Midwife-Witch," *Social History of Medicine* 3:1 (1990): 1–26.

28. Essex Institute, Essex County Court records fol. 15, 61:1, 62:2, 63:1.

29. Hall, *Witch-Hunting*, 20.

30. Massachusetts Archives, Middlesex County Court records, fol. 25.

31. See also Norman Gevitz, "The Devil hath Laughed at the Physicians: Witchcraft and Medical Practice in Seventeenth-Century New England," *Journal of the History of Medicine* 55 (January 2000): 5–36.

32. Selma R. Williams and Pamela Williams Adelman, *Riding the Nightmare: Women and Witchcraft from the Old World to Colonial Salem* (1978; New York: HarperPerennial, 1992), 3.

33. Karlsen, xiii–xv.

34. Unsurprisingly, the powerful and wealthy witch was infrequently represented in fiction before the late twentieth century. An exception of a kind is Lucy Foster Madison's *A Maid of Salem Towne* (1906; New York: Grosset and Dunlap, 1934), where a young girl, Delight English, is accused by her wicked uncle, whose family will inherit her fortune if she is executed.

35. Karlsen, 264, 263. A good example is Wethersfield's Mary Johnson, tried in 1648 and hanged. Mary was traditionally portrayed as "unchaste and light-fingered" (Forrest Morgan, 220), until it was realized that she was being confused with Elizabeth Johnson, who was convicted of adultery. See Holdsworth, "Adultery or Witchcraft?" Karlsen was joined in her analysis by Jane Kamensky, who argued that "the threat of disorderly speech — particularly *female* speech — played a pivotal role in New England's witchcraft beliefs" in "Words, Witches and Woman Trouble: Witchcraft, Disorderly Speech and Gender Boundaries in Puritan New England," *Essex Institute Historical Collections* 128 (1992): 288.

36. Karlsen, 262. See also Elizabeth Reis, *Damned Women: Sinners and Witches in Puritan New England* (Ithaca and London: Cornell University Press, 1997).

37. Norton, 4, 17, 328, 416. For a useful anthology that underscores many of the themes of this chapter, see Elizabeth Reis, ed., *Spellbound: Women and Witchcraft in America* (Wilmington, DE: S.R. Books, 1998).

38. http://extext.virginia.edu/salem/witchcraft/texts/BoySal1.html lists Mary Black and Candy's examinations, and two indictments of Candy for bewitching Mary Walcot and Ann Putnam. Their supposed crimes and their responses to them do not suggest any difference from the kinds of witchcraft of which white people were being simultaneously accused, or any particularly racist motivation among their accusers. However,

Candy's statement about learning witchcraft from her white "owner" in Massachusetts seems a deliberate attempt to rebut accusations of the kind later made against Tituba Indian: namely that she had imported witchcraft from her own culture to America. On black witches, see Timothy J. McMillan, "Black Magic: Witchcraft, Race and Resistance in Colonial New England," *Journal of Black Studies* 25:1 (September 1994): 99–117. Some of McMillan's assertions are unsubstantiated, but the relationship between blackness and witchcraft urgently needs further investigation. A useful selection of culturally diverse scholarship is in Elaine G. Breslaw's *Witches of the Atlantic World: A Historical Reader and Primary Sourcebook* (New York and London: New York University Press, 2000), 169–86.

39. Peterson, 18.
40. William Carlos Williams, 226, 232, 239.
41. Shirley Barker, *Peace My Daughters* (New York: Crown, 1949), 47–52. This mars an otherwise interesting story, which seems a precursor to Updike's *The Witches of Eastwick* (see Chapter Four). Barker also wrote "The Ballad of Betsy Staire" in her volume of poetry *The Dark Hills Under* (New Haven: Yale University Press, 1933), 20–21
42. Hale, 132; Charles W. Upham, xvi, 318, 334–37, 578.
43. See among many others Starkey, *Devil*, 8–9 ("Tituba yielded to the temptation to show the children . . . fragments of something like voodoo" and they paid "almost hypnotic attention to the slurred Southern speech"); Ann Rinaldi, *A Break with Charity* (Orlando, FL: Harcourt Brace, 1992), 19–31; Shirley Barker, 47. These portrayals owe much to Charles W. Upham, something to Hale, but also to Longfellow, whose Tituba is a witch in the tradition of Shakespeare's *Macbeth* ("I, Tituba, an Indian and a slave, / Am . . . mightier than Ministers and Magistrates . . . I have the Evil Eye, the Evil Hand . . . Thus I work vengeance on mine enemies, / Who, while they call me slave, are slaves to me" (*Giles Corey*, 1.1.11–29, and 1.3 *passim*).
44. Castleton, 71–8.
45. Perley spoke of "the ignorance of the Spanish population" (18).
46. Jackson, 14–16.
47. Ann Petry, *Tituba of Salem Village* (New York: HarperTrophy, 1964), 96–98, 106–7, 118–20.
48. Rinaldi, 21–26. See also Milton Meltzer, *Witches and Witch-Hunts: A History of Persecution* (New York: Scholastic, 1999).
49. Maryse Condé, *I Tituba, Black Witch of Salem*, trans. Richard Philcox (1986; New York: Ballantyne Books, 1992) with a Foreword by Angela Y. Davis, 3, 8, 17, 29–34, 51–54, 69, 85, 172, xi. Condé's interview with Ann Armstrong Scarboro is printed as part of an Afterword, 187–225. For a critique of the novel as distorting history see McWilliams 181–4. Like Davis's Foreword, arguments about historical correctness versus imagination are often inflected with anxiety about political correctness or racist assumptions — Davis even suggests that those who first disputed Tituba's African

origin may have been "hoping to stir up enmity between black and Native American women," although there is no evidence of this in the accounts discussed here. An antiracist impulse is more evident.

50. Elaine G. Breslaw, *Tituba, Reluctant Witch of Salem: Devilish Indians and Puritan Fantasies* (New York and London: New York University Press, 1996), xvii, xxi–ii, 13–41

51. Breslaw, *Tituba*, 120, 126, 142. There are other examples where an interesting reading is perhaps given too much weight: *kenaimas* were said by nineteenth-century anthropologists to have a preference for birds as accompaniments or shape-shifting alter egos, and Breslaw suggests the famous yellow bird seen by the afflicted at Salem has its origin in Arawak culture. But bird familiars and omens were also common in other witchcraft cases; it is not possible to be sure where Tituba's ideas on the subject came from, or how securely they may be related to early modern Arawak beliefs.

52. For example, Marc Aronsen, *Witch-Hunt: Mysteries of the Salem Witch Trials* (New York: Simon and Schuster, 2003) and Peggy Saari, *Witchcraft in America* (Detroit: UXL, 2001), both textbooks for schoolchildren that refer to Tituba as Native American (although Saari portrays her as Carib).

53. Norton, 20–21, 48–50, 296–97, 301.

54. Brammer, 141; Stuart Culver, "Growing Up in Oz," *American Literary History* 4:4 (1992): 607–28.

55. L. Frank Baum, *The Wonderful Wizard of Oz* (1900; London, England: Penguin, 1995), 17–18, 94, 111–14, 126, and *The Marvelous Land of Oz* in *Fifteen Books in One*; Baum's involvement with Populism, with its criticism of established American leadership, has been widely discussed: see Henry M. Littlefield, "*The Wizard of Oz*: Parable on Populism," *American Quarterly* 16:1 (1964): 47–58, Timothy E. Cook, "Another Perspective on Political Authority in Children's Literature: The Fallible Leader in L. Frank Baum and Dr. Seuss," *The Western Political Quarterly* 36:2. (1983): 326–36, Gretchen Ritter, "Silver Slippers and a Golden Cap: L. Frank Baum's *The Wonderful Wizard of Oz* and Historical Memory in American Politics." *Journal of American Studies* 31:2 (1997): 171–202.

56. Sally Roesch Wagner, *Matilda Joslyn Gage: She Who Holds the Sky* (Aberdeen, SD: Sky Carrier Press, 1998), 63.

57. Baum, *Wonderful*, 128, 152; Linda Rohrer Paige, "Wearing the Red Shoes: Dorothy and the Power of the Female Imagination in The Wizard of Oz," *Journal of Popular Film and Television* 23:4 (1996): 146–53.

58. John Fricke, Jay Scarfone, and William Stillman, *The Wizard of Oz* (London, England: Hodder and Stoughton, 1989), 19–20, 23, 24. The film creates a "real-world" equivalent for the Wicked Witch in Miss Gulch, adding a dimension of demonization to Baum's original. As Carol Karlsen points out, Myra Gulch is an assertive and propertied woman turned into a witch in Dorothy's imagination (Karlsen, 318). For a continuation of Baum's trajectory, in which the Wicked Witch is herself rehabilitated, see Gregory

Maguire, *Wicked: The Life and Times of the Wicked Witch of the West* (New York: HarperCollins, 1995). For another iconic wicked witch of the period, see *Snow White and the Seven Dwarfs*, producer, Walt Disney, Disney, 1937.

## Chapter 4

1. "Wiccan Army" bumper sticker slogan.
2. Karen Armstrong, "Introduction" to *Frances Hill, A Delusion of Satan: The Full Story of the Salem Witch Trials* (1995; New York: Da Capo, 1997), x.
3. Michelet, 9.
4. Ronald Hutton, *The Triumph of the Moon: A History of Modern Pagan Witchcraft* (Oxford: Oxford University Press, 1999), vii. Hutton comes close to making the same claim on p. 341, but sees feminist Witchcraft as a "contribution" to the wider tradition rather than a distinct creation in its own right, as I am inclined to see it. This chapter is much indebted to his history of British and American paganism. For Wicca, Witchcraft, and paganism generally, and their distinction from Satanism, see Rosemary Ellen Guiley, *The Encyclopaedia of Witches and Witchcraft*, 2nd. ed. (New York: Checkmark, 1999), and Nevill Drury, *Magic and Witchcraft* (London: Thames and Hudson, 2003).
5. Especially "The Breitmann Ballads," from 1868. Charles Godfrey Leland, *Hans Breitmann's Ballads* (1914; New York: Dover, 1965).
6. The major biography is Elizabeth Robins Pennell's *Charles Godfrey Leland*, 2 vols. (Boston and New York: Houghton Mifflin, 1906). Many thanks to Juliette Wood for letting me read her unpublished article "Gypsies, Tramps and Witches: The Pagan Roots of Charles Godfrey Leland's Witchcraft Research."
7. Charles Godfrey Leland, *Aradia: Gospel of the Witches* (1899; Blaine, WA: Phoenix, 1999), xi; *Gypsy Sorcery and Fortune Telling* (1891; New York: Citadel Press, 1962), 6–10, 13, 17. In his *The Algonquin Legends of New England* (Boston, 1884) and later works, Leland believed he had discovered a connection between Native American and Norse myths. See Thomas C. Parkhill, *Weaving Ourselves into the Land: Charles Godfrey Leland, "Indians," and the Study of Native American Religions* (Albany: SUNY Press, 1997), especially 60–63.
8. Charles Godfrey Leland, "The Witchcraft of Dame Darrel of York," Leland papers, Historical Society of Pennsylvania, Box 14A.
9. Leland, "Witch Ballads," Leland papers, Historical Society of Pennsylvania, Box 19.
10. Especially Charles Godfrey Leland, *Etruscan Roman Remains in Popular Tradition* (New York and London, 1892) and *The Gypsies* (1882; Boston and New York: Houghton Mifflin, 1924). See also Regenia Gagnier, "Cultural Philanthropy, Gypsies and Interdisciplinary Scholars: Dream of a Common Language," *19: Interdisciplinary Studies in the Long Nineteenth Century* 1 (2005) at http://www.19.bbk.ac.uk/Issue1articles/RegeniaGagnierarticle.pdf.

11. Robins Pennell documents Leland's involvement with Transcendental thought and Bronson Alcott, vol. 1, 28–29, 33–35.
12. Leland, *Aradia*, vii, 101.
13. Leland, *Aradia*, 6–7.
14. Leland, *Aradia*, 113. See also Ilaria Serra, "Le Streghe Son Tornate: The Reappearance of Streghe in Italian American Queer Writings," *Journal for the Academic Study of Magic* 1 (2003): 131–60 for a queer reading of Aradian myth.
15. Leland, *Aradia*, vi.
16. Robins Pennell, 31–33, 63.
17. Elliot Rose, *A Razor for a Goat* (1989; Toronto, Buffalo, London: University of Toronto Press, 2003), 214–18.
18. Robins Pennell describes many letters and papers sent by Maddalena to Leland (Robins Pennell, 310). Leland himself told her in a letter that Maddalena had sent him "about 200 pages of this folklore" (Robins Pennell, 342).
19. Robert Mathieson, "Charles G. Leland and the Witches of Italy: The Origins of Aradia" in *Aradia or the Gospel of the Witches: A New Translation*, trans. Mario and Dina Pazzaglini (Blaine, WA: Phoenix, 1998), 54–55. Mathieson gives an extremely detailed analysis in his essay and concludes that Leland did have an Italian MS from which to work, and that it did come from Maddalena. One surviving letter of hers is reproduced (471–73).
20. Leland, "Aradia," Leland papers, Box 14.
21. Mario Pazzaglini, "Leland and the Magical World of Aradia," in *Aradia or the Gospel of the Witches: A New Translation*, 84–88. There is some evidence of bowdlerization too.
22. Mathieson, 37–39.
23. Chas. S. Clifton, "The Significance of Aradia" in *Aradia or the Gospel of the Witches: A New Translation*, 65–66, and see also Clifton, "Leland's Aradia and the Revival of Modern Witchcraft," *The Pomegranate* 1 (1997), 2–27. Hutton later acknowledged that he had perhaps stated this view too "crudely" in *Pagan Religions of the British Isles: Their Nature and Legacy* (Oxford: Blackwell, 1991), 301 (*Triumph*, 438).
24. Obituary for Leland by F. York Powell, *Folk-Lore* 14 (1903), 162–64.
25. See for example his Civil War journalism, which concentrated with unusual commitment on women's experience of the war, with sketches such as "A Patriotic Mother," "A Heroine," "Camp Gals," and a piece on "Mrs. General John Morgan," described as "a very bewitching woman." Leland also wrote with genuine shock about the illiteracy of many "Southern belles" (Leland papers, Box 1).
26. Robins Pennell, 15, 61, 71.
27. Leland, *The Gypsies*, 372. Robins Pennell, 378.
28. Robins Pennell, photograph between 310 and 311. In letters, Leland wrote, "I have found all the principal deities of the Etruscans still existing as spirits or folletti in the Romagna. . . . I believe I am the first to find this out! .

.. It turns out that Maddalena was regularly trained as a witch. . . ." (1891 letter to Robins Pennell, 341), "I went with Roma Lister to visit Maddalena, the witch" (1894 letter to Mary A. Owen, 371). Roma Lister mentioned a woman named Margherita, "the heroine of Mr. Leland's Florentine books," and confirmed that she had visited this woman with him (Roma Lister, *Reminiscences Social and Political* [London, England: Hutchinson, 1925], 123–24), cited in Mathieson, 30–31). Robins Pennell confirms that "Maddalena" was a pseudonym (309). While each piece of evidence might be questioned, cumulatively it seems certain that a figure whom Leland called "Maddalena" did exist and did provide him with accounts of Italian witchcraft.

29. Hutton, *Triumph*, 145; Leland, *Aradia*, 102. For further discussion of the name and surviving pagan practices in the Italian context see Carlo Ginzburg, *The Night Battles: Witchcraft and Agrarian Cults in the Sixteenth and Seventeenth Centuries*, trans. John and Anne Tedeschi (1966; Baltimore: Johns Hopkins University Press, 1983) and *Ecstasies: Deciphering the Witches' Sabbath*, trans. Raymond Rosenthal (1989; London, England: Hutchinson Radius, 1990), 200. Ginzburg thought it entirely possible that remnants of a pan-European goddess religion might have been preserved in folk customs and tales, even in the distortions of early modern court records. But he did not think that any accessible tradition still existed, much less a complete text and relegated *Aradia* to a footnote (*Ecstasies*, 89–121, 189, 307). This conclusion is the more striking because Leland's text, if accepted as accurate, would perfectly suit Ginzburg's argument about goddess survivals. For the debate on witchcraft as either pagan survival or the creation of Christian binary thinking, see Norman Cohn, *Europe's Inner Demons*, rev. ed. (1975; London, England: Pimlico, 1993), Stuart Clark, "Inversion, Misrule and the Meaning of Witchcraft," *Past and Present* 87 (1980): 98–127, and *Thinking with Demons*, Muchembled, 139–60. For an overview, see Darren Oldridge, ed., *The Witchcraft Reader* (London and New York: Routledge, 2002), 109–60.

30. Michelet, 41.

31. Leland thinks of witch families and their practices as dating back to "medieval, Roman, or it may be Etruscan times," as if these were historically very alike (*Aradia*, v). He also discusses the Dark Ages on p. 103 as being relevant, too.

32. Leland, *Aradia*, 6–7, 2, 104.

33. Michelet, 49, 53, 48.

34. Leland, *Aradia*, 20. It is this beautiful phraseology that has drawn many modern Witches to Leland and those who have rewritten and publicized his words. Doreen Valiente, who made extensive and acknowledged use of Leland's works (see below), especially liked this particular phrase. She notes it in *The ABC of Witchcraft Past and Present*, 2nd. ed. (1973; London, England: Robert Hale, 1994), 15.

35. Michelet, 59.

36. Leland, *Aradia*, 38.

37. 1889 letter to Mary A. Owen, Robins Pennell, 315.

38. Thomas, 291–300; Owen Davies, *Cunning Folk: Popular Magic in English History* (London and New York: Hambledon and London, 2003), 84–91, 185–86. See also Davies, *A People Bewitched: Witchcraft and Magic in Nineteenth-Century Somerset* (n.p.: Bruton, 1999).

39. Robins Pennell, 311–14, 1889 letters to herself and Mary A. Owen.

40. Robins Pennell, 321–22, 1889 letter to Mary A. Owen. See also Hutton's exploration in *The Triumph of the Moon*, 145–48.

41. Charlotte Perkins Gilman, "When I Was a Witch," in Ann J. Lane. ed., *The Charlotte Perkins Gilman Reader* (London, England: The Women's Press, 1981), 31.

42. Leland, "Prophecies for the Twentieth Century," Leland papers, Box 1.

43. Raymond Buckland, *Witchcraft from the Inside*, 3rd. ed. (1971; St. Paul, MN: Llewellyn, 2001), 93–94.

44. Shekhinah Mountainwater, *Ariadne's Thread: A Workbook of Goddess Magic* (Freedom, CA: The Crossing Press, 1991), 12–15.

45. Phyllis Curott interview in Ellen Evert Hopman and Lawrence Bond, eds., *People of the Earth: The New Pagans Speak Out* (Rochester, VT: Destiny, 1996), 255, and Phyllis Curott, *Book of Shadows* (New York: Broadway Books, 1998), 6–7, 192. For another "Aradia," see Jone Salomonsen, *Enchanted Feminism: The Reclaiming Witches of San Francisco* (London and New York: Routledge, 2002), 109–11.

46. Raven Grimassi, *Italian Witchcraft: The Old Religion of Southern Europe* (1995; St. Paul, MN: Llewellyn, 2003), xv, 88, 281–90. The book was originally published as *Ways of the Strega*. For another Italian Witchcraft heritage, see Leo Martello's many books (listed in Guiley), and the Witches' Liberation Movement, Witches' International Craft Association, and the Witches Anti-Defamation League, founded by Martello to establish rights for Wiccans (Guiley, 222).

47. Anthony Paige, *American Witch: Magick for the Modern Seeker* (New York: Citadel, 2003), 51.

48. Curott, *Book of Shadows*, 83–84, 11.

49. Susan Greenwood, *Witchcraft, Magic and the Otherworld: An Anthropology* (Oxford and New York: Berg, 2000), 128–29.

50. Theodore Mills interview in Evert Hopman and Bond, 108.

51. Curott, *Book of Shadows*, 97, 203–6 and *passim*, and interview in Evert Hopman and Bond, 255; Don Two Eagles Waterhawk interview in Evert Hopman and Bond, 196–203.

52. Philip J. Deloria, *Playing Indian* (New Haven and London: Yale University Press, 1998), 174.

53. See Starhawk (Miriam Simos), *The Spiral Dance: A Rebirth of the Ancient Religion of the Great Goddess* (1979; New York: HarperSanFrancisco, 1999), 42.

54. Celia Rees, *Sorceress* (London, England: Bloomsbury, 2002) and *Witch Child* (London: Bloomsbury, 2000).

55. John Michael Greer and Gordon Cooper, "The Red God: Woodcraft and the Origins of Wicca," *Gnosis Magazine* (Summer 1998): 51–7 and Hutton, *Triumph*, 162–63.
56. A process detailed in Hutton, *Triumph*, 205–40.
57. Valiente, 223–25.
58. A phrase coined by Aidan Kelly in his unpublished 1977 work "The Rebirth of Witchcraft: Tradition and Creativity in the Gardenerian Reform," cited in Margot Adler, *Drawing Down the Moon: Witches, Goddess-Worshippers and Other Pagans in America Today*, 2nd. ed. (Boston: Beacon, 1986), 80. Kelly's book appeared as *Crafting the Art of Magic* in 1991. See also Philip Heselton, *Gerald Gardner and the Cauldron of Inspiration: An Investigation of the Sources of Gardnerian Witchcraft* (Milverton, Somerset, England: Capall Bann, 2003), 206, 229, 285, 291.
59. Gerald Gardner, *Witchcraft Today* (1954; New York: Citadel, 2004). A published version of Gardner's original rites was prepared by Janet and Stewart Farrar with Doreen Valiente and is available as *The Witches' Way* and within Janet and Stewart Farrar, *A Witches' Bible: The Complete Witches' Handbook* (Blaine, WA: Phoenix and London: Robert Hale, 1981, 1984).
60. See note 56.
61. As reported in her book *Witch Blood* (1974) and retold by Janet and Stewart Farrar, "Leaves from the Book of Shadows," 10, in their *The Witches' Bible*.
62. Raymond Buckland, *Buckland's Complete Book of Witchcraft* (St. Paul, MN: Llewellyn, 1999), 14.
63. Buckland was keen to establish his role in bringing Wicca to America (7-8, 229) and has since founded his own Seax-Wica tradition. Sybil Leek brought to the U.S. her own family beliefs and stories of ancient British witchcraft and gypsy lore. Her *Diary of a Witch* (1968; New York: Signet, 1969) describes her reception in "I Discover America," 136–54. Another important British publicizer of Wicca in America was Gavin Frost, with his American wife Yvonne, who founded the Church and School of Wicca, the first recognized Wiccan church in the U.S.A (1972).
64. For example, Allyn Wolfe described his Gardnerian-Alexandrian hybrid tradition in an interview for Evert Hopman and Bond, 48–54.
65. Jessie Wicker Bell, *The Grimoire of Lady Sheba* (1971, 1972; St. Paul, MN: Llewellyn, 2001) incorporates both. It reproduces the coven's Articles of Incorporation, and lists 162 Laws. Lady Sheba's Wicca is a mixture of Gardnerian elements, rites from Britain including from an Arthurian "Camelot Coven," and Kentucky folk traditions. Buckland describes it as "American Celtic Wicca" (225). See also Guiley, 191–92. The Arthurian element in some American Witchcraft may also be related to the understanding of Arthurian myth popularized in Marion (Zimmer) Bradley, *The Mists of Avalon* (London, England: Michael Joseph, 1983).

66. Zsuzsanna Budapest (Zsuzsanna Mokcsay) was an emigrant from Hungary after the 1956 uprising. Budapest describes how her upbringing inspired her to re-create "pagan magic" in *The Grandmother of Time* (San Francisco: HarperSanFrancisco, 1989), xvii–xix. For her influence, see Naomi R. Goldenberg, *Changing of the Gods: Feminism and the End of Traditional Religions* (Boston: Beacon, 1979), 85–100.

67. Starhawk, *The Spiral Dance*. For a history of her tradition, see Goldenberg and Salomonsen (above).

68. Leland, *Aradia*, 111, 114, and also his untitled poem (Leland papers, Box 19), which ends each stanza with a similar phrase to "every Woman is at heart a Witch."

69. Starhawk, *Spiral Dance*, 102–03, 244–45.

70. Starhawk, *Truth or Dare: Encounters with Power, Authority and Mystery* (San Francisco: Harper, 1987), 94.

71. Merlin Stone, *When God Was a Woman* (Orlando, FL: Harcourt, 1976).

72. Gimbutas's work culminated with *The Language of the Goddess* (1989) and *The Civilisation of the Goddess* (1991) and has, as Hutton puts it, been "met with an increasing volume of criticism from fellow archaeologists." But, as he also notes, the interpretation that she placed upon goddess figurines and their contexts, is susceptible of a variety of interpretations (Hutton, *Triumph*, 356–57).

73. Starhawk, *Truth or Dare*, 40–41.

74. Starhawk, *Truth or Dare*, 29–30.

75. Starhawk, *Truth or Dare*, 2.

76. Starhawk, *Spiral Dance*, 5-6, 62, 214–15.

77. Starhawk, *Spiral Dance*, 203 and 258–59.

78. Starhawk, *Spiral Dance*, 14.

79. Starhawk, *Spiral Dance*, 278, 203.

80. Starhawk, *Spiral Dance*, 13, 8.

81. A phrase of Merlin Stone's, although Stone explicitly said that she was "not suggesting a return or revival of the ancient female religion" (228, xxv). For Starhawk's other inspirations in Victor and Cora Anderson's Fairy or Feri lore see Margaret A. Murray, *The God of the Witches* (1931; Oxford: Oxford University Press, 1970), 46–64, and *My First Hundred Years* (London: William Kimber, 1963); Anna Korn interview, Francesca Dubie interview, Victor Anderson interview in Evert Hopman and Bond, eds., 64–91; Starhawk, *Spiral Dance*, 28–29, 233, 264–65.

82. Starhawk, *Dreaming the Dark: Magic, Sex and Politics* (1982; Boston: Beacon, 1997).

83. Starhawk, *Spiral Dance*, 4.

84. Listed in Guiley, 65–66.

85. Oriethyia interview in Evert Hopman and Bond, eds., 131. See also her contribution to Adler, 463–65.

86. Not my own phrase, unfortunately, but the title of Lucy Summers's magic manual *Hex and the City: Sophisticated Spells for the Urban Witch* (London, England: Quarto/Barrons, 2003).

87. Cynthia Eller, *Living in the Lap of the Goddess: The Feminist Spirituality Movement in America* (Boston: Beacon, 1993), 83, 146.

88. Eller, 145.

89. Tannin Schwartzstein and Raven Kaldera, *The Urban Primitive: Paganism in the Concrete Jungle* (St. Paul, MN: Llewellyn, 2002), x.

90. Christopher Penczak, *City Magick: Urban Rituals, Spells and Shamanism* (York Beach, ME: Red Wheel/Weiser, 2001), xiv, 2.

91. Penczak, 55–56, 63, 65.

92. Penczak, 68–69.

93. Penczak, 112–13, 115.

94. Penczak, 81.

95. Penczak, 77, 52.

96. Penczak, 176–82, 184.

97. Penczak, 269, 192.

98. Penczak, xiv, 3–5.

99. Schwartzstein and Kaldera, 24, 83.

100. Eller, 18–20.

101. Schwartzstein and Kaldera, xi, 26.

102. Schwartzstein and Kaldera, 187–88.

103. Schwartzstein and Kaldera, 83, 26, 24.

104. Schwartzstein and Kaldera, 48–52, 69.

105. Schwartzstein and Kaldera, 48–49. This continues genuine ancient tradition: see, for example, Daniel Ogden, "Binding Spells: Curse Tablets and Voodoo Dolls in the Greek and Roman Worlds," in Valerie Flint, Richard Gordon, Georg Luck, and Daniel Ogden, *Witchcraft and Magic in Europe: Ancient Greece and Rome* (London, England: Athlone, 1999), 4–90, especially 23, 38–39.

106. Curott, for example, invoked goddesses from many different countries and faiths in the 1970s.

107. Schwartzstein and Kaldera, 55–68.

108. Quoted in Adler, 98.

109. Adler, 88, 80–82; Hutton, *Triumph*, 207, 381, 385.

110. Schwartzstein and Kaldera, 184.

111. Helen A. Berger, *A Community of Witches: Contemporary Neo-Paganism and Witchcraft in the United States* (Columbia, SC: University of South Carolina Press, 1999), 114–20.

112. Judy Harrow interview in Evert Hopman and Bond, eds., 252.

113. Adler, viii.

114. Adler, x.

115. Adler, 137–38.

116. Eller, 23.

117. Adler, 443–47.

118. Adler, 457, 453.
119. Laurie Cabot with Tom Cowan, *Power of the Witch* (New York: Delta, 1989), 231–33.
120. Cabot, 82.
121. Cabot, 234.
122. For a popular history/anthropology of modern witches, vampires and other "magical" groups, see Christine Wicker, *Not in Kansas Anymore: A Curious Tale of How Magic is Transforming America* (San Francisco: HarperSanFrancisco, 2005).
123. Adler, 453.
124. *Rosemary's Baby*, dir. Roman Polanski, Paramount, 1968.
125. Thomas Potts, *The Wonderfull Discoverie of Witches* (London, England, 1612) L2v, B4–B4v, D3.
126. Reginald Scot, *The Discoverie of Witchcraft* (1584) in Gibson, ed., *Witchcraft and Society*, 88.
127. Kramer and Sprenger, 21, 26.
128. Kramer and Sprenger, 26.
129. Louise Huebner, *Witchcraft for All* (1969; London, England: Universal-Tandem, 1971), 25. This book is known in the U.S. as *Power through Witchcraft*.
130. *The Witches of Eastwick*, dir. George Miller, Warner, 1989; John Updike, *The Witches of Eastwick* (London, England: Andre Deutsch, 1984)
131. See Linda C. Badley, "Spiritual Warfare: Post-feminism and the Cultural Politics of the Blair Witch Craze," Intensities 3 at http://www.cultmedia.com/issue3/Abad.htm; Tanya Krzywinska, *A Skin for Dancing In: Possession, Witchcraft and Voodoo in Film* (Trowbridge: Flicks Books, 2000), 131–34; Rachel Moseley, "Glamorous Witchcraft: Gender and Magic in Teen Film and Television." *Screen* 43:4. (2002): 413–15.
132. Andrew Fleming at http://www.sonypictures.com/movies/thecraft/chat.html.
133. Starhawk, *Spiral Dance*, 56, 269.
134. Cabot, 84–85.
135. Buffy was played by Kristy Swanson in the film *Buffy the Vampire Slayer*, dir. Fran Rubel Kuzui, Twentieth-Century Fox, 1992.
136. Rhonda V. Wilcox, "Who Died and Made Her the Boss? Patterns of Mortality in *Buffy*," in Rhonda V. Wilcox and David Lavery, eds., *Fighting the Forces: What's At Stake in Buffy the Vampire Slayer?* (Lanham, MD: Rowman and Littlefield, 2002), 13.
137. "I Robot . . . You Jane" (28.04.97). J. P. Williams, "Choosing Your Own Mother: Mother-Daughter Conflicts in *Buffy*" summarizes Willow's filial relationship with Jenny in Wilcox and Lavery, eds., 70.
138. "Becoming (Part One)" (12.05.98) and "Becoming (Part Two)" (19.05.98).
139. Tanya Krzywinska, "Hubble-Bubble, Herbs and Grimoires: Magic, Manichaeanism, and Witchcraft in Buffy," in Wilcox and Lavery, eds., 188.
140. "Hush" (14.12.99).

141. "New Moon Rising" (02.05.00).
142. On Whedon's motivation, see Justine Larbalestier, "*Buffy*'s Mary Sue is Jonathan: *Buffy* Acknowledges the Fans," in Wilcox and Lavery, eds., 227.
143. This is Teresa De Lauretis's word, from *The Practice of Love: Lesbian Sexuality and Perverse Desire* (Bloomington: Indiana University Press, 1994), 191. It has even been argued, by scholars such as Thomas Lacquer [*Making Sex: Body and Gender from the Greeks to Freud* (Cambridge, MA: Harvard University Press, 1990]) and Lillian Faderman (*Surpassing the Love of Men: Romantic Friendship and Love between Women from the Renaissance to the Present* [New York: William Morrow, 1981]), that same-sex desire between women did not exist before the eighteenth or nineteenth centuries in any detectable, or actual, way. Others, such as Valerie Traub, have retorted that it certainly did exist, and that there are traces of it that that have traditionally been overlooked by scholars because they are coded or ambiguous. For Traub's readings of Shakespeare see "Desire and the Difference it Makes," in Valerie Wayne, ed., *The Matter of Difference: Materialist Feminist Criticism of Shakespeare* (Ithaca: Cornell University Press, 1991), 81–114, and "The (In)significance of 'Lesbian' Desire in Early Modern England," in Susan Zimmerman, ed., *Erotic Politics: Desire on the Renaissance Stage* (New York: Routledge, 1992), 150–69. For portrayals of witches as heterosexual, see Lene Dresen-Coenders, "Witches as Devils' Concubines: On the Origin of Fear of Witches and Protection Against Witchcraft," in Dresen-Coenders, ed., *Saints and She-Devils* (London, England: Rubicon, 1987), 59–82 and Charles Zika, "Fears of Flying: Representations of Witchcraft and Sexuality in Early Sixteenth-Century Germany," *Australian Journal of Art* 8 (1989/1990), 19–47.
144. For lesbian witches in pornography, see, for example, F. Solano Lopez and Barreiro, *The Young Witches* (Seattle: Eros Comix, 1992). For lesbian Witches as celebrating sex, see D'vora and Annie Sprinkle interviews in Evert Hopman and Bond, eds., 140–46, 146–51. For discussion, see Andrea Dworkin, *Pornography: Men Possessing Women* (New York: G.P. Putnam, 1979); Robin Morgan, "Theory and Practice: Pornography and Rape," in L. Lederer, ed., *Take Back the Night* (New York: William Morrow, 1980); and Susan Griffin, *Pornography and Silence: Culture's Revenge against Nature* (New York: Harper and Row, 1981). A useful anthology is Lynne Segal and Mary McIntosh, eds., *Sex Exposed: Sexuality and the Pornography Debate* (London, England: Virago, 1992).
145. Joss Whedon interview with David Bianculli on Fresh Air, National Public Radio, 09.05.2000 archived at http://www. buffyguide.com/extras/josswt.shtml.
146. Farah Mendlesohn, "Surpassing the Love of Vampires: Or, Why (and How) a Queer Reading of the Buffy/Willow Relationship is Denied," in Wilcox and Lavery, eds., 59.
147. "Who Are You?" (29.02.00).
148. "All the Way," "Once More With Feeling," "Tabula Rasa," "Smashed."

149. Sara Crosby, "The Cruelest Season: Female Heroes Snapped into Sacrificial Heroines," in Sherrie A. Inness, ed., *Action Chicks: New Images of Tough Women in Popular Culture* (New York and Basingstoke, England: Palgrave Macmillan, 2004), 165.

150. Joss Whedon at The Bronze chat room, 29.01.2000, archived at www.buffyguide.com/extras/josswt.shtml.

151. "Seeing Red" (07.05.02), "Two to Go" (14.05.02), "Villains," and "Grave" (21.05.02).

152. Jane Czyzselska, "What Amber Did Next," *Diva* (March 2003), 51.

153. Czyzselska, 51. The extent to which the show's fans invest emotionally in *Buffy* is explored more generally in Geraldine Bloustien, "Fans with a Lot at Stake: Serious Play and Mimetic Excess in Buffy the Vampire Slayer," in *The European Journal of Cultural Studies* 5:4 (2002): 427–49.

154. Willowlicious and Kyraroc, "The Dead/Evil Lesbian Cliche" at http://www.xtreme-gaming.com/theotherside/cliche.php and elsewhere; Jennifer Greenman, "Witch Love Spells Death" at xtreme-gaming.com/theotherside/witchlove.php and elsewhere.

155. Dana Heller, "Found Footage: Feminism Lost in Time," *Tulsa Studies in Women's Literature* 21:1 (Spring 2002): 85–98; Chris. J Cowan, "If You Go Out in the Woods Today": Approaching *The Blair Witch Project* as Western Mythology," *49th Parallel* 4 (Winter 2000) at http://www.49thparallel.bham.ac.uk/back/issue4/cowan.htm.

156. Jane Roscoe correctly identifies her as the "monstrous-feminine" in "*The Blair Witch Project*: Mock-Documentary Goes Mainstream," *Jump Cut* 43 (2000): 7.

157. Both the DVD commentary and Dana Heller make this point, and Heller offers a striking analysis of the film's misogyny. See also Joseph S. Walker, "Mom and the Blair Witch: Narrative, Form and the Feminine," in Sarah L. Higley and Jeffrey Andrew Weinstock, *Nothing That Is: Millennial Cinema and the* Blair Witch *Controversy* (Detroit: Wayne State University Press, 2004), 163–80.

158. Badley, "Spiritual warfare" at http://www.cult-media.com/issue3/Abad.htm suggests J. Hoberman, "Screaming and Kicking," *The Village Voice* (July 14–20, 1999), as one of the first reviews to see Heather as witch.

159. Director's commentary on the DVD version of *Blair Witch Two*. See Peg Aloi, "Be Afraid, Be Very Afraid, of the Dark" at http://www.witchvox.com/media/blairwitch_review.html for a more positive response, and Berlinger's interview for *The Witches' Voice* at witchvox.com/media/blairwitch2_interview.html.

160. Erica Leerhsen was the actress's real name. In an interview included in the DVD package, she says that she was invited back during the casting process to read the part of Tristen, and was offered the role of "the witch." Berlinger says in his commentary that he had intended her for the part of Kim. Whether the director noticed the aptness of her name during the casting process is unclear.

161. Director's commentary. Berlinger explains his admiration for the first film but also stresses his reservations about its marketing as a real documentary. He adds that in his opinion Myrick and Sanchez, despite being named as executive producers of *Blair Witch Two*, did not like his director's cut and had little to do with the film.

162. Explored in Sarah L. Higley, "'People Just Want to See Something': Art, Death and Document in Blair Witch, The Last Broadcast and Paradise Lost,'" in Higley and Weinstock, eds., 87–110.

163. http://www.dykesvision.com/en/articles/homophobia.html.

## Chapter 5

1. Roseanne Barr, *Roseanne: My Life as a Woman* (1989: London, England: Collins, 1990), 159. A witch logo ends every episode of Barr's comedy show, *Roseanne*.

2. Mara Leveritt, "The Witch Trial: Witch on Death Row," Arkansas Writers' Project at http://www.arktimes.com/trial2.htm.

3. *Paradise Lost*, dir. Joe Berlinger, HBO, 1996.

4. Jay Rogers, "Child Sacrifice in the New Age: Salem's Witch Cult and America's Abortion Industry" at http://forerunner.com/champion/X0039_Child_ Sacrifice_in_t.html; Pat Robertson, fund-raising letter: now available at geocities.com/CapitolHill/7027/quotes.html and numerous other sites. See also *Season of the Witch (Jack's Wife)*, dir. George A. Romero, Latent Image, 1973.

5. http://www.pjcomix.com/hillarywitch.html and http://www.wickedwitch. org/.

6. Scott Lehigh "We Used to Keep Religion Out of Politics," *Boston Globe* (27.06.1999): F01.

7. Ann Coulter, "Godless Causes Liberals to Pray . . . for a Book Burning" at http://www.anncoulter.com/cgi-local/printer_friendly.cgi?article=135 (21 June 2006, accessed 5 October 2006). See also Kirsten Anderberg, "Watch Lists or Witch Hunts: American Terrorist Lists" (2004) at http://www.indy-media.org.uk/en/2004/01/283437.html (accessed 18 October 2006).

8. Drew Mackenzie, "They're Calling My Daughter a Teenage Witch," *Sunday* magazine, *News of the World* (25.02.2001): 15–16; http://archive.aclu.org/ court/blackbear_complaint.html.

9. Richard Abanes, *Harry Potter and the Bible* (Camp Hill, PA: Christian Publications, 2001), 21.

10. J. K. Rowling, *Harry Potter and the Philosopher's Stone* (London: Bloomsbury, 1998); Levine quoted in Sean Smith, *J. K. Rowling: A Biography*, rev. ed. (London: Arrow, 2002), 181; figures from Julia Eccleshare, *A Guide to the Harry Potter Novels* (London and New York: Continuum, 2002), 13.

11. See, for example, Gareth Roberts, *The Mirror of Alchemy* (London: British Library, 1994). Its power was, however, easily abused by the wicked seeker, as Ben Jonson's *The Alchemist* (1610) shows.

12. Connie Neal, *What's a Christian to do with Harry Potter?* (Colorado Springs: Waterbrook Press, 2001), 195.
13. http://www.exposingsatanism.org/harrypotter.htm.
14. American Library Association, *Library Journal* (07.02.2000), quoted in Abanes, 4–5.
15. Abanes, 23–24, 33–39, 57–59, 89–91, 97–99, 136–38.
16. Abanes, 177–86, 205–23.
17. Gary Greenwald, *Satan's Trojan Horse* (Eagles Nest Ministries, n.d.).
18. Robert McGee, "First-Person: Parents Should See Harry Potter without the Kids" (16.11.2001) at http://www.baptistpress.org/bpnews.asp?ID12190; Tobin Perry, "Harry Potter Movie Lamented as Kid's First Look at the Occult" (12.11.2001) at http://www.baptistpress.org/news.asp?ID12138.
19. Charlie Warren, "Arkansas Baptists Support 2000 SBC Beliefs Statement," *Baptist Press,* 09.11.2001, archived at http://www.baptistpress.org/bpnews.asp?ID=12127.
20. "Harry Potter: A $7 Ticket Straight to Hell," http://www.bettybowers.com/harrypotter.html.
21. Quoted in Neal, 104–05. The material originated at onion.com.
22. http://www.exposingsatanism.org/harrypotter.htm and numerous other sites. This quotation headlines Scholastic's official J. K. Rowling interview (www2.scholastic2.com/teachers/authorsandbooks/authorstudies/authorhome.jhtml?authorID=821&collateralID=5276&displayName=Biography) included in its teachers' pages.
23. Judy Corman, speaking for Scholastic, quoted in Jim Galloway and Chris Burritt, "School Lets Hero Off Hook," *Atlanta Journal* (13.10.1999), np; J. K. Rowling, in an interview with Michele Hatty, "Harry Potter Author Reveals the Secret of Getting Kids to Read as Children's Book Week Kicks Off," *USA Weekend Online* (14.11.1999), both quoted in Abanes, 5; Eccleshare, 73–74; Philip Nel, *J. K. Rowling's Harry Potter Novels* (London and New York: Continuum, 2001), 44, 63.
24. BBC2, *Newsnight* (19.06.2003).
25. Martin Savidge, "Bubbling Troubles Trail Harry," *CNN,* 06.07.2000, archived at http://edition.cnn.com/2000/books/news/07/06/trouble.harry/index.html).
26. Lindsey Fraser, *Telling Tales: An Interview With J. K. Rowling* (London, England: Mammoth, 2000), 31.
27. Sean Smith, 209.
28. See Pico Iyer, "The Playing Fields of Hogwarts," *New York Times Book Review* (10.11.1999) and David K. Steege, "Harry Potter, Tom Brown and the British School Story: Lost in Transit?" in Lana A. Whited, ed., *The Ivory Tower and Harry Potter: Perspectives on a Literary Phenomenon* (Columbia and London: University of Missouri Press, 2002), 140–56.
29. Hutton, *Triumph*, vii, 253–86.
30. Charles Colson, "Witches and Wizards: The Harry Potter Phenomenon," *BreakPoint* (2.11.1999), n.p.
31. Abanes, 62.

32. Berit Kjos, "Harry Potter Lures Kids to Witchcraft with Praise from Christian Leaders," http://www.crossroads.to/text/articles/Harry&Witchcraft.htm.

33. Neal, 65–67.

34. For example, Thomas Heyward and Richard Brome, *The Late Lancashire Witches* (London, 1634), Thomas Shadwell, *The Lancashire Witches* (London, 1681).

35. Thorne Smith (completed by Norman Matson), *The Passionate Witch* (1942; London, England: Tandem, 1966), 39.

36. Sylvia Townsend Warner, *Lolly Willowes* (1926; Chicago: Academy Chicago Publishers, 1979) in which an English spinster becomes a witch to escape from the suffocating demands of men; Esther Forbes, *A Mirror for Witches* (1928; Bath: Cedric Chivers, 1973), a parody of a seventeenth-century tract denouncing witches, where the superstitious stupidity of the witch's accusers is both the joke and the tragedy of the plot, and the young "witch" is herself deluded into accepting her own guilt.

37. Kramer and Sprenger, 43.

38. Thorne Smith, 56.

39. *I Married a Witch*, dir. Rene Clair, United Artists, 1942.

40. The name's spelling was changed for the film.

41. Authorship was already divided between Smith and Matson, and the fact that the film employed four other writers suggests problems with narrative and tone. They were: Marc Connelly, Andre Rigaud, Dalton Trumbo, and Robert Pirosh.

42. Smith, 40, 130, 105.

43. Theatrical trailer for *Bell, Book and Candle*, dir. Richard Quine, Columbia, 1958. On the DVD version of the film, 2002.

44. Smith, 59, where "sex not hex" is the witch's supposed crime.

45. The German Web site http://home.swipnet.se/stephanSE/bellbookandcandle.htm even argues that *Bell, Book and Candle* is an alternative "third" ending for Stewart and Novak's characters, "a repetition and continuation of *Vertigo*."

46. John van Druten, *Bell, Book and Candle* (New York: Dramatists' Play Service, 2003), 36.

47. Matthew Hopkins, *The Discovery of Witches* (London, 1647). There is even an illustration of Pyewacket. *The Undead*, dir. Roger Corman, A.I.P., 1957 shows that the traditional formula for wicked sexy witches could still be played out, alongside such new ventures as *Bell, Book and Candle*.

48. *I Am a Camera* was running in New York in 1951 and its composition is closely associated with *Bell, Book and Candle*.

49. Van Druten, 44.

50. First aired 17.09.1964.

51. Interview with William Asher at http://www.bewitched.net/asherinterv.htm.

52. Elyce Rae Helford, ed., *Fantasy Girls: Gender in the New Universe of Science Fiction Television* (Lanham, Boulder, Oxford, New York: Rowman and Littlefield, 2000), 2.

53. Joseph N. Bell, "A Witch to Watch," *Pageant* (April 1965), available at http://www.harpiesbizarre.com/vintage-witch2watch.htm.

54. For example, "Help, Help, Don't Save Me" (15.10.1964) and "Witch or Wife" (12.11.1964).

55. For example, "Illegal Separation" (06.05.1965) and "Double Tate" (17.02.1966), where the Kravitzes and Tates respectively find themselves in marital disharmony.

56. The *Lancashire Witch* was build by Robert Stephenson in 1828, there were several *Water Witches*, one of whom sailed Lake Champlain from 1832, and W.I.T.C.H. stood for Wolverhampton Instrument for Teaching Computing from Harwell and was a vast computer built in 1948.

57. "Remember the Main" (20.05.1965).

58. Jean Bodin, *De le Demonomanie des Sorciers* (Paris, 1587), Book 2, Chapter 5, Reginald Scot, *The Discoverie of Witchcraft* (London, 1584), Book 3, Chapter 2.

59. Kramer and Sprenger, 63.

60. For example, "Remember the Main" (20.05.1965) and "Pleasure O'Reilly" (18.03.1965).

61. "This Little Piggie" (25.02.1971), "Darrin Goes Ape" (11.03.1971), "Trick or Treat" (28.10.65) "Darrin on a Pedestal" (22.10.1970), "If The Shoe Pinches" (26.03.1970).

62. Scot, Book 5, Chapter 3.

63. Harry Ackerman's original treatment was called "The Witch of Westport," Herbie J. Pilato, *Bewitched Forever* (Irving, TX: Summit, 1996), 14.

64. 11.03.1965; "Tabitha's Very Own Samantha" (29.01.1970); "Double, Double, Toil and Trouble" (28.09.1967). Endora's birthplace is discussed in "A Nice Little Dinner Party" (28.01.1965).

65. Susannah Sheldon against Bridget Bishop and others, from the Records of the Court of Oyer and Terminer 1692, in the Phillips Library, Peabody Essex Museum at Salem, Massachusetts.

66. See also "It's Nice to Have a Spouse Around the House" (24.10.1968) and others.

67. 01.04.1965.

68. Mather Papers, Boston Public Library MS AM 1502 v1, no. 28, v. 2, no. 3, v. 3, no. 45; Samuel Wyllys Papers, Connecticut State Library; Mather, *Memorable Providences*. See chapters 1 and 2.

69. "And Then There Were Three" (13.01.1966).

70. Wyllys Papers Box 1, 344–45; Pynchon Notebook, NYPL 13; Miller, *The Crucible in Plays: One* (London, England: Methuen, 1988), 235.

71. "It Shouldn't Happen To a Dog" (01.10.1964), "Aunt Clara's Victoria Victory" (09.03.1967), "Business, Italian Style" (21.09.1967).

72. "Abner Kadabra" (15.04.1965), "A Most Unusual Wood Nymph" (13.10.1966), "I'd Rather Twitch Than Fight" (17.11.1966).

73. "Driving Is the Only Way to Fly" (25.03.1965).

74. Durward Grinstead, *Elva* (New York: Covici Friede, 1929). *Maid of Salem* was a "historical" narrative, in which a pair of fictional lovers also fall victim to the witchcraft craze sweeping the town. Written by Grinstead, Walter Ferris, and Bradley King, it starred Claudette Colbert.

75. Originally the stridently named "Victor," he was renamed, more meekly, "Maurice" ("Just One Happy Family" [19.11.1964]).

76. Pilato, 58.

77. Interview with Asher at bewitched.net/asherinterv.htm.

78. "They Tried to Take My Baby Away From Me," interview with Stanley Cooper in *TV Photo Story* (October, 1965). Available at harpiesbizarre.com/vintagetab.htm.

79. Tabitha was also spelled "Tabatha" in error in the show's credits.

80. "And Then There were Three," above.

81. Pilato, 39.

82. Pilato, 5.

83. ABC's *Tabitha*, starring Lisa Hartman (1977).

84. Columbia press pack text available at http://www.users.globalnet.co.uk/~zap/Bewitchedintro.htm.

85. Quentin Tarantino, screenplay for *Pulp Fiction* (London and Boston: Faber and Faber, 1994), 47. This scene was shot, but cut from the movie.

86. Pilato, xvi.

87. "The Legend of Lizzie" in *The Advocate* (July 30, 1992), harpiesbizarre.com/advocatearticle.htm.

88. "Elizabeth Montgomery: The Good Witch," in *The New York Times Magazine* (December 31, 1995), harpiesbizarre.com/goodwitch.htm.

89. "Remember the Main," above.

90. 19.11.1964.

91. "Sisters at Heart" (24.12.1970); Pilato, 9–11, 197.

92. harpiesbizarre.com/thoughts.htm.

93. Pilato, 13–14.

94. Pilato, 25.

95. Pilato, 31.

96. Pilato, 21–22.

97. "George Washington Zapped Here, Parts 1 and 2" (19 and 26.02.1972), "My Friend Ben" (08.12.1966) and "Samantha for the Defense" (15.12.1966), "Paul Revere Rides Again' (29.10.1970).

98. "The Witches Are Out" (29.10.1964), "The Safe and Sane Halloween" (26.10.1967), "To Trick or Treat or Not to Trick or Treat" (30.10.1969).

99. "Samantha's Thanksgiving to Remember" (23.11.1967); Pilato, 9.

100. Pilato, x.

101. Alice Hoffman, *Practical Magic* (1995; London: Vintage, 2002), 6.

102. DVD commentary for *Practical Magic*, dir. Griffin Dunne, Warner, 1998.

103. Their mother does appear in a time-travel story "That 70s Episode" (07.04.1999). In apparent reminiscence of *Bewitched*, their father is called Victor. See also the episode "Lost and Bound" (31.1.2002). The show was created by Constance M. Burge.
104. http://www.thewb.com/Shows/Show/0,7353,%o7c%7c156,00.html.
105. 04.05.2000.
106. "Power Outage" (16.11.2000).
107. "Long Live the Queen" and "Womb Raider" (02.05.2002, 09.05.2002).
108. http://www.popmatters.com/tv/reviews/c/charmed.html.
109. See Badley "Spiritual Warfare" at http://www.cult-media/issue3/Abad.htm for another exploration of this domestication. Despite this, *Charmed* does offer pleasures to feminists, Wiccans, and historians with its attempts to challenge conventional portrayals of women and witches, its borrowings from Doreen Valiente, and its witty play with witchcraft history (episode titles such as "Animal Pragmatism"). See N. E. Genge, *The Book of Shadows: The Unofficial* Charmed *Companion* (New York: Three Rivers Press, 2000) for a popular exploration of the relationship between *Charmed* and Wicca.
110. Griffin Dunne's commentary, *Practical Magic*.
111. Hoffman, 279.
112. Helford, ed., 27.
113. Susan Spillman, "Her Magic Touch," cited in Helford, ed., 15.
114. 1 Samuel 15:23.
115. Mather, *Wonders*, 15.
116. *Bewitched*, dir. Nora Ephron, Columbia, 2005. The film was disliked by about three quarters of the reviewers that I have encountered, who thought it too clever and possibly too feminist, although no one was brave enough to say so. Isabel (Nicole Kidman) might be too sweet for some feminist viewers, but the film is a worthy successor to the series.
117. Starhawk, *The Spiral Dance*, 269.

# BIBLIOGRAPHY

Archives and Manuscripts: original trial material and other major collections of papers

New Haven Colony Historical Society, Whitney Library collections
Massachusetts Archives, especially records of Middlesex County Court, Suffolk County Court
Historical Society of Pennsylvania, Leland Papers
New York Public Library, John Pynchon Notebook,
Essex Institute: especially files of Essex County Court
Connecticut State Library, Hartford: especially County Court/Particular Court Books, Records of the Court of Assistants, Samuel Wyllys Papers
Brown University, John Hay Library, Wyllys Papers
Library of Virginia: especially Princess Anne County Order Books, Minutes of Council
Boston Public Library: especially Mather Papers, Prince Collection.
Wethersfield Historical Society collections
Houghton Library, Harvard University, especially Trials for Witchcraft in New England collection
Historic Northampton
Connecticut Valley Historical Museum, Springfield, especially records of Hampshire County Court

## Printed Sources

Abanes, Richard. *Harry Potter and the Bible* (Camp Hill, Pennsylvania.: Christian Publications, 2001)
Abbot, Abiel. *History of Andover* (Andover, Massachusetts, 1829)

Adams, Hannah. *A Summary History of New England* (Dedham, Massachusetts, 1799)

Adams, Sherman W. and Henry R. Stiles, *The History of Ancient Wethersfield* vol. 1 (1904; Wethersfield: New Hampshire Publishing and Wethersfield Historical Society, 1974)

Adler, Margot. *Drawing Down the Moon: Witches, Goddess-Worshippers and Other Pagans in America Today*, 2nd. ed. (Boston: Beacon, 1986)

Allen, Neal W., "A Maine Witch," *Old-Time New England* 61 (Winter 1971) 75-81

Anderson, Elaine M. "Eleanor Roosevelt and the Bok Peace Prize," *Historical Perspectives* (March 2004) 1-14

Anderson Jones, Mary Jeanne. *Congregational Commonwealth: Connecticut* (Middletown, Connecticut: Wesleyan University Press, 1968)

Anon., *The Witches: A Tale of New England* (Bath, 1837)

Anon, *Connecticut's Courts* revised ed. (Hartford, Connecticut: State of Connecticut Judicial Branch, 1999)

Anon, *Salem Witchcraft*, published serially in *The New York Literary Journal and Belles-Lettres Repository* (September-November 1820) 3-4, 329-35, 417-20 and 17-27

Anon, *The Witch of New England: A Romance* (Philadelphia, 1824)

Apkarian-Russell, Pamela E. *A Collector's Guide to Salem Witchcraft and Souvenirs* (Atglen, Pennsylvania: Schiffer, 1998)

Aronsen, Marc. *Witch-Hunt: Mysteries of the Salem Witch Trials* (New York: Simon and Schuster, 2003)

Bancroft, George. *History of the Colonization of the United States* vol. 3, 9th ed. (1840; Boston, 1841)

Barker, Shirley. *The Dark Hills Under* (New Haven: Yale University Press, 1933)

_____. Peace My Daughters (New York: Crown, 1949)

Barr, Amelia E., *The Black Shilling* (New York: Dodd, Mead and Co., 1903)

Barr, Roseanne. *Roseanne: My Life as a Woman* (1989; London: Collins, 1990)

Baum, L. Frank. *The Wonderful Wizard of Oz* (1900; London: Penguin, 1995)

_____. Fifteen Books in One: The Original Oz Series (n.p: Shoes and Ships and Sealing Wax, 2005)

Bell, Stuart. *When Salem Came to the Boro: The True Story of the Cleveland Child Abuse Cases* (London: Pan, 1988)

Beale Davis, Richard 'The Devil in Virginia in the Seventeenth Century', *Virginia Magazine of History and Biography* 65 (1957) 131-49

Beard, George M. *The Psychology of the Salem Witchcraft Excitement of 1692 and its Practical Application to our own Time* (1882; Stratford, Connecticut: John E. Edwards, 1971)

Beattie, J.M. *Crime and the Courts in England 1660-1800* (Oxford: Clarendon, 1986).

Bell, Jessie Wicker. *The Grimoire of Lady Sheba* (1971, 1972; St. Paul, Minnesota: Llewellyn, 2001)

Berger, Helen A. *A Community of Witches: Contemporary Neo-Paganism and Witchcraft in the United States* (Columbia, South Carolina: University of South Carolina Press, 1999)

____. *Witchcraft and Magic in Contemporary North America* (Philadelphia: University of Pennsylvania Press, 2005)

Bloustien, Geraldine. "Fans With a Lot at Stake: Serious Play and Mimetic Excess in Buffy the Vampire Slayer" in *The European Journal of Cultural Studies* 5.4. (2002) 427-449

Bodin, Jean. *De le Demonomanie des Sorciers* (Paris, 1587)

Booth, Sally Smith. *The Witches of Early America* (New York: Hastings House, 1975)

Bostridge, Ian. *Witchcraft and its Transformations c. 1650-c.1750* (Oxford: Clarendon, 1997)

Bowen, Jesse N. "Lecture to the Lawyers' Round Table of Maryland," 7 December 1929, Maryland Historical Society

Bowyer, James T. *The Witch of Jamestown* (Richmond, 1890)

Boyer, Paul and Stephen Nissenbaum. *Salem Possessed: The Social Origins of Witchcraft* (Cambridge, Massachusetts and London: Harvard University Press, 1974)

Bradey, Marion (Zimmer). *The Mists of Avalon* (London: Michael Joseph, 1983)

Brammer, Leila R. *Excluded from Suffrage History: Matilda Joslyn Gage, Nineteenth-Century American Feminist* (Westport, Connecticut: Greenwood Press, 2000)

Breslaw, Elaine G. *Tituba, Reluctant Witch of Salem: Devilish Indians and Puritan Fantasies* (New York and London: New York University Press, 1996)

____. ed. *Witches of the Atlantic World: A Historical Reader and Primary Sourcebook* (New York and London: New York University Press, 2000)

Brown, David C. *A Guide to the Salem Witchcraft Hysteria of 1692* (n.p.: n.p., 1984)

Bruce, Philip A. *Institutional History of Virginia in the Seventeenth Century* (1910; Gloucester, Massachusetts: Peter Smith, 1964)

Buckland, Raymond. *Buckland's Complete Book of Witchcraft* (St. Paul, MN: Llewellyn, 1999)

____. *Witchcraft From the Inside* 3rd. ed. (1971; St. Paul, Minnesota: Llewellyn, 2001)

Budapest Z. (Zsuzsanna Mokcsay) *The Grandmother of Time* (San Francisco: HarperSanFrancisco, 1989)

Buell, Lawrence. *New England Literary Culture: From Revolution through Renaissance* (Cambridge: Cambridge University Press, 1986)

Burr, George Lincoln, *Narratives of the New England Witchcraft Cases* (1914; Mineola, New York: Dover, 2002)

____. "New England's Place in the History of Witchcraft," in Ronald H. Bainton, George Lincoln Burr, His Life with Lois Oliphant Gibbons, ed., *Selections from his Writings* (Ithaca and New York: Cornell University Press, 1943) 352-77

_____. "The Literature of Witchcraft" *Papers* of the American Historical Association 4:4 (1889-90) 37-66

Cabot, Laurie with Tom Cowan, *Power of the Witch* (New York: Delta, 1989)

Calef, Robert, *More Wonders of the Invisible World* (London, 1700)

Caporeal, Linnda, "Ergotism: The Satan Loosed in Salem," *Science* 192 (April 2, 1976) 21-6

Carey, George C. *Maryland Folklore and Folklife* (Cambridge, Maryland: Tidewater, 1970)

Castleton, D.R. *Salem: A Tale of the Seventeenth Century* (New York: 1874)

Caulfield, Ernest, "Pediatric Aspects of the Salem Witchcraft Tragedy," *American Journal of Diseases of Children* 65 (May 1943) 788-802

Chews, Ed. "A Shadowy Side of Early American History: Witch Bottles, Hidden Shoes, Amulets and Charms," *Colonial Williamsburg* (Summer 2001) 23:2 32-7

Child, Frank Samuel. *A Colonial Witch: Being a Study of the Black Art in the colony of Connecticut* (New York, 1897)

Churchwell, Sarah. *The Many Lives of Marilyn Monroe* (London: Granta, 2004)

Clark, Stuart. "Inversion, Misrule and the Meaning of Witchcraft," *Past and Present* 87 (1980) 98-127

_____. *Thinking with Demons: The Idea of Witchcraft in Early Modern Europe* (Oxford: Clarendon, 1997)

Clifton, Chas. S. "The Significance of *Aradia*" in *Aradia or the Gospel of the Witches: A New Translation* 59-80

_____. "Leland's *Aradia* and the Revival of Modern Witchcraft," *The Pomegranate* 1 (1997) 2-27

Cockburn, J.S. *Introduction to Calendar of Assize Records. Home Circuit Indictments. Elizabeth I and James I* (London: HMSO, 1985)

Cohn, Norman. *Europe's Inner Demons*, rev. ed. (1975; London: Pimlico, 1993)

Colson, Charles. "*Witches and Wizards: The Harry Potter Phenomenon*," BreakPoint (2.11.1999) n.p.

Condé, Maryse. *I Tituba, Black Witch of Salem* trans. Richard Philcox (1986; New York: Ballantyne Books, 1992) with a Foreword by Angela Y. Davis and Afterword by Ann Armstrong Scarboro

*Connecticut Historical Society Collections Volume 2: Particular Court 1639-1663* (Hartford, Connecticut: CHS and the Society of Colonial Wars in the State of Connecticut, 1928)

Cook, Timothy E. "Another Perspective on Political Authority in Children's Literature: The Fallible Leader in L. Frank Baum and Dr. Seuss," *The Western Political Quarterly* 36:2. (1983) 326-336

Cortesi, Lawrence. "Was Mercy Desborough In League With the Devil?," *Connecticut* (October 1972) 27, 46

_____. "The Beautiful Witch of Fairfield," *Cobblestone* (January 1981) 16-19

Cotton, Josiah. "Some Observations Concerning Witchcraft," MS Am 1165, Houghton Library, Harvard University

Crosby, Sara. "The Cruelest Season: Female Heroes Snapped into Sacrificial Heroines" in Sherrie A. Inness, ed., *Action Chicks: New Images of Tough Women in Popular Culture* (New York and Basingstoke: Palgrave Macmillan, 2004) 153-78

Cross, Tom Peete. "Witchcraft in North Carolina," *Studies in Philology* 16:3 (July 1919) 217-87

Crowley, John W. "James Nelson Barker in Perspective," *Educational Theatre Journal* 24:4 (December 1972) 363-9

Culver, Stuart. "Growing Up in Oz," *American Literary History* 4:4 (1992) 607-628

Curott, Phyllis. *Book of Shadows* (New York: Broadway Books, 1998)

Czyzselska, Jane. "What Amber Did Next," *Diva* (March 2003) 51

Dabney Coleman, Elizabeth. "The Witchcraft Delusion Rejected," *Virginia Cavalcade* (Summer 1956) 6:1 28-34

Dahlgren, Madeleine Vinton. *South Mountain Magic* (Boston, 1882)

Dana, Marvin. *A Puritan Witch: A Romance* (New York: Smart Set Publishing, 1903)

Davies, Owen. *A People Bewitched: Witchcraft and Magic in Nineteenth-Century Somerset* (np: Bruton, 1999)

_____. *Cunning Folk: Popular Magic in English History* (London and New York: Hambledon and London, 2003)

Davis, Dona L. "George Beard and Lydia Pinkham: Gender, Class and Nerves in Late Nineteenth-Century America," *Health Care for Women International* 10:2/3 (1989) 93-114

Deetz, James and Patricia Scott Deetz, *The Times of Their Lives: Life, Love and Death in the Plymouth Colony* (New York: W.H. Freeman, 2000)

De Forest, John W. *Witching Times*, ed. Alfred Appel (serialized 1856-7; New Haven: College and University Press, 1967)

De Lauretis, Teresa. *The Practice of Love: Lesbian Sexuality and Perverse Desire* (Bloomington: Indiana University Press, 1994)

Deloria, Philip J. *Playing Indian* (New Haven and London: Yale University Press, 1998)

Demos, John Putnam,. *Entertaining Satan: Witchcraft and the Culture of Early New England.* Oxford: Oxford University Press, 1982

_____. "Underlying Themes in the Witchcraft of Seventeenth-Century New England," *The American Historical Review* 75:5 (June 1970) 1311-26

*Dictionary of American Biography*, ed. Dumas Malone (New York: Charles Scribner's Sons, 1936) and supplements

Disbrow, Michael S. *Descendants of Thomas and Mercy* (Holbridge) Disbrow (Manton, MI: Disbrow Family Association, 1992

Dow, George Francis, ed., *Records and Files of the Quarterly Courts of Essex County, Massachusetts* vol. 1 (Salem: Essex Institute, 1911)

Drake, Frederick C. "Witchcraft in the American Colonies 1647-1662," *American Quarterly* 20:4 (Winter 1968) 694-708

Drake, Samuel G. *Annals of Witchcraft in New England and Elsewhere in the United States* (1869; n.p.: Kessinger, 2006)

_____. *The Witchcraft Delusion in New England* 3 vols. (Roxbury, 1866)

Dresen-Coenders, Lene. "Witches as Devils' Concubines: On the Origin of Fear of Witches and Protection Against Witchcraft" in Lene Dresen-Coenders, ed., *Saints and She-Devils* (London: Rubicon, 1987) 59-82

Drury, Nevill. *Magic and Witchcraft* (London: Thames and Hudson, 2003)

Dworkin, Andrea. *Pornography: Men Possessing Women* (New York: G.P.Putnam, 1979)

Eccleshare, Julia. *A Guide to the Harry Potter Novels* (London and New York: Continuum, 2002)

Ehrenreich, Barbara and Deirdre English, *Witches, Midwives and Nurses: A History of Women Healers* (New York: The Feminist Press at the City University of New York, 1973)

Elam, W.C. "Old Times in Virginia and a Few Parallels," *Putnam's Magazine* 14:20 (1869) n.p.

Eller, Cynthia. *Living in the Lap of the Goddess: The Feminist Spirituality Movement in America* (Boston: Beacon, 1993)

Erikson, Kai, *Wayward Puritans: A Study in the Sociology of Deviance* (New York: John Wiley and Sons, 1966)

Esten Cooke, John. "Grace Sherwood, the One Virginia Witch," *Harper's Magazine* (June 1884) 99-102

Evert Hopman, Ellen and Lawrence Bond, eds., *People of the Earth: The New Pagans Speak Out* (Rochester, VT: Destiny, 1996)

Faderman, Lillian. *Surpassing the Love of Men: Romantic Friendship and Love between Women from the Renaissance to the Present* (New York: William Morrow, 1981)

Farrar, Janet and Stewart Farrar. *A Witches' Bible: The Complete Witches' Handbook* (Blaine, WA: Phoenix and London: Robert Hale, 1981, 1984)

Fischer, David Hackett. *Albion's Seed: Four British Folkways in America* (Oxford: Oxford University Press, 1989)

Forbes, Esther. *A Mirror for Witches* (1928; Bath: Cedric Chivers, 1973)

Francis, Richard. *Samuel Sewall's Apology* (London: Fourth Estate, 2005)

Franklin, Benjamin, untitled article, *Pennsylvania Gazette* (October 22, 1730) 3-4

_____. "Melancholy Effects of Credulity in Witchcraft," *The Gentleman's Magazine* 1 (January 1731) 29-30

Fraser, Lindsey. *Telling Tales: An Interview With J.K. Rowling* (London: Mammoth, 2000)

Fricke, John, Jay Scarfone, and William Stillman, *The Wizard of Oz* (London: Hodder and Stoughton, 1989)

Frost, Robert. *Selected Poems* (New York and Avenel, New Jersey: Gramercy, 1992)

Galloway Jim, and Chris Burritt, "School Lets Hero Off Hook," *Atlanta Journal* (13.10.1999) n.p.

Gardner, Gerald. *Witchcraft Today* (1954; New York: Citadel, 2004)

Gardner, Richard A. *Sex Abuse Hysteria: Salem Witch Trials Revisited.* Cresskill, New Jersey: Creative Therapeutics, 1991

Geis, Gilbert and Ivan Bunn, *A Trial of Witches: A Seventeenth Century Witchcraft Prosecution.* London and New York: Routledge, 1997

Genge, N.E. *The Book of Shadows: The Unofficial Charmed Companion* (New York: Three Rivers Press, 2000)

Gevitz, Norman. "The Devil Hath Laughed at the Physicians: Witchcraft and Medical Practice in Seventeenth-Century New England," *Journal of the History of Medicine* 55 (January 2000) 5-36

Gibson, Marion. *Reading Witchcraft: Stories of Early English Witches.* London and New York: Routledge, 1999

_____. *Early Modern Witches: Witchcraft Cases in Contemporary Writing.* London and New York: Routledge, 2000

_____. "Understanding Witchcraft: Accusers' Stories in Print in Early Modern England," Stuart Clark, ed., *Languages of Witchcraft: Narrative, Ideology and Meaning in Early Modern Culture* (Basingstoke: Macmillan, 2001) 41-54

_____, ed., *Witchcraft and Society in England and America 1550-1750* (Ithaca and London: Cornell University Press and Continuum, 2003)

Ginzburg, Carlo. *Ecstasies; Deciphering the Witches' Sabbath.* Trans. Raymond Rosenthal. London: Hutchinson Radius, 1990

_____. *Myths, Emblems and Clues.* Trans. J. and A. Tedeschi. London: Hutchinson Radius, 1986

_____. *The Night Battles: : Witchcraft and Agrarian Cults in the Sixteenth and Seventeenth Centuries.* Trans. John and Anne Tedeschi. 1966; Baltimore: Johns Hopkins UP, 1992

Godbeer, Richard, "Chaste and Unchaste Covenants: witchcraft and Sex in Early Modern Culture" in Peter Benes, ed., *Wonders of the Invisible World 1600-1900* (Boston: Boston University Press, 1995) 53-72

_____. *Escaping Salem: The Other Witch Hunt of 1692* (Oxford: Oxford University Press, 2005)

Goldenberg, Naomi R. *Changing of the Gods: Feminism and the End of Traditional Religions* (Boston: Beacon, 1979)

Goodell, Abner C. *Further Notes on the History of Witchcraft in Massachusetts* (Cambridge, Massachusetts, 1884)

Goodrich, Charles A. *A History of the United States of America* (New York, 1829)

Gorman, Herbert. *The Place Called Dagon* (1927; New York: Hippocampus, 2003)

Gottfried, Martin. *Arthur Miller: A Life* (New York: Da Capo, 2003)

Gough, Isobel. "Witchcraft - Northumberland County Style," *Northumberland County Historical Society Bulletin* 5 (1968) 52-7

Gould, Philip. *Covenant and Republic: Historical Romance and the Politics of Puritanism* (Cambridge: Cambridge University Press, 1996)

____. "New England Witch-Hunting and the Politics of Reason in the Early Republic," *New England Quarterly* 68:1 (March 1995) 58-82

Gragg, Larry, *The Salem Witchcraft Crisis* (New York: Praeger, 1992)

Greene, David L., "Salem Witches I: Bridget Bishop," *American Genealogist* 57:3 (July 1981) 129-38

Greenwald, Gary. *Satan's Trojan Horse* (Eagles Nest Ministries, n.d)

Greenwood, Susan. *Witchcraft, Magic and the Otherworld: An Anthropology* (Oxford and New York: Berg, 2000)

Greer, John Michael and Gordon Cooper, "The Red God: Woodcraft and the Origins of Wicca," *Gnosis Magazine* (Summer 1998) 51-7

Griffin, Susan. *Pornography and Silence: Culture's Revenge against Nature* (New York: Harper and Row, 1981)

Grimassi, Raven. *Italian Witchcraft: The Old Religion of Southern Europe* (1995; St. Paul, MN: Llewellyn, 2003)

Grinstead, Durward. *Elva* (New York: Covici Friede, 1929).

Guiley, Rosemary Ellen. *The Encyclopaedia of Witches and Witchcraft* 2nd. ed. (New York: Checkmark, 1999)

Guskin, Phyllis J. "The Context of Witchcraft: The Case of Jane Wenham 1712," *Eighteenth-Century Studies* 15:1 (Autumn, 1981) 48-71

Hale, John. *A Modest Enquiry Into the Nature of Witchcraft* (Boston, 1702). *Witchcraft in Europe and America*, Reel 48. Woodbridge, Connecticut: Research Publications

Hall, David D., "Witchcraft and the Limits of Interpretation," *New England Quarterly* 59:2 (June 1985) 253-81

____. *Witch-hunting in Seventeenth-Century New England: A Documentary History 1638-1693*. 2nd. ed. Boston: Northeastern University Press, 1999.

Hansen, Chadwick, "Salem witches and DeForest's *Witching Times*," *Essex Institute Historical Collections* 104:2 (April 1968) 89-108

Harley, David, "Explaining Salem: Calvinist Psychology and the Diagnosis of Possession," *American Historical Review* 101 (April 1996) 307-30

____. "Historians as Demonologists: The Myth of the Midwife-Witch," *Social History of Medicine* 3.1 (1990): 1-26.

Hawthorne, Nathaniel. *The House of the Seven Gables* (1851; London: Dent, 1970)

____. *The Scarlet Letter* ed. Seymour Gross, Sculley Bradley, Richmond Croom Beatty and E. Hudson Long (1850; New York and London: W.W. Norton, 1988)

____. "Young Goodman Brown" in Charles L. Crow, ed., *American Gothic: An Anthology 1787-1916* (Oxford: Blackwell, 1999) 113-20

____. "Alice Doane's Appeal" in Crow, ed. 106-13

Haynie, W. Preston. "Witchcraft - An Outcry of Public Hysteria, Paranoia or a Belief of the Time?," *Bulletin of the Northumberland County History Society* 28 (1991) 33-9

Hayward, Rhodri. "Demonology, Neurology and Medicine in Edwardian Britain," *Bulletin of the History of Medicine* 78:1 (March 2004) 37-58

Helford, Elyce Rae ed., *Fantasy Girls: Gender in the New Universe of Science Fiction Television* (Lanham, Boulder, Oxford, New York: Rowman and Littlefield, 2000)

Heller, Dana. "Found Footage: Feminism Lost in Time," Tulsa *Studies in Women's Literature* 21:1 (Spring 2002) 85-98

Herbert, Henry William. *The Fair Puritan: An Historical Romance of the Days of Witchcraft* (Philadelphia, 1875)

Heredia, Christopher. "Joel Dorius — Gay Professor in '60s Porn Scandal," *Chronicle* 19 February 2006 (obituary) n.p.

Herr, Karl. *Hex and Spellwork: The Magical Practices of the Pennsylvania Dutch* (Boston and York Beach, Maine: Weiser Books, 2002)

Heselton, Philip. *Gerald Gardner and the Cauldron of Inspiration: An Investigation of the Sources of Gardnerian Witchcraft* (Milverton, Somerset: Capall Bann, 2003)

Hester, Marianne. *Lewd Women and Wicked Witches*. London and New York: Routledge, 1992

Jackson, Shirley, *Witchcraft in Salem Village* (New York: Random House, 1956)

Heyward, Thomas and Richard Brome, *The Late Lancashire Witches* (London, 1634)

Higley, Sarah L. "People Just Want to See Something: Art, Death and Document," in *Blair Witch, The Last Broadcast* and *Paradise Lost* in Higley and Weinstock, eds., 87-110

Hill, Frances. A *Delusion of Satan: The Full Story of the Salem Witch Trials*. 1995; New York: Da Capo, 1997

_____, ed., *The Salem Witch Trials Reader*. New York: Da Capo, 2000

_____. *Hunting for Witches: A Visitor's Guide to the Salem Witch Trials* (Beverly, Massachusetts: Commonwealth Editions, 2002)

Hoadly, Charles J. "A Case of Witchcraft in Hartford," *Connecticut Magazine* 5:11 (November 1899) 557-61

Hoffer, Peter Charles. *The Salem Witchcraft Trials: A Legal History*. Lawrence: University of Kansas Press, 1997

Hoffman, Alice. *Practical Magic* (1995; London: Vintage, 2002)

Holbert Tucker, George. *Virginia Supernatural Tales: Ghosts, Witches and Eerie Doings* (Norfolk, Virginia: Donning, 1977)

Holdsworth, William K. "Law and Society in Colonial Connecticut 1636-1672," unpublished Ph.D. thesis, Claremont Graduate School, 1974

_____. "Adultery or Witchcraft? A New Note on an Old Case in Connecticut," *New England Quarterly* 48:3 (September 1975) 394-409

Holland, Josiah Gilbert. *The Bay Path: A Tale of New England Colonial Life* (New York, 1891)

_____. *Wanted* (New York, 1872)

Hood, Lynley. A *City Possessed: The Christchurch Civic Creche Case* (Dunedin: Longacre, 2001)

Hopkins, Matthew. *The Discovery of Witches* (London, 1647)

Hudson, Carson O. *These Detestable Slaves of the Devil: A Concise Guide to Witchcraft in Colonial Virginia* (Haverford, Pennsylvania: Infinity Publishing, 2001)

Huebner, Louise. *Witchcraft For All* (1969; London: Universal-Tandem, 1971)

Hutton, Ronald. *The Triumph of the Moon: A History of Modern Pagan Witchcraft* (Oxford: Oxford University Press, 1999)

_____. *Pagan Religions of the British Isles: Their Nature and Legacy* (Oxford: Blackwell, 1991)

Hyder, Clyde Kenneth. *George Lyman Kittredge, Teacher and Scholar* (Lawrence, Kansas: University of Kansas Press, 1962)

Ingle, Edward. "A Virginia Witch," *Magazine of American History* 10:5 (November 1883) 425-7

Innes, Stephen. *Labor in a New Land: Economy and Society in Seventeenth-Century Springfield* (Princeton: Princeton University Press, 1983)

Irving, Washington. *The Complete Tales of Washington Irving*, ed. Charles Neider (New York: Doubleday, 1975)

Jackson, Shirley, *The Witchcraft of Salem Village* (1956; New York: Random House, 2001)

James, Edward W. "Grace Sherwood the Virginia Witch," *William and Mary Quarterly Historical Magazine* 3:2 (1894) 96-101

_____. "Grace Sherwood the Virginia Witch," *William and Mary Quarterly Historical Magazine* 3:3 (1895) 190-2

_____. "Grace Sherwood the Virginia Witch," *William and Mary Quarterly Historical Magazine* 3:4 (1895) 242-5

_____. "Grace Sherwood the Virginia Witch," *William and Mary Quarterly Historical Magazine* 4:1 (1895) 18-22

_____. "Witchcraft in Virginia," *William and Mary Quarterly* 2:1 (July 1893) 58-60

_____. "Witchcraft in Virginia," *William and Mary Quarterly* 1:3 (January 1893) 127-9

Johnston, Richard Malcolm. "Our Witch," *Century Magazine* 53 (n.s. 31) (March 1897) 760-66

Joslyn Gage, Matilda. W*oman, Church and State* (1893; Amherst, NY: Prometheus Books, 2002)

Kamensky, Jane. "Words, Witches and Woman Trouble: Witchcraft, Disorderly Speech and Gender Boundaries in Puritan New England," *Essex Institute Historical Collections* 128 (1992) 286-307

Karlsen, Carol F. *The Devil in the Shape of a Woman: Witchcraft in Colonial New England*. 2nd. ed. 1987; New York and London: W.W. Norton, 1998

Kerr, Howard and Charles L. Crow, eds., *The Occult in America: New Historical Perspectives* (Urbana and Chicago: Universityof Illinois Press, 1986)

Kittredge, G.L, "Notes on Witchcraft" in the *Proceedings of the American Antiquarian Society*, new series 18 (1907) 148-212

_____. *Witchcraft in Old and New England*. Cambridge, Mass.: Harvard UP, 1929.

Klaits, Joseph. *Servants of Satan: The Age of the Witch Hunts* (Indiana UP: Bloomington, 1985)

Kramer, Heinrich and Jacob Sprenger, *Malleus Maleficarum* (1486), ed. and trans. Montague Summers (1928; London and New York: Dover, 1971)

Krzywinska, Tanya. *A Skin for Dancing In: Possession, Witchcraft and Voodoo in Film* (Trowbridge: Flicks Books, 2000)

____. "Hubble-Bubble, Herbs and Grimoires: Magic, Manichaeanism, and Witchcraft in *Buffy*" in Wilcox and Lavery, eds. 178-204.

Kyle, Louisa Venable. *The Witch of Pungo* (Virginia Beach: Four O'Clock Farms Publishing, 1973)

Lacquer, Thomas. *Making Sex: Body and Gender from the Greeks to Freud* (Cambridge, Massachusetts: Harvard University Press, 1990)

Larbalestier, Justine. "*Buffy*'s Mary Sue is Jonathan: *Buffy* Acknowledges the Fans" in Wilcox and Lavery, eds. 227-238

Larner, Christina. *Enemies of God*. London: Chatto and Windus, 1981

____. *Witchcraft and Religion*. Ed. Alan Macfarlane. Oxford: Blackwell, 1984

Laulainen Schein, Diana Lyn, unpublished Ph.D. thesis "Comparative Counterpoints: Witchcraft Accusations in Early Modern Lancashire and the Chesapeake," University of Minnesota, 2004

Lawson, Deodat. *A Brief and True Narrative of Some Remarkable Passages Relating to Sundry Persons Afflicted by Witchcraft*. Boston, 1692

Le Beau, Bryan F. *The Story of the Salem Witch Trials*. Upper Saddle River, New Jersey: Prentice-Hall, 1998

Leek, Sybil. *Diary of a Witch* (1968; New York: Signet, 1969)

Lehigh, Scott. "We Used to Keep Religion Out of Politics," *Boston Globe* (27.06.1999) F01

Levack, Brian P. "State-Building and Witch-Hunting in Early Modern Europe," in Jonathan Barry, Marianne Hester and Gareth Roberts, eds., *Witchcraft in Early Modern Europe: Studies in Culture and Belief* (Cambridge: Cambridge University Press, 1996) 96-115

Leland, Charles Godfrey. *Algonquin Legends of New England* (Boston, 1884)

____. *Hans Breitmann's Ballads* (1914; New York: Dover, 1965)

____. *Aradia: Gospel of the Witches* (1899; Blaine, WA: Phoenix, 1999)

____. *Aradia or the Gospel of the Witches: A New Translation,* trans. Mario and Dina Pazzaglini (Blaine, WA: Phoenix, 1998)

____. *Gypsy Sorcey and Fortune Telling* (1891; New York: Citadel Press, 1962)

____. *Etruscan Roman Remains in Popular Tradition* (New York and London, 1892)

____. *The Gypsies* (1882; Boston and New York: Houghton Mifflin, 1924)

Levermore, Charles H. "Witchcraft in Connecticut," *New England Magazine* 12:5 (July 1892) 636-44

____. "Witchcraft in Connecticut," *The New Englander and Yale Review* 44:189 (1885) 788-817

Lister, Roma. *Reminiscences Social and Political* (London: Hutchinson, 1925)

Littlefield, Henry M. "The Wizard of Oz: Parable on Populism," *American Quarterly* 16:1 (1964) 47-58

Lofficer, Jean-Marc and Randy. *Into the Twilight Zone: The Rod Serling Programme Guide* (London: Virgin, 1995)

Longfellow, Henry Wadsworth, *Giles Corey of the Salem Farms in The New England Tragedies* (London, 1868)

Love, Philip. "Witch of St. Mary's Moll Dyer Lives on in Legend — and a Rock," *Baltimore Sun supplement* (October 20 1974) 24-6

Lowell, James Russell. "Witchcraft" in *Among My Books* (1870; London and Toronto: Dent, 1925) 64-116

Lunsford, Virginia. "The Witch in Colonial Virginia: A Question of Gender and Family Relations," *Northern Neck Historical Magazine* 43:1 (1993) 5007-16

Macfarlane, Alan. *Witchcraft in Tudor and Stuart England* (1970. Prospect Heights, Illinois: Waveland Press, 1991)

Mackie, Pauline Bradford. *Ye Lyttle Salem Maide: A Story of Witchcraft* (1898; Boston: L.C.Page, 1903)

Madison, Lucy Foster. *A Maid of Salem Towne* (1906; New York: Grosset and Dunlap, 1934)

Maguire, Gregory. *Wicked: The Life and Times of the Wicked Witch of the West* (New York: HarperCollins, 1995)

Mappen, Mark. *Witches and Historians: Interpretations of Salem.* 2nd. ed. Malabar, Florida: Krieger Publishing, 1996

Marcus, Ronald. *Elizabeth Clawson: Thou Deservest to Die* (Stamford: Stamford Historical Society, 1976)

Martine, James J. T*he Crucible: Politics, Property and Pretense* (New York: Twayne, 1993)

Mather, Cotton. *Wonders of the Invisible World* (Boston and London, 1692) in *Cotton Mather on Witchcraft.* New York: Dorset Press, 1991

_____. "Memorable Providences," *Relating to Witchcrafts and Possessions* (Boston, 1689)

Mather, Increase. *Cases of Conscience* (Boston, 1693). *Witchcraft in Europe and America,* Reel 66. Woodbridge, Connecticut: Research Publications

Mathieson, Robert. "Charles G. Leland and the Witches of Italy: The Origins of *Aradia*" in *Aradia or the Gospel of the Witches: A New Translation,* trans. Mario and Dina Pazzaglini (Blaine, WA: Phoenix, 1998) 25-57

Matossian, Mary Kilbourne. *Poisons of the Past: Molds, Epidemics, and History* (New Haven and London: Yale University Press, 1989) 113-22

H.R. McIlwaine, *Minutes of the Council and General Court of Colonial Virginia 1622-32 and 1670-6,* ed. Jon Kukla, 2nd. ed. (1924; Richmond: Virginia State Library, 1979)

McManus, Edgar J. *Law and Liberty in Early New England: Criminal Justice and Due Process 1620-1692* (Amherst: University of Massachusetts Press, 1993)

McMillan, Timothy J. "Black Magic: Witchcraft, Race and Resistance in Colonial New England," *Journal of Black Studies* 25:1 (September 1994) 99-117

McWilliams, John. *New England's Crises and Cultural Memory: Literature, Politics, History and Religion 1620-1860* (Cambridge: Cambridge University Press, 2004)

Meltzer, Milton. *Witches and Witch-Hunts: A History of Persecution* (New York: Scholastic, 1999)

Mendlesohn, Farah. "Surpassing the Love of Vampires: Or, Why (and How) a Queer Reading of the Buffy/Willow Relationship is Denied" in Wilcox and Lavery, 45-60

Michelet, Jules. *La Sorciere,* retitled *Satanism and Witchcraft,* trans. A.R.Allinson (1862; London: Tandem, 1965)

Middlekauff, Robert. *The Mathers: Three Generations of Puritan Intellectuals 1596-1728* 2nd. ed. (1971; Berkeley: University of California Press, 1999)

Miller, Arthur. *The Crucible* (1952) in *Plays:One* (London: Methuen, 1988)

____. "Why I Wrote *The Crucible,*" *The New Yorker* (October 21 and 28, 1996)

____. *The Crucible: A Screenplay* (London: Methuen, 1996)

Miller, Perry. *The New England Mind: From Colony to Province* 2nd. ed. (1953; Boston: Beacon, 1961)

Moore, G.H. Final Notes on *Witchcraft in Massachusetts* (New York, 1885).

Morgan, Forrest. "Witchcraft in Connecticut," *American Historical Magazine* 1 (1906) 216-38

Morgan, Robin. "Theory and Practice: Pornography and Rape" in L. Lederer, ed., *Take Back the Night* (New York: William Morrow, 1980)

Morse, Jedidiah, and Elijah Parish. *A Compendious History of New England* (London, 1808)

Moseley, Rachel. "Glamorous Witchcraft: Gender and Magic in Teen Film and Television," *Screen* 43:4. (2002) 403-422

Mountainwater, Shekhinah. *Ariadne's Thread: A Workbook of Goddess Magic* (Freedom, California: The Crossing Press, 1991)

Muchembled, Robert. "Satanic Myths and Cultural Reality" in Bengt Ankarloo and Gustav Henningsen, eds, *Early Modern European Witchcraft: Centres and Peripheries* (1990; Oxford: Clarendon, 1993) 139-160

Murray, Margaret. *The Witch Cult in Western Europe.* Oxford: Clarendon, 1921.

____. *The God of the Witches* (1931; Oxford: Oxford University Press, 1970)

____. *My First Hundred Years* (London: William Kimber, 1963)

Neal, Connie. *What's a Christian to Do with Harry Potter?* (Colorado Springs: Waterbrook Press, 2001)

Neal, John. *Rachel Dyer* (1828; Amherst, New York: Prometheus Books, 1996)

Nel, Philip. *J.K. Rowling's Harry Potter Novels* (London and New York: Continuum, 2001)

Nelson Barker, James. *The Tragedy of Superstition* in Arthur Hobson Quinn, ed., *Representative American Plays from 1767 to the Present* (New York: Appleton Century Crofts, 1953)

Noel Hume, Ivor. "Witchcraft and Evil Spirits: Weird Sisters, Hand in Hand," *Colonial Williamsburg* (Autumn 1998) 21:1 14-19

Norton Mary Beth. *In the Devil's Snare: The Salem Witchcraft Crisis of 1692* (New York: Alfred A. Knopf, 2002)

Ogden, Daniel. "Binding Spells: Curse Tablets and Voodoo Dolls in the Greek and Roman Worlds" in Valerie Flint, Richard Gordon, Georg Luck and Daniel Ogden, *Witchcraft and Magic in Europe: Ancient Greece and Rome* (London: Athlone, 1999) 4-90

Oldridge, Darren ed. *The Witchcraft Reader* (London and New York: Routledge, 2002)

Orians, G.Harrison, "New England Witchcraft in Fiction," *American Literature* 2 (March 1930) 54-71

Orne Jewett, Sarah. "In Dark New England Days" in Jessica Amanda Salmonson, ed., *Lady Ferry and Other Uncanny People* (Ashcroft, British Columbia: Ash-Tree Press, 1998) 26-41

Paige, Anthony. *American Witch: Magick for the Modern Seeker* (New York: Citadel, 2003)

Paige, Linda Rohrer. "Wearing the Red Shoes: Dorothy and the Power of the Female Imagination in The Wizard of Oz," *Journal of Popular Film and Television* 23:4 (1996) 146-153

Paige, Lucius. *History of Cambridge, Massachusetts, 1630-1877* (Boston, 1877)

Palfrey, John Gorham. *History of New England* (Boston, 1877)

Parke, Francis Neal. *Witchcraft in Maryland* (np: np, nd), Maryland Historical Society

Parkhill, Thomas C. *Weaving Ourselves into the Land: Charles Godfrey Leland, 'Indians', and the Study of Native American Religions* (Albany: SUNY Press, 1997)

Patrick, Mike. "Within the Circle of the Craft," *Connecticut Post* 11 August 1996 A1, A12-13

Pazzaglini, Mario. "Leland and the Magical World of Aradia" in Leland, *Aradia ... A New Translation* 81-103

Penczak, Christopher. *City Magick: Urban Rituals, Spells and Shamanism* (York Beach, Maine: Red Wheel/Weiser, 2001)

Perkins Gilman, Charlotte. "When I Was a Witch" in Ann J. Lane. ed., *The Charlotte Perkins Gilman Reader* (London: The Women's Press, 1981)

Perley, M.V.B. *A Short History of the Salem Village Witchcraft Trials* (1911; n.p.: Kessinger, 2005)

Peterson, Henry. *Dulcibel: A Tale of Old Salem* (Philadelphia: John C. Winston, 1907)

Petry, Ann, *Tituba of Salem Village* (New York: HarperTrophy, 1964)

Pilato, Herbie J. *Bewitched Forever* (Irving, Texas: Summit, 1996)

Poole, William F. "Cotton Mather and Salem Witchcraft," *North American Review* 108 (April 1869) 337-97

_____. *Cotton Mather and Salem Witchcraft: Two Notices of Mr. Upham his Reply* (1870; np: Kessinger, 2006)

Potts, Thomas. *The Wonderfull Discoverie of Witches* (London, 1612)

Powell, F. York. Charles Godfrey Leland, obituary. *Folk-Lore* 14 (1903) 162-164

Purkiss, Diane. *The Witch in History: Early Modern and Twentieth Century Representations*. London and New York: Routledge, 1996

Putnam, A.P., *Address at the Dedication of a Tablet in Honor of Forty Friends of Rebecca Nurse of Salem Village* (Boston, 1894)

Ravenwolf, Silver. *American Folk Magick: Charms, Spells and Herbals* (St. Paul, Minnesota: Llewellyn, 1999)

Rees, Celia. *Witch Child* (London: Bloomsbury, 2000)

____. *Sorceress* (London: Bloomsbury, 2002)

Reis, Elizabeth. *Damned Women: Sinners and Witches in Puritan New England* (Ithaca and London: Cornell University Press, 1997)

____, ed., *Spellbound: Women and Witchcraft in America* (Wilmington, Delaware: S.R. Books, 1998)

Ann Rinaldi, *A Break with Charity* (Orlando: Harcourt Brace, 1992)

Riordan, Timothy B. *The Plundering Time: Maryland and the English Civil War 1645, 1646* (Baltimore: Maryland Historical Society, 2004)

Ritter, Gretchen. "Silver Slippers and a Golden Cap: L. Frank Baum's The Wonderful Wizard of Oz and Historical Memory in American Politics," *Journal of American Studies* 31:2 (1997) 171-202

Roach, Marilynne K. *The Salem Witch Trials: A Day-by-Day Chronicle of a Community Under Siege* (Lanham, Maryland, New York, Dallas, Boulder, Colorado, Toronto, Oxford: Taylor Trade Publishing, 2002)

Roberts, Gareth. *The Mirror of Alchemy* (London: British Library, 1994).

Robertson, Alice. "A Biographical Study of George Lyman Kittredge," M.A. thesis, University of Maine, 1947

Robins Pennell, Elizabeth. *Charles Godfrey Leland*, 2 vols. (Boston and New York: Houghton Mifflin, 1906)

Robinson, Enders A. *The Devil Discovered: Salem Witchcraft 1692* (Prospect Heights, Illinois: Waveland Press, 1991)

Roesch Wagner Sally. *Matilda Joslyn Gage: She Who Holds the Sky* (Aberdeen, South Dakota: Sky Carrier Press, 1998)

Roper, Lyndal. *Oedipus and the Devil* (London and New York: Routledge, 1994)

Roscoe, Jane. "*The Blair Witch Project*: Mock-Documentary Goes Mainstream," *Jump Cut* 43 (2000) 7

Rose, Elliot. *A Razor for a Goat* (1989; Toronto, Buffalo, London: University of Toronto Press, 2003)

Rosen, Barbara. *Witchcraft in England 1558-1618*. 1969 (Amherst: University of Massachusetts Press, 1991)

Rosenthal, Bernard. *Salem Story: Reading the Witch Trials of 1692* (Cambridge: Cambridge UP, 1993)

Rowling, J.K. *Harry Potter and the Philosopher's Stone* (London: Bloomsbury, 1998)

Rushton, Peter. "Texts of Authority: Witchcraft Accusations and the Demonstration of Truth in Early Modern England" in Stuart Clark, ed. *Languages of Witchcraft: Narrative, Ideology and Meaning in Early Modern Culture* (Basingstoke: Macmillan, 2001) 21-39

Saari, Peggy. *Witchcraft in America* (Detroit: UXL, 2001)

Salomonsen, Jone. *Enchanted Feminism: The Reclaiming Witches of San Francisco* (London and New York: Routledge, 2002)

Schissel, Wendy. "Re(dis)covering the Witches in Arthur Miller's *The Crucible*: A Feminist Reading," *Modern Drama* 37 (1994) 461-473

Schlosser, S.E. *Spooky South: Tales of Hauntings, Strange Happenings, and Other Local Lore* (Guilford, Connecticut: Globe Pequot Press, 2004)

Schwartzstein, Tannin and Raven Kaldera. *The Urban Primitive: Paganism in the Concrete Jungle* (St.Paul, MN: Llewellyn, 2002)

Scot, Reginald. *The Discoverie of Witchcraft* (London, 1584)

Sedgwick, Catharine Maria. *Hope Leslie: Or, Early Times in the Massachusetts* (1827; New York: Penguin, 1998)

Segal, Lynne and Mary McIntosh, eds., *Sex Exposed: Sexuality and the Pornography Debate* (London: Virago, 1992)

Serra, Ilaria. "Le Streghe Son Tornate: The Reappearance of Streghe in Italian American Queer Writings," *Journal for the Academic Study of Magic* 1 (2003) 131-160

Sewall, Samuel. *The Diary of Samuel Sewall* ed. M. Halsey Thomas, 2 vols. ( New York: Farrar, Straus and Giroux, 1973)

Shadwell, Thomas. *The Lancashire Witches* (London, 1681)

Shapira, Ian "After Toil and Trouble, Witch is Cleared," *The Washington Post*, Metro section 12 July 2006, B1-2

Sharpe, J.A. *Instruments of Darkness: Witchcraft in England 1550-1750*. London: Hamish Hamilton, 1996

_____. "Witchcraft and Women in Seventeenth Century England: Some Northern Evidence," *Continuity and Change* 6.2 (1991): 179-99

Shurtleff, N.B. ed. *Records of the Governor and Company of the Massachusetts Bay* 5 vols. (Boston, 1853-4)

Silverman, Kenneth. *The Life and Times of Cotton Mather* (New York: Welcome Rain, 1984)

Smith, Joseph. *Colonial Justice in Western Massachusetts 1639-1702* (Cambridge, Massachusetts: Harvard University Press, 1961)

Smith, Sean. *J.K. Rowling: A Biography*. Rev. ed. (London: Arrow, 2002)

Smith, Thorne (completed by Norman Matson), *The Passionate Witch* (1942; London: Tandem, 1966)

Solano Lopez, F. and Barreiro, *The Young Witches* (Seattle: Eros Comix, 1992).

Spanos, Nicholas P. and Jack Gottlieb, "Ergotism and the Salem Village Witch Trials," *Science* 194 (24 December 1976) 1390-4

Speare, Elizabeth George. *The Witch of Blackbird Pond* (1958; New York: Bantam Doubleday, 1987)

Starhawk (Miriam Simos), *The Spiral Dance: A Rebirth of the Ancient Religion of the Great Goddess* (1979; New York: HarperSanFrancisco, 1999)

_____. *Truth or Dare: Encounters with Power, Authority and Mystery* (San Francisco: Harper, 1987)

_____. *Dreaming the Dark: Magic, Sex and Politics* (1982; Boston: Beacon, 1997)

Starkey, Marion L. *The Devil in Massachusetts: A Modern Inquiry into the Salem Witch Trials* (1949; New York: Time Inc., 1963)

_____. *The Visionary Girls: Witchcraft in Salem Village* (Boston and Toronto: Little, Brown, 1973)

Steege, David K. "Harry Potter, Tom Brown and the British School Story: Lost in Transit?" in Lana A. Whited, ed., *The Ivory Tower and Harry Potter: Perspectives on a Literary Phenomenon* (Columbia and London: University of Missouri Press, 2002) 140-156

Stone, Merlin. *When God Was a Woman* (Orlando: Harcourt, 1976).

Summers, Lucy. *Hex and the City: Sophisticated Spells for the Urban Witch* (London: Quarto/Barrons, 2003)

Tarantino, Quentin. *Pulp Fiction* (London and Boston: Faber and Faber, 1994)

Taylor, John M. *The Witchcraft Delusion in Colonial Connecticut 1647-1697* (New York: Grafton, 1908)

Taylor Squires, Stephen. "Search for Westport Relative Uncovers Truth about Witches," *Fairfield Minuteman* (9 March 1995) 3, 30

_____. "Man Finds Odd Coincidences in Family History," *Fairfield Minuteman* (26 October 1995) B3, B6

Thomas, Keith, *Religion and the Decline of Magic*. 1971. London: Peregrine, 1978

Toksvig, Sandi. *The Gladys Society: A Personal American Journey* (London: Little, Brown, 2002)

Tomlinson, R.G. *Witchcraft Trials of Connecticut* (Hartford: Bond Press, 1978)

Townsend Warner, Sylvia. *Lolly Willowes* (1926; Chicago: Academy Chicago Publishers, 1979)

Trask, Richard B. *The Devil Hath Been Raised: A Documentary History of the Salem Village Witchcraft Outbreak of March 1692.* Rev. ed. (Danvers, Massachusetts: Yeoman Press, 1997)

Traub, Valerie. "Desire and the Difference it Makes" in Valerie Wayne, ed., *The Matter of Difference: Materialist Feminist Criticism of Shakespeare* (Ithaca: Cornell University Press, 1991) 81-114

_____. "The (In)significance of 'Lesbian' Desire in Early Modern England" in Susan Zimmerman, ed., *Erotic Politics: Desire on the Renaissance Stage* (New York: Routledge, 1992) 150-69

Trumbull, J. Hammond, ed. *The Public Records of the Colony of Connecticut* vol. 1 (Hartford: Brown and Parsons, 1850)

Trumbull, Annie E. "One Blank of Windsor," *Hartford Courant Literary Supplement* (December 3 1904) 11

Turner, Florence Kimberley. *Gateway to the New World: A History of Princess Anne County, Virginia 1607-1824* (Easley, South Carolina: Southern Historical Press, 1984) 78-82

Updike, John. *The Witches of Eastwick* (London: Andre Deutsch, 1984)

Upham, Caroline E. *Salem Witchcraft in Outline* (Salem, 1891)

Upham, Charles W. *Salem Witchcraft* ed. Bryan F. Le Beau (1867; Mineola, New York: Dover, 2000)

\_\_\_\_. *Salem Witchcraft and Cotton Mather: A Reply* (Morrisana, New York, 1869)

Upham, William P. *Account of the Rebecca Nurse Monument* (Salem, Massachusetts, 1886)

Valente, Joseph. "Rehearsing the Witch Trials: Gender Injustice in *The Crucible*," *New Formations* 32 (1997) 120-134

Valiente, Doreen. *The ABC of Witchcraft Past and Present* 2nd. ed. (1973; London: Robert Hale, 1994)

van Druten, John. *Bell, Book and Candle* (New York: Dramatists' Play Service, 2003)

W.,W. *A true and just Recorde* (London, 1582)

Walker, Joseph S. "Mom and the Blair Witch: Narrative, Form and the Feminine" in Sarah L. Higley and Jeffrey Andrew Weinstock, *Nothing That Is: Millenial Cinema and the Blair Witch Controversy* (Detroit: Wayne State University Press, 2004) 163-180

Waters, Stanley. "Witchcraft in Springfield, Massachusetts," *New England Historical and Genealogical Register* 35 (1881) 152-3

Weinberg, Alyce T. *Spirits of Frederick* (Frederick, Maryland: Studio 20, 1979)

Weisberg, Barbara. *Talking to the Dead: Kate and Maggie Fox and the Rise of Spiritualism* (New York: HarperSanFrancisco, 2004)

Weisman, Richard. *Witchcraft, Magic and Religion in Seventeenth-Century Massachusetts*. Amherst: University of Massachusetts Press, 1984

Wentersdorf, Karl P. "The Element of Witchcraft in The Scarlet Letter," *Folklore* 83 (Summer 1972) 132-53

Whitney, Annie Weston and Caroline Canfield Bullock, *Folk-Lore from Maryland* (New York: American Folklore Society, 1925)

Whittier, John Greenleaf. *Legends of New England* (1831; Gainesville, Florida: Scholar's Facsimiles and Reprints, 1965)

Wicker, Christine. *Not in Kansas Anymore: A Curious Tale of How Magic is Transforming America* (San Francisco: HarperSanFrancisco, 2005)

Wilcox, Rhonda V. and David Lavery, eds. *Fighting the Forces: What's At Stake in* Buffy the Vampire Slayer? (Lanham, Maryland: Rowman and Littlefield, 2002)

Wilcox, Rhonda V. "Who Died and Made Her the Boss? Patterns of Mortality in *Buffy*" in Wilcox and Lavery, eds. 3-17

Wilkins (Freeman), Mary E. *Giles Corey, Yeoman* (New York, 1893)

Willard, Samuel. Samuel Willard, "A Brief Account of a Strange and Unusual Providence" Ms.Am.1502 v.2, no. 3

\_\_\_\_. *Some Miscellany Observations on Our Present Debates Respecting Witchcrafts* (Philadelphia, 1692)

Williams, J.P. "Choosing Your Own Mother: Mother-Daughter Conflicts in *Buffy*" in Wilcox and Lavery, eds. 61-72

Williams Selma R. and Pamela Williams Adelman, *Riding the Nightmare: Women and Witchcraft from the Old World to Colonial Salem* (1978; New York: HarperPerennial, 1992)

Williams, William Carlos. "Tituba's Children" (1948) in *Many Loves and Other Plays* (New York: New Directions, 1961)

Wilson, Mary. "Witchcraft and Witches" in *A Story of Fairfield: Esseys Delivered by the Honor Students of the Class of 1932* (Fairfield: Roger Ludlowe High School, n.d.)

Witt, John. "Story of Accused Sorceress' Trial by Water in State is Bewitching Tale," *Richmond Times-Dispatch* 31 October 1989 n.p.

Wood, Juliette. Unpublished article "Gypsies, Tramps and Witches: The Pagan Roots of Charles Godfrey Leland's Witchcraft Research." Courtesy of the author.

Woodward, William Elliot. *Records of Salem Witchcraft* (Roxbury, Massachusetts, 1864)

Wright, John Hardy. *Sorcery at Salem* (Charleston, South Carolina: Arcadia, 1999)

Yoder, Don. *Discovering American Folklife: Essays on Folk Culture and the Pennsylvania Dutch* (Mechanicsburg, Pennsylvania: Stackpole Books, 1990)

Zika, Charles. "Fears of Flying: Representations of Witchcraft and Sexuality in Early Sixteenth-Century Germany," *Australian Journal of Art* 8 (1989/1990) 19-47

## Websites

Aloi, Peg. "Be Afraid, Be Very Afraid, of the Dark" http://www.witchvox.com/media/blairwitch_review.html

Anderberg, Kirsten. "Watch Lists or Witch Hunts: American Terrorist Lists" (2004) at http://www.indymedia.org.uk/en/2004/01/283437.html

Badley, Linda C. "Spiritual warfare: Post-feminism and the Cultural Politics of the Blair Witch Craze," Intensities 3 at http://www.cult-media.com/issue3/Abad.htm

Bell, Joseph N. "A Witch to Watch," *Pageant* (April, 1965) available at http://www.harpiesbizarre.com/vintage-witch2watch.htm

Berlinger, Joe, interview, The Witches' Voice at witchvox.com/media/blairwitch2_interview.html

Campbell, Beverly. "When Virginia Ducked Milady Witch," *Richmond Times-Dispatch* 30 December 1934 at http://richmondthenandnow.com/Newspaper-Articles/Witch-Grace-Sherwood.html

Carlson, I. Marc, online list of "Witches in History" at http://www.personal.utulsa.edu/~marc-carlson/witchtrial/na.html

Coulter, Ann. "Godless Causes Liberals to Pray... For a Book Burning" at http://www.anncoulter.com/cgi-local/printer_friendly.cgi?article=135

Cowan, Chris. J "'If You Go Out in the Woods Today': Approaching The Blair Witch Project as Western Mythology." 49th Parallel 4 (Winter 2000) at http://www.49thparallel.bham.ac.uk/back/issue4/cowan.htm

Dishneau, David. "Witchcraft as a Part of Maryland's Past," *Washington Times* 11 October 2004 at http://washingtontimes.com/metro/20041010-102416-3747r.htm

El-Khoury, Tamara. "Witchduck Witch Ducked for Re-Enactment," *The Virginian-Pilot* 11 July 2003 at http://home.hamptonroads.com/stories/story.cfm?story=56802&ran=28970

Gagnier, Regenia. "Cultural Philanthropy, Gypsies and Interdisciplinary Scholars: Dream of a Common Language," 19: Interdisciplinary Studies in the Long Nineteenth Century 1 (2005) at http://www.19.bbk.ac.uk/Issue1articles/RegeniaGagnierarticle.pdf

Gummere, Amelia Mott. "Witchcraft and Quakerism: A Study in Social History" (Philadelphia, 1908) at http://www.strecorsoc.org/gummere/contents.html

harpiesbizarre.com/advocatearticle.htm

harpiesbizarre.com/goodwitch.htm

harpiesbizarre.com/thoughts.htm

harpiesbizarre.com/vintagetab.htm

http://ccbit.cs.umass.edu/parsons/goodyparsons

http://ccbit.cs.umass.edu/parsons/hnmockup/

http://home.swipnet.se/stephanSE/bellbookandcandle.htm

http://www.adeaw.us/

http://www.bettybowers.com/harrypotter.html

http://www.bewitched.net/asherinterv.htm

http://www.buffyguide.com/extras/josswt.shtml

http://www.dykesvision.com/en/articles/homophobia.html

http://www.exposingsatanism.org/harrypotter.htm

http://www.nationalgeographic.org/salem

http://www.pbs.org/independentlens/greatpinkscare

http://www.pjcomix.com/hillarywitch.html

http://www.pem.org/visit/ed_curriculum.php

http://www.popmatters.com/tv/reviews/c/charmed.html

http://www.sonypictures.com/movies/thecraft/chat.html

http://www.thewb.com/Shows/Show/0,7353,%o7c%7c156,00.html

http://www.users.globalnet.co.uk/~zap/Bewitchedintro.htm

http://www.wam.umd.edu/~dschloss/Legends/index.htm

http://www.wickedwitch.org/

http://www.xtreme-gaming.com/theotherside/cliche.php

http://www2.scholastic2.com/teachers/authorsandbooks/authorstudies/authorhome.jhtml?authorID=821&collateralID=5276&displayName=Biography

Kjos, Berit. "Harry Potter Lures Kids to Witchcraft with Praise from Christian Leaders," http://www.crossroads.to/text/articles/Harry&Witchcraft.htm

Leveritt, Mara. "The Witch Trial: Witch on Death Row," Arkansas Writers' Project at http://www.arktimes.com/trial2.htm

Mackenzie, Drew. "They're Calling My Daughter a Teenage Witch," Sunday magazine, News of the World (25.02.2001) 15-16; http://archive.aclu.org/court/blackbear_complaint.html

Maryland State Archives at http://guide.mdarchives.state.md.us

McGee, Robert. "First-Person: Parents Should See Harry Potter Without the Kids" (16.11.2001) at http://www.baptistpress.org/bpnews.asp?ID12190

Newman, Kim. "The McCarthy Witch Hunt" at http://www.infinityplus.co.uk/stories/mccarthy.htm

Public Records of the Colony of Connecticut from April 1636 to October 1776 15 vols. (Hartford, 1850-90) http://www.colonialct.unconn.edu (consulted 20 June 2006)

Records of the Salem Witchcraft Trials, at http://extext.virginia.edu/salem/witchcraft/

Rogers, Jay. "Child Sacrifice in the New Age: Salem's Witch Cult and America's Abortion Industry" at http://forerunner.com/champion/X0039_Child_Sacrifice_in_t.html

Robertson, Pat, fund-raising letter: now available at geocities.com/CapitolHill/7027/quotes.html

Savidge, Martin. "Bubbling Troubles Trail Harry," CNN 06.07.2000, archived at http://edition.cnn.com/2000/books/news/07/06/trouble.harry/index.html).

Tobin, Perry. "Harry Potter Movie Lamented as Kid's First Look at the Occult" (12.11.2001) at http://www.baptistpress.org/news.asp?ID12138

Warren, Charlie. "Arkansas Baptists Support 2000 SBC Beliefs Statement," Baptist Press 09.11.2001, archived at http://www.baptistpress.org/bpnews.asp?ID=12127

Whedon, Joss. Interview with David Bianculli on "Fresh Air," National Public Radio, 09.05.2000

## Films, Theatre and Television Productions

*Accused, The.* dir. Albert McCleery, written by William L. Stuart, *Hallmark Hall of Fame*, 1 March 1953

*Bell, Book and Candle*, dir. Richard Quine, Columbia, 1958

*Bewitched*, ABC, 1964-72

*Bewitched*, dir. Nora Ephron, Columbia, 2005

*Blair Witch Project, The.* dir. Daniel Myrick and Eduardo Sanchez, Artisan, 1999

*Blair Witch Two: Book of Shadows*, dir. Joe Berlinger, Artisan, 2000

*Buffy the Vampire Slayer*, dir. Fran Rubel Kuzui, Twentieth-Century Fox, 1992

*Buffy the Vampire Slayer, Mutant Enemy*, 1997-2003

*Charmed*, Warner, 1998-

*Craft, The*, dir. Andrew Fleming, Columbia, 1996

*Great Pink Scare, The* dir. Tug Tourgrau and Dan Miller (PBS/Independent Lens, premiered 6 June 2006)

Hudson, Carson. *Cry Witch!*, performance at Colonial Williamsburg 5 July 2006

*I Married A Witch*, dir. Rene Clair, United Artists, 1942

*Practical Magic,* dir. Griffin Dunne, Warner, 1998

*Rosemary's Baby*, dir. Roman Polanski, Paramount, 1968

*Sabrina the Teenage Witch*, Hartbreak Films, 1996-2003

*Season of the Witch* (Jack's Wife), dir. George A. Romero, Latent Image, 1973

*'Still Valley' The Twilight Zone*, dir. James Sheldon, 24 November 1961

*Tabitha*, Columbia/ABC, 1977

*Undead, The.* dir. Roger Corman, A.I.P., 1957

*Three Sovereigns for Sarah*, dir. Philip Leacock, Night Owl Productions/American Playhouse/National Endowment for the Humanities, 1985

*Witches of Eastwick, The.* dir. George Miller, Warner, 1989

*Wizard of Oz, The.* dir. Victor Fleming, MGM, 1939.

# INDEX